Justifying New Labour Policy

Justifying New Labour Policy

Judi Atkins
*Research Officer, Department of Political and Cultural Studies,
Swansea University, UK*

palgrave
macmillan

First published 2011 by
PALGRAVE MACMILLAN

Palgrave Macmillan in the UK is an imprint of Macmillan Publishers Limited, registered in England, company number 785998, of Houndmills, Basingstoke, Hampshire RG21 6XS.

Palgrave Macmillan in the US is a division of St Martin's Press LLC, 175 Fifth Avenue, New York, NY 10010.

Palgrave Macmillan is the global academic imprint of the above companies and has companies and representatives throughout the world.

Palgrave® and Macmillan® are registered trademarks in the United States, the United Kingdom, Europe and other countries.

ISBN: 978–0–230–27911–7 hardback

This book is printed on paper suitable for recycling and made from fully managed and sustained forest sources. Logging, pulping and manufacturing processes are expected to conform to the environmental regulations of the country of origin.

A catalogue record for this book is available from the British Library.

Library of Congress Cataloging-in-Publication Data

Atkins, Judi, 1975–
     Justifying New Labour policy / Judi Atkins.
       p. cm.
     Includes index.
       ISBN 978–0–230–27911–7 (hardback)
       1. Labour Party (Great Britain) 2. Communication in politics – Great Britain. 3. Ideology – Great Britain. 4. Great Britain – Politics and government – 1997–2007. 5. Great Britain – Social policy – 1979– I. Title.
JN1129.L32A83 2011
324.24107—dc22   2011004883

10 9 8 7 6 5 4 3 2 1
20 19 18 17 16 15 14 13 12 11

Printed and bound in the United States of America

This book is dedicated to my family with love and gratitude

Contents

Part II The Case of New Labour

Acknowledgements

My first acknowledgement is to Steve Buckler, in the Department of Political Science and International Studies, University of Birmingham, for his patience and constructive criticism of my work. I also wish to thank Michael Freeden and Lou Cabrera, for their insightful comments on an earlier draft of this book. Although I have benefited greatly from the advice and encouragement of many people over the past few years, I would particularly like to thank Mike Adkins, Stephen Bates, Jethro Butler, Emma Foster, Simon Griffiths, Oz Hassan, Clare Heywood, Kevin Hickson, Lee Jarvis, Laura Jenkins, Caroline Kenny, Peter Kerr, Barbara Morazzani, David Norman, Richard North, Richard Shorten, Ben Taylor and Cai Wilkinson. I am especially indebted to Alan Finlayson for his encouragement and enthusiasm, and for his generosity in sharing with me his extensive knowledge of rhetoric. He also gave me my first academic job, and I hope I have gone some way towards repaying his faith in me.

I would also like to express my gratitude to the ESRC for providing the initial funding for my research (award number PTA-030-2005-00628) and the Leverhulme Trust for its support in the later stages of this project (grant number F/00 391O). At Palgrave Macmillan, I wish to thank Alison Howson for commissioning the book, and Liz Blackmore and Amber Stone-Galilee for seeing it through to completion. Finally, this book draws on and develops the arguments presented in two earlier articles, 'Moral Argument and the Justification of Policy: New Labour's Case for Welfare Reform', *British Journal of Politics and International Relations*, 12, 408–24, and 'How Virtue Theoretic Arguments may be used in the Justification of Policy', *Politics*, 28, 129–37. Both articles are available through www.interscience.wiley.com and I am grateful to Wiley-Blackwell for granting me permission to use this material.

However, my greatest debt is owed to my family, particularly to Rhianydd. Your kindness, patience and generosity of spirit never cease to amaze me, and you really are the best daughter I could wish for. Another special debt is due to my parents, sister and step-father. You always believed in me and you never let me give up, even when completing this project seemed like an impossible task. My final debt is to my close friends, Julia and Ian Garrett, who have become like family over the years and who have supported me unstintingly throughout this endeavour. This book would not have been written without the love, patience and encouragement of these most important people, and for that reason I dedicate it to them.

Introduction

The justification of policy is an integral part of democratic politics. From the annual party conference to the House of Commons, a television interview, or a general election manifesto, politicians seek to win support for their party's legislative and policy programme in a variety of settings. There is a range of justificatory strategies available, and a politician may attempt to sell a policy by claiming, for instance, that it is justified on pragmatic grounds, by reference to tradition, or perhaps because public opinion demands it (Cook, 1980, pp. 514–16). The stakes involved are high, as a well-chosen argument can ensure the successful passage of legislation through Parliament or help to secure an election victory. To maximize its chances of success, a party must consider a number of factors when formulating an argumentative strategy to promote a new policy initiative. They include the history of the policy area or programme, the need for consistency between their chosen argument and the party's core values, the prevailing political climate, and the audience they will address. By the same token, scholars must take these same factors into consideration if they are to supply a full account of the dynamics of political justification.

Politicians often appeal to moral principles and arguments in their efforts to sell new policy programmes. Thus, they typically make the case for initiatives in the area of welfare by reference to the increase in well-being – or, more generally, the positive consequences – the policy will produce, and they frequently invoke human rights or liberties when seeking to persuade people to back constitutional reforms. The promotion of community responsibilities, meanwhile, is most often justified by reference to the fostering of civic virtue and the common good. However, it is important to note that in making arguments of this kind, politicians are not seeking to claim that a policy is morally right

1

in the sense that it fulfils the criteria supplied by a particular moral theory. Rather, their goal is to achieve a consensus in the policy area concerned, and moral arguments – used in conjunction with various rhetorical strategies – can enable them to do so. On this basis, the book examines these argumentative strategies from the perspective of politics, as opposed to the standpoint of moral philosophy, and therefore seeks to offer a 'politicized' conception of moral argument.

Given the prevalence of moral language in contemporary political argument, it is surprising that its role has to date received little attention from scholars. The primary task of this book, therefore, is to facilitate exploration of this topic by proposing a theoretical framework that will enable us to disaggregate and reconstruct the process by which politicians select, formulate and employ moral arguments to win support for their policies. To demonstrate the utility of this approach, the book applies the framework to the case of New Labour and the argumentative strategies it employed across the policy areas of welfare, rights and constitutional reform, community, and foreign policy. This combination of theoretical innovation with a detailed empirical analysis of the ideas, language and policy of New Labour means that the book will be of interest to scholars and students within the areas of political theory, discourse analysis, ideology studies and British politics, as well as to policy makers and those involved in the presentation of policy.

The methodologies employed in current analyses of political discourse

Despite the importance of language in political life, 'rhetorical and linguistic approaches, indeed interpretivism in general, are not widely adopted approaches to the study of contemporary government' (Finlayson, 2004, p. 529). One exception to this rule is Paul Chilton's use of critical discourse analysis and cognitive linguistics to investigate how humans think and act politically. Chilton identifies three strategic functions of language in political discourse, which he terms coercion, legitimization (of the self) and delegitimization (of the other), and representation and misrepresentation, and I now examine them in turn. Coercion depends upon the power and resources of the speaker and, as such, is not merely a linguistic function. In a political context, Chilton writes, coercion consists in 'setting agendas, selecting topics in conversation, positioning the self and others in specific relationships, making assumptions about realities that hearers are obliged to at least temporarily accept in order to process the text or talk' (2004, p. 45).

Moreover, coercion can be emotive or propositional. Emotive coercion may be said to take place when particular uses of language induce emotional effects – such as fear, hope, anger or pity – in an audience. In many cases, we can reasonably assume that the speaker knows their words are likely to stir particular emotions, and that this response is not necessarily within the control of their listeners. On this basis, therefore, we can view this technique as a form of coercion (Chilton, 2004, p. 118). Propositional coercion induces hearers to make certain inferences in the course of processing a speech. Enoch Powell's notorious 'rivers of blood' speech, in which he warned of the harmful effects of immigration on the majority white population of Britain, provides an illustration of how this strategy is used. Here, Powell described how 'they found themselves made strangers in their own country... their homes and neighbourhoods changed beyond recognition' (quoted in Chilton, 2004, p. 122). Chilton explains that the passive construction of these phrases was intended to suggest that the changes concerned were made to the lives of Britain's 'existing population' by an unspecified active agent, namely the immigrant. So, although Powell did not explicitly blame immigration for these changes, his listeners were nonetheless invited to make this inference from his speech (2004, p. 122).

Chilton identifies two types of legitimization, of which the first is epistemic. In using this technique, a politician will claim to have superior knowledge of a situation, and hence to be more 'impartial' or more 'rational' than his or her opponents. Claims of this kind are typically supported by sources that the speaker believes his or her audience will accept as authoritative, such as lists, independent reports and statistics. The second form of legitimization is deontic, in which feelings and 'factual' representations overlap. To establish authority in this way, a speaker will seek to provoke in an audience basic emotional, intuitive responses such as protectiveness, fear or – more fundamentally still – the schema of self versus other. If successful, the speaker is able to ground his or her position in moral intuitions or feelings that nobody will challenge, and on this basis to claim – whether explicitly or implicitly – to be 'right' in both a cognitive and a moral sense (Chilton, 2004, p. 117).

Delegitimization is the opposite of legitimization and involves the negative representation of an opponent through, for instance, speech acts of insulting, accusing, blaming or scape-goating, attacking their rationality or moral character, and the invocation of notions of difference (Chilton, 2004, p. 47). Finally, the third strategic function of language in political speech is representation and misrepresentation. As Chilton explains, 'political control involves the control of information, which is by definition a matter of discourse control'. Thus, people can be prevented from giving information (censorship) or receiving it (secrecy), or they can be given information that is insufficient for their needs, perhaps because it is not entirely accurate. Other means of distorting information, such as omission, euphemism, lying and denial, are also found in political speech and are classed as qualitative misrepresentation (2004, p. 46).

Chilton employs this framework to explore how language is used within such political institutions as Parliament and the political interview, and the ways in which political actors talk about topics such as religion and international politics. While his analysis is of considerable interest, it overlooks the influence of ideology on a politician's choice of language and is, therefore, incomplete. Jonathan Charteris-Black's study of rhetoric and metaphor in political speech goes some way towards rectifying this oversight. In this work, he examines how politicians use these linguistic strategies to create an appearance of ethical integrity, communicate policies, incite an emotional response in hearers, and activate political myths. For Charteris-Black, ideology 'appeals through *consciously* formed sets of beliefs, attitudes and values while myth appeals to our emotions ... through *unconsciously* formed sets of beliefs, attitudes and values' (2005, p. 13). The role of metaphor is to mediate between these cognitive and emotional modes of persuasion, and thus to generate a moral viewpoint on life. It also helps a social group to use a particular belief system – or ideology – to create the meanings through which it can justify its own existence to itself. Ideology is frequently communicated via myth, a story that supplies an explanation for those things which people need explaining. As Charteris-Black puts it, myth supplies a 'narrative-based representation of intangible experiences that are evocative because they are unconsciously linked to emotions such as sadness, happiness and fear' (2005, p. 23).

Charteris-Black's conception of myth bears a close resemblance to Chilton's concept of emotive coercion; indeed, both are deployed in political discourse with the aim of achieving or maintaining power. This goal is evident in the speeches of Winston Churchill, in which he used the technique of personification to create an emotive link between Britain and heroic qualities such as bravery, and between Germany and the characteristics of the villain, which include treachery. These personifications were based on the conceptual metaphor THE NATION IS A PERSON[1] and, together with Churchill's use of light and dark metaphors to supply moral evaluations of the two nations respectively, contributed to a heroic myth in which 'Britain and her Allies are constructed as a force for goodness while Germany was constructed as a force of evil' (Charteris-Black, 2005, p. 56). Although a key purpose of this myth was to unify the nation and raise the morale of the British people, the combination of the myth of BRITAIN IS A HERO and first-person references such as 'we' and 'us' also enabled Churchill to create a myth of himself as a heroic leader, which in turn enhanced his authority (2005, pp. 35, 42).

Charteris-Black also analyses the discourse of Tony Blair, identifying as a key feature his use of colloquial phrases to create an informal communication style. Interestingly, Blair used these phases not only when addressing the public via television, but also in the more formal context of the political speech, where he employed it to legitimize his party's policies. This, Charteris-Black suggests, was his 'unique innovation in political speaking' (2005, p. 146). Blair was also noted for his ethical discourse, in which he used the conceptual metaphor POLITICS IS ETHICS, together with rhetorical contrasts between right and wrong, good and evil (which themselves imply the conceptual metaphor MORALITY IS CONFLICT), to create a Conviction Rhetoric whose primary purpose was 'self-legitimization as a source of moral and ethical authority' (2005, pp. 148–52), and hence the reinforcement of his leadership. Although Charteris-Black's analysis undoubtedly yields some valuable insights, Blair's speeches are not situated within the wider context of the New Labour project. Consequently, ideology is reduced to a mere abstraction, and its influence on New Labour discourse and policy is left unacknowledged.

Norman Fairclough offers a critical discourse analysis of the language of New Labour, which focuses on Blair's rhetorical style, the construction of the Third Way as a political discourse, and the ways in which language is utilized in the process of governing. Like Charteris-Black, he identifies a great strength of Blair's style as his capacity to blend 'formality and informality, ceremony and feeling, publicness and privateness'. This enabled Blair to compensate somewhat for the swagger and deceptions that characterize political life by continually reasserting his ordinary, likeable personality, which he achieved primarily by combining the language of politics with the language of the normal person (Fairclough, 2000, pp. 7–8). Also in common with Charteris-Black, Fairclough notes Blair's fondness for ethical discourse, observing that under New Labour, the concept of 'community' has been recast in moral terms that emphasize a reciprocal relationship between rights and responsibilities (2000, p. 38).

Fairclough defines the Third Way as an 'ongoing representation of the world as it is now, of the world as it might be and should be according to New Labour, and of government itself as a process of acting to change the world' (2000, p. 9). It also contains representations of work, of the family, of crime, of the economy, and so on. On the basis of this representative function, Fairclough classes the Third Way not as an ideological position, but as a political discourse. This discourse, he asserts, incorporates elements from both 'Old' Labour and Thatcherism, while at the same time claiming to have transcended the traditional antagonism of left and right through the reconciliation of such hitherto incompatible concepts as economic efficiency and social justice (2000, p. 22). However, by reducing ideology to a discourse, Fairclough fails to consider it in its own right, and thus disregards its impact on the choice of argumentative strategies and its potential to guide political action.

While the three works examined above make an important contribution to the literature on political language, none can be said to offer a comprehensive account of the process of justification. Their discussions of the various linguistic strategies available to politicians are of considerable interest – and indeed inform the analysis offered in this book – but they do not include an assessment of the effectiveness of these strategies. Moreover, the relationship between ideology and rhetoric is under-theorized, with Fairclough treating the former as a discourse and Chilton overlooking it altogether. While Charteris-Black assigns a role to ideology, he treats it as an abstraction and, in so doing, overlooks its action-guiding possibilities. He also fails to explain how ideological concepts both feature in and influence political rhetoric.

The question arises, therefore, of why these three scholars neglect the role of ideology in their work. One explanation may be the perception that ideologies are 'closed', in the sense that they 'are often presented (by their proponents as well as scholars) as being informed by some underlying necessity' (Bastow and Martin, 2003, p. 15). This perceived closure violates the anti-essentialist impulse of discourse theory, and thus leads to the marginalization of ideology in those studies that adopt this analytical approach. A further reason may be that ideology is often regarded as irrelevant in the post-Cold War world. This viewpoint is linked to the 'end of ideology' thesis (Bell, 2000; Fukuyama, 1992) and the recent move towards the centre-ground of politics. However, Andrew Heywood counters this position by pointing out that the thesis is itself ideological, on the ground that it attempts to portray a 'particular set of political ideas and values as superior to all its rivals, and to do so by predicting its ultimate triumph' (2003, p. 326). This in turn demonstrates that ideological change and development is very much an ongoing process, and that ideology remains relevant in contemporary politics as a body of ideas and a guide to action.

One scholar who recognizes the relationship between ideology and language in political life is Steve Buckler. In a recent paper, he proposes a framework that identifies three 'levels' of political discourse, which he terms 'theory,' 'ideology' and 'rhetoric.' The 'context of theory' denotes scholarly discourse of the kind found in academic debate, while the 'context of ideology' relates to the use of ideas as 'elements in an integrated and coherent ideological platform with action-guiding potential.' Finally, the 'context of rhetoric' is concerned with the debate that takes place between actors in their efforts to win power, and thus to secure hegemonic advantage over their opponents (Buckler, 2007, p. 37). Buckler deploys this framework to examine the idea of 'community' as it appears in contemporary political discourse, notably that of New Labour. He demonstrates that, by linking community to its core values of equality of opportunity and equal worth, New Labour was able to present this idea as 'constituting an enabling partnership from the point of view of citizens' (2007, p. 49). In turn, this conception of community enabled New Labour to frame personal responsibilities as those that attach to the citizens of a just society in which economic individualism is tempered by fairness. Such a society places limited moral demands on its citizens, and thus contrasts with the Conservatives' traditionalist notion of a community built around 'Victorian values' that found expression in illiberal policies. Consequently, Buckler believes, New Labour could seek rhetorical advantage by accusing the Conservatives of using lazy stereotypes as the basis for policies that exacerbated the exclusion of certain social groups (2007, p. 50).

Although there are similarities between Buckler's framework and the approach taken here, they differ in their application. While Buckler explores the role of ideas in politics, a goal that invites consideration of how these ideas feature in Political Theory, this book examines the use of moral arguments in the justification of policy. As such, the 'context of theory' is not pertinent to this study and is replaced by a 'context of argumentation', which is concerned with the various modes of moral argument that are available to politicians. Meanwhile, the 'context of rhetoric' is broadened into a 'context of hegemonic competition', thus bringing to the fore the 'competitive' aspect of political discourse contained within this component of Buckler's approach. This new framework will enable us to disaggregate and reconstruct the process by which politicians select, formulate and articulate moral arguments, an aspect of political justification that – despite its prevalence in contemporary politics – has to date received little attention from scholars.

The structure of the book

A core assumption of the book is that the formulation of moral justifications is mediated by three factors, which may be said to make up a general 'context of justification'. They are a *context of ideology*, a *context of argumentation*, and a *context of hegemonic competition*, and their elaboration is the task of Part I of this volume. Chapter 1 draws on Michael Freeden's work to characterize the 'context of ideology'. Here, the key themes are the 'morphological' character of ideology, and the processes of conceptual 'decontestation' and integration that are involved in the formation of an ideological position. These features will allow us to analyse the selection of argumentative strategies in the light of two factors, namely a requirement for ideological integration or consistency, and the forms of decontestation to which those arguments might be subject.

In Chapter 2, I explore the 'context of argumentation', which demands consideration of how particular forms of moral argument may be deployed to win support for specific types of policy. Here, I introduce the three major traditions of Western moral philosophy – namely consequentialism, deontology and virtue theory – and draw on the work of Brian Barry, Ronald Dworkin and Alasdair MacIntyre to examine how each form of moral reasoning can be deployed in actual political argument. Next, Chapter 3 examines the 'context of hegemonic competition', in which the questions of how to secure advantage in moral and political 'wars of position' and achieve victory in rhetorical competitions may further influence the selection and modification of argumentative strategies. The discourse theory of Ernesto Laclau and Chantal Mouffe provides a starting-point for this discussion, which is illustrated with examples from Stuart Hall's influential analysis of Thatcherism. I also explore the role played by moral discourse in hegemonic politics, and demonstrate that it offers politicians an important weapon in the struggle for rhetorical advantage.

Chapter 4 brings together the previous three and uses this account of the 'context of justification' as a starting-point for the construction of a threefold analytical framework. This framework will enable us to disaggregate and reconstruct the process by which political actors select, adapt and utilize moral principles and arguments to promote their policies in different areas.

In Part II of the book, I employ the theoretical framework to examine the argumentative strategies that New Labour formulated across the policy areas of welfare, rights and constitutional reform, community, and foreign policy during Tony Blair's ten years as Prime Minister. These areas tend to invoke consequentialist, deontological, virtue theoretic and mixed justifications respectively, so the range of modes of moral argument considered is maximized. This approach will enable us to identify any changes in the relationship between New Labour's ideological position, its policy programmes, and the arguments it used to support them over a clearly defined period. It will also help us to explain any tensions that arise within New Labour's justificatory strategies.

Next, Chapter 5 outlines the assumptions that underpinned New Labour's ideological platform and draws on Freeden's morphological approach to examine the concepts that comprise its core cluster. These concepts are equal worth, equality of opportunity, community, and rights and responsibilities, and I explain how their meanings were decontested in relation to one other to form a coherent ideological position. The findings of this chapter supply the ideological component of the 'context of justification', which will enable me to assess the extent to which New Labour's chosen argumentative strategies in the four policy areas were consistent with its early ideological commitments. It will also allow me to identify any changes in New Labour's ideology that may have occurred during its time in government. The chapter then examines the emergence of New Labour as a hegemonic enterprise and identifies some of the similarities it shared with 'Old' Labour and Thatcherism, as well as some of the features that distinguished it.

In the following four chapters, I apply the theoretical framework elaborated in Part I to investigate how New Labour used moral principles and arguments to make the case for policy initiatives in the four areas identified above. Thus, Chapter 6 examines New Labour's case for the New Deals, which were designed primarily to realize its core value of equality of opportunity. This programme was New Labour's flagship welfare policy and was justified by means of a consequentialist argument. Meanwhile, Chapter 7 focuses on the Human Rights Act of 1998, which was an important initiative in the area of rights and constitutional reform. As we will see, New Labour offered a deontological argument to promote this policy, which invoked its core concepts of equal worth and rights and responsibilities. Chapter 8 assesses New Labour's argumentative strategy for its anti-social behaviour agenda, which resonated strongly with virtue theoretic reasoning and emphasized the values of community and reciprocal responsibility. Finally, Chapter 9 considers Blair's case for the Iraq war of 2003, which utilised mixed justifications and drew on the notions of community and human rights. In each chapter, I examine the rhetorical techniques that New Labour used to support its arguments, and assess the extent to which it succeeded in winning hegemonic advantage in the four policy areas. The book concludes with a general account of New Labour's argumentative strategy during Blair's premiership. Here, I demonstrate that the four case studies, when taken together, yield a comprehensive account of how New Labour selected, modified and applied the moral principles and arguments that constituted its justificatory strategies in the policy areas concerned. Next, I provide an overview of the argumentative strategies used by Gordon Brown's government in these areas and compare them to those employed by Blair. The book therefore offers a complete retrospective study of the strategies that New Labour utilized to promote its initiatives in the four policy areas throughout its 13 years in office. Finally, I highlight the implications of the case of New Labour for our understanding of the process of political justification.

Part I
The Context of Justification

1
The Context of Ideology

In his book *Ideologies and Political Theory*, Michael Freeden (1996) proposes a framework through which we can understand and analyse the various manifestations of ideologies in the social world. He proceeds from the assumption that the political concept is the object of study in political thought, and argues that ideologies are clusters of political concepts arranged in a distinctive way. These conceptual configurations, or 'morphologies', link together such notions as equality and justice and, in so doing, bestow upon each a decontested meaning. The process of decontestation plays a key role in Freeden's account of ideological consistency and integration. Indeed, he employs it to explain the attribution of meaning not only at the micro-level of the political concept, but also at the macro-level of the ideology itself. I begin the chapter by discussing these two levels in turn. Next, I examine the notion of ideological decontestation, and the distinction between essential and effective contestability. Finally, I consider and reject some objections to Freeden's approach.

The political concept and its constituents

Freeden defines political concepts as 'complex ideas that inject order and meaning into observed or anticipated sets of political phenomena and hold together an assortment of related notions' (1996, p. 52). As such, they are the building blocks of ideologies. Any ideology will, Freeden claims, contain all of the main political concepts, which he identifies as equality, justice, rights, liberty, democracy and power. In turn, each of these principal concepts will include such categories as a conception of moral ends, a view of social structure, a unit of political analysis, and an account of human nature. However, the interpretations attached to these components – and indeed to the concepts themselves – are not fixed. Rather, they are derived from a potentially limitless and essentially contestable assortment of meanings, and thus will exhibit a wide range of variations (Freeden, 1996, pp. 54–66).

A concept can be described as 'essentially contested' if its proper use is the subject of irresolvable controversy among its users.[1] This description certainly applies to political concepts, whose content and uses differ – to a greater or lesser extent – from one ideology to another. In Freeden's words, a concept can 'properly be designated as essentially contestable not just when the norms and values it contains are contestable, but crucially, when all or any of its components are contestable' (1996, p. 57). As a result, we need to express a cultural preference, or make an analytical judgement, regarding the elements that are to be included within a particular concept. In turn, these preferences or judgements are applicable to two essentially contestable areas, namely the range of the elements to be contained within the concept, and the indeterminacy of several of these elements, which allows them to be described in a number of different ways once they are included within that concept. For this reason, Freeden argues, we must appreciate that a concept is the 'product of various judgements concerning how to assemble and describe its components, as well as incorporating any subsequent evaluation of them' (1996, p. 58).

The question then arises of how these elements are arranged within the concept. Freeden's view is that the formation of intensions – the properties that are included in a concept – is, to a great extent, 'a matter of temporal and spatial conventions: hence our analytical judgements concerning intension may be vitally affected by our cultural preferences' (1996, p. 58).[2] In particular, these judgements about the meaning of a word or concept are influenced by the ways in which it is used. Consequently, an empirical approach is required if we are to determine meaning. As noted previously, Freeden identifies several key political concepts. To the extent that these concepts recur in both everyday and academic discourse, this tradition of usage broadly indicates the presence (or otherwise) of a given concept, but not its accepted content. It can also accommodate the possibility that new political concepts can emerge as society changes. Thus, by acknowledging this relationship between meaning and usage, Freeden's theory allows us to 'relate empirically to those concepts that exist as linguistic and cultural artefacts and that are … in reasonable general use' (1996, p. 61).

Freeden then proposes that our analysis of the morphology of political concepts should proceed from the assumption that the principal political concepts possess both ineliminable and quasi-contingent features. It is important to note, he says, that the ineliminable components are neither logically necessary to, nor inherent in, the meaning of the word to which they join, but arise from the way in which they are used in a real-world context.[3] In other words, the ineliminable component remains a constant feature of the concept in all its uses; indeed, 'to eliminate it means to fly against all known usages of the concept (though this does not rule out its removal in future)' (Freeden, 1996, p. 63). So, the ineliminable component is central to a concept only in a conventional – as opposed to a logical – sense. It is for this reason, Freeden claims, that political concepts do not possess fixed cores, though a core may be present as a structural feature (1996, pp. 53–4). However, this undifferentiated core cannot support the concept by itself; rather, the ineliminable component must be fleshed out with other elements if it is to have any meaning at all. It is at this point that the importance of the quasi-contingent constituents of a concept becomes clear.

The quasi-contingent components of the main political concepts are, Freeden writes, '*individually* dispensable, [but they] occupy *categories* that are not' (1996, p. 66). As we have seen, each political concept contains several categories, one of which is a conception of human nature. This category is a necessary component of any of the main political concepts and can include a range of contingent instances, such as self-interest, rationality, altruism and autonomy. Consequently, we can select different combinations of instances from within the various categories, and thereby assign meaning and content to the ineliminable component. However, Freeden points out that 'although the concrete instances of each category will be contingent, their broad permutations may be limited' (1996, p. 67). Thus, a conception of human nature, for example, can include only human attributes, and no others. The indeterminate variety of meanings suggested by essential contestability is, in practice, limited.

The notion of logical adjacency also serves to constrain this indefinite range of meanings. A concept is said to be logically adjacent to the ineliminable component if it is one of the necessary permutations that comes into play in any attempt to flesh out the core concept. For example, the ineliminable component of the concept of liberty is non-constraint, so some aspect of the adjacent concepts of autonomy, self-development, self-determination and power will necessarily be available to play a part in the concretization of any concept of liberty (Freeden, 1996, p. 68). If we accept that the adjacent concepts are essentially contestable, then we cannot be certain which of their constituents will be manifested within the main political concept itself. Nonetheless, the idea of quasi-contingency allows us to note that some feature of each adjacent concept will necessarily be present therein. Moreover, Freeden says, 'some instances of these logically adjacent categories will be locked into the ineliminable and integral component of the concept' (1996, p. 68). In other words, they will constitute additional elements of the concept, in whose absence the concept would be devoid of meaning. It is unclear at this point whether Freeden is discussing logical adjacency with respect to the constituents of a concept, or to those of an ideology. Given the context of the discussion, it is reasonable to assume that Freeden is referring to the former, though it will become apparent in the next section that the claims he makes here are equally applicable to the latter.

Cultural adjacency imposes additional constraints on conceptual morphology and comes in two forms. The first type of cultural adjacency functions as a constraint within the framework of logical adjacency. Freeden explains that, because the ineliminable component of the concept entails numerous additional elements, and thereby overfills the concept with more components than it can contain (due to possible conflicts between them), cultural adjacency is needed to impose limits on these logical connections and thus maintain the integrity of the concept. By doing so, it allows us both to favour one logical connection over another based on cultural preference, and to contain the practical contradictions that are present within the concept. On this basis, Freeden believes that ideologies are, to a degree, immune to logical criticism (1996, pp. 70–1). The second type of cultural adjacency refers, Freeden says, to 'elements that do not follow logically from the ineliminable components of a concept, but are regarded in ordinary usage as legitimate, if not indispensable' (1996, p. 71). For instance, a particular combination of words may contain a logical contradiction, but it is nonetheless acceptable from a cultural point of view. Similarly, cultural adjacency may permit two seemingly contradictory elements to be present within a concept, on the ground that this 'paradox' is culturally permissible. So, to sum up, cultural adjacency relates to a geographical and historical usage of language and ideas that may be either conventional or innovative.

According to Freeden, the existence of a concept is dependent upon its skeletal structure, which comprises the ineliminable component and the categories logically adjacent to it. This structure, he writes, imposes limits upon the composition of the concept, and hence is 'culturally privileged, by dint of accepted or common usage, over the other components of a political concept' (1996, p. 75). However, the presence of the skeletal structure alone is insufficient for the concept to have meaning. Rather, political concepts will acquire meaning from the ideational context in which they are found. This process is made possible by the permeable boundary of a concept, which permits the passage of ideas from its intension to its idea-environment, and vice versa. Further, the nature of this boundary means that we should understand the majority of a concept's contingent components as externalized, free-floating elements that can join onto the skeletal structure in a variety of different ways (Freeden, 1996, p. 73). It is thus that Freeden's theory can account for the variations in the meaning of a concept between different ideological formations.

The configuration of concepts, or ideology

For Freeden, any given ideology will include most – if not all – of the main political concepts, and will tie together a particular conception of moral ends, a particular view of social structure, of equality, of justice, and so on.[4] His central claim is that ideologies have a 'morphological' character and consist of core, adjacent and peripheral concepts. As is the case in conceptual morphology, the ineliminable core is a structural – as opposed to a substantial – feature of an ideology, and embodies those 'detectable features of common usage without which a particular ideology simply would not continue to be that ideology' (Freeden, 2003, p. 11). As Freeden points out, this is an assessment of the cultural and political feasibility of an ideological family, and focuses not on its novelty or its truth value, but on its discursive usefulness. Hence the core consists not of a single concept, but of a cluster of concepts whose components can be assigned greater or lesser importance by members of the same ideological family. For example, the adherents of one version of socialism will identify equality as the principal core concept of their ideology, while the proponents of other variants will emphasize creativity, welfare, or the achievement of species-being. Nonetheless, all four of these concepts may be present in different versions of the core cluster of socialism (Freeden, 1996, p. 84). So, Seliger writes, the 'formation of doctrines that go together with the formation of parties requires adjustments between the beliefs of constituent members or groups', a process that continues in perpetuity (1976, pp. 98–9).

Freeden terms the dispute over the internal weighting of the distinguishing core concepts of an ideology 'flexible coherence'. In this context, ideas become coherent by virtue of their firm attachment to each other, and not necessarily because they are rationally consistent. These morphological compatibilities are explicable in terms of convention, experience, cultural preferences, and perhaps even fear. For this reason, Freeden writes, coherence 'requires interpretation in the light of plausible links, connections and interdependencies [between concepts], all the while acknowledging the multiple logical paths such coherence can take' (2005, p. 4).[5] In other words, we should understand the relationships between the components of an ideology in terms of logical and cultural adjacency. The location of concepts within a single ideological system may also be contested. Freeden explains that, in some variations of a particular ideology, a concept may initially have been part of the core but, over time, has travelled to a peripheral location. Other versions of the same ideology, in contrast, may retain this concept in their core (1996, p. 84). Consequently, the cores of an ideology are structurally necessary, but their contents are not fixed.

For Freeden, it is important to note that to identify some concepts, opinions and ideas as peripheral 'is not to pronounce upon their importance as ideas and values. It is simply a statement about their structural positioning within a given ideological morphology' (2003, p. 3). Indeed, these concepts can play a vital role in the composition of an ideology, as the core concepts acquire their unique content through their relationship to the concepts adjacent to them. It is at this point that the importance of logical and cultural adjacency in the process of decontestation becomes clear. As Freeden explains, the numerous 'skeletal or "thin" concepts develop elements, both logically and culturally, that form overlapping and shared areas, which then react back on their separate ineliminable components to constitute full but mutually dependent concepts' (1996, p. 78). This interdependence gives an ideology its distinctive character, for an ideology – like a concept – possesses concept-categories that are logically and culturally necessary for its continued existence, though the specific instances of these categories are once more contingent.

Freeden divides the peripheral elements of an ideology into two types. The first is the margin, which comprises those concepts and ideas that are of little emotional and intellectual importance relative to the core. Because a concept may travel from the margin to the core and vice versa, changes on the level of significance are frequently 'longer term arrangements, reflecting accumulative changes, though they may occasionally be triggered off by cataclysmic events in the non-ideational environment of an ideology' (Freeden, 1996, pp. 78–9). A marginal idea or concept may sometimes be detrimental to an ideology, as nationalization was to the projects of socialist governments in the West. Alternatively, a concept may be on the margin of an ideology only because other ideologies have forced it to be so; its presence there is accepted grudgingly.

The second peripheral element is the perimeter, which consists of those concepts and ideas that 'straddle the interface between the conceptualisation of social realities and the external contexts and concrete manifestations in and through which those conceptualisations occur' (Freeden, 1996, p. 79). In other words, they link the concepts that comprise an ideology to the social world. The perimeter components are often policy-proposals or ideas, as opposed to complete concepts, and they may be both particular and ephemeral. However, this specificity allows them to function both as channels for the cultural limitations that affect ideological morphology, and as 'conduits of structural and logical constraints already available in the ideological grouping in question, through which social facts and concrete events are construed' (Freeden, 1996, p. 80). In this way, the perimeter performs a vital function in the process of assigning a decontested meaning to the constituent concepts of an ideology.

According to Freeden, the perimeter demands that, for an ideology to have relevance, it should accommodate, and attempt to influence the course of, actual events. By doing so, an ideology acts as a bridge between the realms of political philosophy and political action, thereby fulfilling one of its primary purposes. It is also possible for an institution, event, or practice to be absorbed into the ideology via the perimeter. This process is vital to the decontestation of the core and, to a lesser degree, of the adjacent concepts. While these concepts afford an ideology the flexibility it needs if it is to survive, the perimeter components allow the ideology to acquire relevance for the real world, to incorporate and respond to social change, and to supply the high level of precision needed to understand the core and adjacent concepts (Freeden, 1996, pp. 76–80).

The process of decontestation

For Freeden, the process of decontestation is the ideological response to conceptual indeterminacy, on the ground that it aims to assign a specific meaning to each of the concepts contained within a given ideology. Decontestation is effected primarily through logical and cultural adjacency and involves, Freeden says, the rotation of each of the concepts in an ideology 'through a range of meanings until one of those meanings is held *vis-à-vis* the similarly held, or decontested, meanings of every other concept' (1996, p. 83). Any available meanings that are logically and/or culturally incompatible with those of the other concepts present within the ideology are therefore rejected. Perhaps the most important aspect of ideological morphology is the lack of definite boundaries dividing the components of ideological systems. This fluidity means that different ideologies can use the same idea in different ways, thereby giving rise to such ideological hybrids as liberal socialism and conservative liberalism.[6] On this basis, Freeden argues that any attempt to compartmentalize ideologies into 'prefabricated categories called socialism or liberalism flies in the face of the evidence' (1996, p. 88).

While morphology plays a key role in the process of decontestation, it is not the only factor involved. As Freeden puts it, 'the morphology of an ideology is not a hermetically sealed network of conceptual relationships' (1996, p. 96), and is, therefore, open to such external influences as the temporal and cultural context in which the ideology is situated. Freeden identifies four reasons why history is important to the analyst of ideologies, the first of which is that history – like geography – supplies the context necessary for the concretization of the meanings of political concepts and ideologies. As we have seen, this process occurs via the ideas and concepts on the perimeter. Second, the inclusion of history allows us to recognize that the main political concepts are heavily laden with associations, prejudices and debates that often go back to ancient times, all of which influence and contribute to their meanings. These two reasons are based, Freeden says, on an understanding of history as a 'concrete framework within which meaning can be located' (1996, p. 99).

Freeden's third ground for claiming a key role for history in the analysis of ideologies is that the idea of change is itself a sociopolitical concept that is included within the intension of an ideology. The notion of progress, for example, will influence the process of change within an ideology, reacting with other adjacent concepts to form a particular interpretation of rationality, liberty, or welfare. For this reason, a conservative idea of gradual change will either stem the development of adjacent concepts, or view them through the lens of organic change. Fourth, Freeden continues, 'broad theories of history may themselves be a factor affecting the configurations of political concepts,' and thus will influence the way in which these concepts are decontested (1996, p. 99). Underpinning both of these reasons is the assumption that history is a value-laden, abstract concept that affixes itself to an ideological configuration and influences the meanings of the concepts adjacent to it.

The cultural context in which an ideology is situated also plays a vital part in the process of decontestation, on the ground that it forms the basis of the notion of cultural adjacency. On Freeden's view, culture consists of customs, beliefs, discourses, institutional patterns, systems of ethics, technologies, and dominant theories. An ideology is inextricably embedded in this context and, as a result, its morphology mirrors the 'social practices of conversation and discourse in which individuals participate with variable, and mutually shaped, input' (Freeden, 1996, p. 107). This wide individual variation, together with the numerousness of these practices, can also explain the broad variations that exist within the dominant ideational and structural type of the ideology concerned. In this way, it allows us to appreciate that cultural factors are fundamental both to the essential contestability of concepts and to their decontestation. So, to sum up, the meanings of both ideologies and the main political concepts are decontested, and ultimately obtained, on the three dimensions of space, time and morphology.

Essential and effective contestability

The discussion so far highlights the important role played by the claim that concepts are contestable in Freeden's morphological account of ideology. However, the question arises of how we are to understand this notion of contestability, and the present section seeks to address it. Christine Swanton defines the essential contestability thesis as follows:

> ECT: There are certain key concepts in political argument, which are essentially such that they both (a) admit of a variety of interpretations, and (b) are disputable. (1980, pp. 813–14)

This is a philosophical definition of essential contestability, according to which the possibility of disagreement is inherent in the concept. The interpretative claim that ECT offers can be strengthened, Newey writes, by Mason's *reasonable disagreement thesis*:

> RDT: The concepts' interpretations may be (a) mutually inconsistent (b) individually reasonable, and (c) such that there is none which is justifiably regarded as superior to its rivals. (quoted in Newey, 2001, p. 247)

However, Newey argues that RDT is seriously flawed because it contravenes plausible limits on the conditions of concept-possession. Further, he claims, it effectively depends upon either an 'esoteric doctrine which short-circuits the thesis's original explanatory rationale, or on an error theory which cannot do the explanatory job the thesis requires' (2001, p. 245). I now outline these objections in turn.

Newey begins his first argument by suggesting that a convincing account of the criteria that anyone who is in possession of a particular concept *C* needs to meet should include the following:

> *P*: It is a necessary condition of the distinctness of any given concept *C* that it is individuated by its possession-condition(s). (2001, p. 248)

On the basis of this claim, it follows from the distinctness of any particular concept *C* that any person who possesses *C* does so by fulfilling a set of possession-conditions that is unique to it. Newey then demonstrates the plausibility of *P* by assuming, contrary to this assumption, that there are two different concepts that share the same set of possession-condition(s). In this case, there is a single set of possession-conditions, by virtue of which we can say that a person has mastered both concepts. If the concepts are distinct, however, their distinctness must, at least in theory, be apparent in specific in-principle possible situations. As Newey explains, this distinctness might become manifest when two competent concept-users assign different truth-values to 'pairs of propositions differing only in that the term(s) referring to *C* are uniformly replaced by one(s) referring to another concept *C'*, or vice versa'. But if this is the case, the possession-conditions cannot supply a complete account of concept-mastery because they relate indifferently to both *C* and *C'*, and thus cannot supply – even in theory – an account of 'differential recognition by concept-users of those conditions in which one concept, but not the other, applies' (Newey, 2001, p. 248). On Newey's view, the concepts cannot fulfil the possession-conditions outlined in *P* because the use of possession-conditions to differentiate between concepts is incompatible with ECT. Even if we assume that two people with conflicting definitions of the concept both satisfy the same set of possession-conditions for the concept concerned, they will still differ in a range of dispositions, which may include the concept's referent or 'patterns of assent to sample propositions referring to the concept under dispute.' But for each party to the disagreement, continues Newey, we can extrude a different concept, which is defined in such a way that *its* set of possession-conditions replicates those of the concept the party is referring to – the concept in question 'simply being *defined* as that whose possession-conditions give rise to the differential patterns of assent and dissent' (2001, p. 249). However, they will differ from each other, so the concept that ECT defines as contested will not, against *P*, be distinguished by its possession-conditions.

Newey's second argument against ECT centres on its explanatory redundancy. He begins by assuming that two people disagree about a matter of justice, and asks how we can say that they are disagreeing over a single concept *justice*, and not simply talking past one another. There may, he suggests, be a 'common conceptual core to justice, in virtue of which both can be said to have provided a theory of justice' – an example of which could be 'the procedures which should govern the methods for determining the holdings of scarce goods in society' (2001, p. 249). It therefore follows that if the conflict is to be about a single concept *justice*, then we need to assign to this concept an essential core. However, if we accept both this view and the claim that there were other features of the concept about which the two parties disagreed, it does not follow that *justice* is essentially contestable. The possibility of disagreement would need to be integral to the concept, as a constituent part of its essence. If this were the case, the ECT thesis states that the two parties would either have to agree that the alternative interpretation was possible, or face changing the subject, in which case the concept would cease to be contestable. The only way the parties could fail to reach an agreement is by being in error, or by being ignorant of the character of the concept. If *justice* is an essentially contested concept, it is so by virtue of certain properties which entail the possibility of disagreement. If we deny this possibility, Newey argues, we also deny the claim of the ECT theorists that *justice* possesses certain essential properties, and so 'the concept of which the parties' conceptions *are* conceptions cannot be identical with that which those theorists have in view' (2001, p. 250).

It seems, therefore, that ECT cannot provide us with a satisfactory account of political disagreement. If the claim that the thesis is explanatorily redundant is correct, Newey says, it must be dependent upon an esoteric doctrine. This is the case irrespective of whether it is read as ECT or RDT. If it is RDT, he argues, then the fact that it sanctions numerous interpretations will be unable to account for the parties' perception that they are disagreeing, as opposed to arriving at a difference without disagreement. Alternatively, if it is read as ECT, and there is one interpretation that is more reasonable than its rivals, then a difference of this kind would not arise, given that the parties should agree on that; by hypothesis, there are more compelling grounds to adopt this interpretation than any of its rivals. However, any failure to recognize this entails the use of an error theory which will necessarily *not* employ the explanatory thesis itself. Thus, the explanatory power of the thesis can be maintained only by an esoteric doctrine. Such a doctrine consists of W.B. Gallie's philosophical claim concerning the structure of the contested concepts, namely that they are inherently evaluative; they can be used both defensively and aggressively; they possess manifold criteria of application, the relative weightings of which are debatable or unclear; and so on. 'In its efforts to understand the political', concludes Newey, 'the thesis in fact succeeds in moving the locus of explanation out of the political and into the philosophical realm' (2001, p. 252).

In response to Newey's arguments, Freeden changed his position and now endorses a political notion of contestability, which he terms 'effective contestability' (EFC). He explains that a concept can be described as effectively contestable because its contestability is not an essential characteristic of the concept, but a feature of political discourse. If this contestability were eliminated, then the discourse and its constituent concepts would be fixed in a way that both deviates from past practices and is unimaginable in any future practice. Such a development would effect fundamental changes in the nature of the political discourse in question, insofar as its distinguishing properties would be destroyed and it would therefore cease to be recognizable as a political discourse. For this reason, Freeden claims, the effective contestability thesis 'is as strong a statement [for the student of politics] as EC is for the logician' (2004, p. 5).

Freeden offers three arguments in support of EFC, the first of which he terms the 'argument from history'. Here, Freeden asserts that the circumstances in which political decisions are made will never be identical, and that the political realm is always changing. It therefore follows that to concur with Gallie's view that historical understandings are a divergence from an exemplar is to accept the assumptions that any given political concept has a definite origin, and that any changes in its meaning will defile its original purity. The first of these assumptions falls down, Freeden claims, because it is impossible to identify the precise moment at which a concept emerged. Meanwhile, the second assumption appeals to the idea of authenticity. Here, Freeden notes that arguments from replication are taken from scientists, who carry out experiments with the aim of replicating a particular finding. Political discourse, in contrast, is impossible to replicate; indeed, Freeden argues, experiments in deliberative democracy can only succeed if researchers hold too many variables constant, and found their case on the macroanalysis of concepts while ignoring their micro-analysis. Hence the overlapping consensus that the proponents of deliberative democracy both aspire to, and claim to create collapses under close examination and, further, relies on a refusal to pursue arguments beyond a given point (Freeden, 2004, pp. 8–9).

The 'argument from context' is Freeden's second argument in support of EFC. While the argument from history is founded on the premise that the passage of time is an objective phenomenon, this second argument appeals to our *experience* of time, in which the human memory performs an extremely selective role. On this basis, Freeden claims, we can say that both temporal and spatial contexts are to a certain extent the outcome of agency, which is relatively unknown to us. The first clause of this statement suggests that political discourses and concepts are situated within environments that are chosen, rather than given. Although spatial and temporal environments exist objectively, Freeden writes, these environments nonetheless contain 'infinite numbers of factors among which we have to choose when constructing our thoughts' (2004, p. 9). Political concepts, therefore, are always found in this context rather than in another, and even in this holism rather than in another.

In light of the permeability of the perimeter of a concept and its role in allowing actual events to affect the core, the flexibility of context supports the EFC thesis. When interpreting a particular concept or discourse, we need to choose a context in which to do so. If we do not make this decision, we neglect the other contexts in which the concept or discourse can acquire rather different meanings. Given that these contexts do not disappear even if we ignore them, Freeden claims that the choice between them is effectively contestable; after all, neither has, as yet, been proved either wrong or mistaken. The EFC thesis is thus partially dependent on an 'as yet' condition, but this is an inevitable consequence of ineliminability. As Freeden explains, the 'as yet' condition is not an expectation but a part of speech, and 'were the effective contestability of this example to be made eliminable, the world would be unrecognisable and assume the features of a laboratory' (2004, p. 9).

The choice of context is not entirely ours, however, given that the second clause of Freeden's statement posits contexts unbeknown to us. This clause gives expression to the central claim of hermeneutics, which states that, through the process of recontextualization, we can discover within a discourse or text meanings hitherto concealed from its author. In this case, the EFC thesis is concerned with the inevitability of the emergence of many different readings of the text or discourse, both over space and time and within any given moment. This ineliminability suggests, Freeden says, that we can only envisage 'the impossibility of conferring on a political discourse a new reading, or a reading that is not identical to a previous one' in a 'laboratory of thought-experiments' (2004, p. 10).

Freeden calls his third argument for EFC the 'argument from ambiguity'. He begins by stating that, contrary to popular belief, the term 'ambiguity' does not apply only to situations in which a particular word has different meanings attached to it, an example of which is 'band' (denoting a musical group or a ring). This misunderstanding arose because analytical philosophers, in regarding ambiguity as a failure of either reasoning or defining, and aiming to substitute precision for ambiguity, overlook the fact that the construction of ambiguity is a crucial characteristic of political discourse. The outcome is effectively contestable insofar as rallying people to a cause is a key political activity, and insofar as a multiplicity of ideas and opinions is a characteristic of political societies. Ambiguity, therefore, 'is not only the inevitable by-product of polysemy, but it is a recipe for political co-existence' (Freeden, 2004, p. 10). From this perspective, Freeden claims, the argumentative and articulatory precision that many philosophers wish to impose upon political thought serves not to promote consensus, but to worsen disagreement. The level of precision they seek results in the sharp demarcation of positions in both substantive and methodological terms, and the likelihood of political conflict is increased dramatically as a result. For Freeden, the fact that words can contain many, related but different meanings is vital for the proper functioning of ideological and political orders. 'And if we are still justifiably concerned about political conflict', Freeden writes, 'the challenge becomes the humanising of conflict, not its impossible elimination' (2004, p. 10).

Overall, it is clear that EFC thesis yields a better account of political disagreement than does ECT. This is because EFC can accommodate the particularity of space and time, the locations in which actual political debate happens, and, in so doing, removes the notion of contestability from the abstract realm of analytic philosophy and makes it applicable in a political context. Furthermore, EFC enables Freeden to demonstrate that there are 'additional methods of claiming that political concepts are contestable in indefeasible, permanent ways, without having to fall back on a notion of essentialism' (2004, p. 7). This new anti-essentialist approach to the study of ideology neutralizes the conflict that previously existed between Freeden's analysis and discourse theory, and thus enables me to use both perspectives in this book. Chapter 3 draws on discourse theory to examine the 'context of hegemonic competition', but in the meantime, I discuss some criticisms of Freeden's theory.

Some objections to Freeden's approach

A critic of the morphological approach is Mark Bevir, who objects that Freeden's model of ideologies is reified and, as a result, exhibits two major problems. First, Bevir argues, Freeden's definition of ideologies as sets of concepts leads him to describe any given ideology by matching its components with the core elements of a range of traditions and ideologies. Although this model is flexible, and thus enables us to provide a detailed and subtle description of a particular ideology, Bevir asserts that the question of how to explain its ideas remains unanswered. Surely, he asks, we cannot simply assume that a particular ideology took its components from the traditions Freeden specifies? Bevir's second claim is that even if we give an affirmative response to this question, we would still not know why the ideology concerned adopted this particular combination of concepts rather than another. Given that Freeden views an ideology as a collection of concepts that can be joined together in various ways, Bevir continues, he concentrates on explicating how they have been combined. Further, because the constituent components of the ideology are 'static, albeit contested,' they appear to determine, or at least impose limits on, the combinations that are available. 'Surely,' asks Bevir, 'people can reject concepts, modify old ones and create new ones in unlimited ways?' (2000, p. 281).

However, Bevir's first objection is founded on the incorrect belief that Freeden asks us to accept that the proponents of any given ideology have simply taken elements from existing traditions and joined them together to form a new one. After all, it is clear from the preceding discussion that Freeden is fully aware that ideologies develop and change over time. This awareness is apparent in both the important role that Freeden assigns to history in his description of the process of decontestation, and in his account of the process by which the new ideological cluster of multiculturalism emerged.[7] As Freeden explains, this development occurred in response to changes relating to 'practices involving liberty' – in this case the free movement of individuals – that took place at the periphery of liberalism and were impelled by 'draconian restrictions on the recent waves of economic and political migrants from countries that are poor and that are suffering political upheaval' (2003, p. 5). From this explanation, it is clear that Freeden views multiculturalism as an offshoot of liberalism that emerged in response to changes in the social world, and not as a construct that its proponents assembled from various elements of existing ideologies.

Bevir's second objection, which states that Freeden views as static the constituent components of an ideology, is also founded on a misrepresentation of the morphological approach. As noted above, Freeden holds that concepts can change in both their content and their position within the ideological system, due to such factors as effective contestability, human agency, and spatial and historical circumstance. He also claims that ideologies 'construct fleeting, temporary and strictly circumscribed consistencies out of more fundamental, abstract and purist inconsistencies' (2000, p. 13). On this basis, Freeden explains, we should understand an ideology as an 'internal arena of competition, indeterminacy and uncertainty over the key meanings of the political values and concepts with which it engages' (1999, p. 50). If we take these claims together, it is clear that Freeden does not view the constituents of an ideology as static, and that Bevir's charge of reification is therefore unfounded.

If we accept Freeden's argument that the constituent concepts of ideologies are not static, and his claim that there is 'constant intercourse between political conceptualisation and the real world to which it relates and from which it springs' (1996, p. 39), then a further problem seems to arise. As we have seen, Freeden holds that the perimeter components of an ideology are often ideas and policy-proposals. So, by introducing new policy programmes, a political party will effect changes in the perimeter of their ideology. These new initiatives will, in turn, need to be decontested in relation to their neighbouring concepts if inconsistency within the ideology is to be kept to a minimum. As a result, the periphery is in a state of constant flux, though the degree of change that occurs in the core cluster may be negligible. Given this high degree of mutability, any attempt to pin down and analyse an ideology would appear difficult, if not impossible.

Freeden resolves this apparent problem in his discussion of methodology. He asserts that we need to superimpose 'diachronic on synchronic analysis and multiple synchrony on the examination of a single system' if we are to fully appreciate the role played by temporal, spatial and cultural factors in the attribution of meaning to a given ideology (1996, p. 5). More specifically, we can use diachronic analysis to trace the history of the meaning of political concepts, while 'the continuity of an ideological tradition – which is assumed, rightly or wrongly, by the continuity of the words that denote those concepts – can only be put to the test by examining multiple synchronic states, over time and space (Freeden, 1996, p. 52). Such an examination will enable us to pin down an ideology at various stages of its development, and consequently to map its morphology. These snapshots can then be compared and any changes investigated, taking into account the impact of events occurring in the social world. This in turn will allow us to analyse ideological systems while still recognizing their extreme mutability. In the following chapter, we will see how the requirements of argumentation – which are themselves part of the social realm – may supply additional reference points for decontestation.

2
The Context of Argumentation

The 'context of argumentation' is concerned with the way in which different modes of argument may be utilized to promote specific types of policy. This aspect of justification encompasses the three main forms of moral argument, namely consequentialism, deontology and virtue theory. From a philosophical perspective, each of these approaches claims to offer an exhaustive account of our moral judgements. However, the purpose of this chapter is to examine the use of moral language within the political arena, where such arguments have currency regardless of whether they give an adequate description of moral justification. Thus, the first section provides the standard definitions of consequentialism, deontology and virtue theory that moral philosophers would accept, while the following three sections draw on the work of Barry, Dworkin and MacIntyre to explore how each theory may be employed in actual political argument.

The three major traditions of Western moral philosophy

Consequentialism states that the rightness of an act is determined by whether it brings about the best consequences, as judged from an impartial perspective that gives equal consideration to the interests of all (Scheffler, 1988, p. 1). Most of the theories in this family share the following five features. First, they are welfarist, meaning that they are concerned with the welfare of human beings. The term 'welfare' can be understood in a number of different ways, with Jeremy Bentham and the early utilitarians defining it in terms of pain and pleasure. However, many contemporary theorists favour a broader notion of welfare that emphasizes the living of a fulfilling life. Second, the theories are consequentialist, in the sense that the moral worth of any action is always found in the consequences it produces. As Bernard Williams writes, 'it is by reference to their consequences that actions, and indeed such things as institutions, laws and practices, are to be justified if they can be justified at all' (1973, p. 79). The third feature shared by consequentialist moral theories is the notion that welfare can be aggregated. In other words, it is possible to calculate the welfare of all human beings to yield an overall total. Fourth, consequentialism incorporates a maximization component, which states that agents should maximize the net balance of welfare within their society. This element is linked to the consequentialist criterion of rightness, so we can say that the greater the amount of welfare an action produces, the better it is. Fifth, consequentialists endorse the notion of universalism, according to which every person's interest counts in equal measure. In James Rachels's words, 'no one's happiness is to be counted as more important than anyone else's. Each person's welfare is equally important' (1999, p. 107).

Deontology, meanwhile, states that an action is morally good if, and only if, it is performed from a sense of duty. Central to this theory is Immanuel Kant's notion of the categorical imperative, an unconditional requirement for action from which our moral duties are derived. The categorical imperative has several formulations, the first of which is 'I ought never to act except in such a way that I could also will that my maxim should become a universal law' (Kant, 1997, p. 15). In other words, an act is only permissible if the maxim on which it is based is acceptable to all rational agents. Thus, the maxim 'always keep promises' is universally applicable because we can imagine everyone acting on it, while the maxim 'make false promises if it is convenient to do so' yields an impossible situation when we try to universalize it, and is therefore prohibited. Kant's second formulation of the categorical imperative demands 'So act that you use humanity, whether in your own person or in the person of any other, always at the same time as an end, never merely as a means' (1997, p. 38). Here, 'humanity' denotes the particular qualities that characterize us as human, such as autonomy and rationality, and we are required to acknowledge and respect it in all persons including ourselves. In this way, persons are distinguished from things, which *can* be regarded as means to an end. As Roger Scruton notes, this distinction forms the basis of the notion of a 'right'. So, if someone asks if a stone or a rabbit, for instance, has rights, they are asking whether this second version of the categorical imperative applies to it (2001, p. 86). The third formulation of the categorical imperative is 'the idea of the will of every rational being as a will giving universal law' (Kant, 1997, p. 40). This version emphasizes our status as makers – as opposed to followers – of universal laws. In giving such laws, we act as free, rational beings, while the laws themselves obligate us to respect the rationality and autonomy of others. It is this freedom to make laws that Kant identifies as 'the ground of the dignity of human nature and of every rational nature' (1997, p. 43).

Deontologists also hold that the right and the good are distinct, with the former being prior to the latter. Indeed, as Geoffrey Scarre points out, contemporary deontological theories tend to emphasize concepts of natural rights over concepts of duty. This tendency is clearly evident in popular moral and political discourse, in which notions of rights – both individual and collective – are now firmly embedded. However, rights are accompanied by obligations, and we must accept these limits on our freedom of action in exchange for the privilege of exercising our rights. For instance, an individual's right to life imposes on others the obligation not to kill him, even if doing so might, in some situations, prevent the occurrence of a greater evil (Scarre, 1996, p. 12). The pairing of rights and obligations is also a feature of many international human rights instruments, one example being the American Convention on Human Rights. This document commits its signatories to uphold a range of rights and freedoms, including the right to humane treatment (Article 5) and the right to freedom of association (Article 16), and to protect them against abuse. In return, Article 32 of the Convention provides that every individual has responsibilities to their family, their community and to all of humankind and, further, that 'the rights of each person are limited by the rights of others, by the security of all, and by the just demands of the general welfare, in a democratic society' (Organization of American States, 1969).

Virtue theory is characterized by its emphasis on the 'virtuous individual and on those inner traits, dispositions, and motives that qualify her as being virtuous' (Slote, 1997, p. 177). These features set it apart from consequentialism and deontology, which focus primarily on the rightness or wrongness of an action, and consider the qualities of the moral agent only derivatively. Consequently, the virtue theorist is primarily interested in the question 'What sort of person should I be?' while that of 'Which action should I perform?' matters only because the action concerned expresses a particular virtue or vice. An early proponent of virtue ethics was Aristotle, who based his approach on the 'doctrine of the mean.' According to this doctrine, a virtue is a 'mean between two vices, that which depends on excess and that which depends on defect' (Aristotle, 1998, p. 39). So, the virtue of courage, for example, is the mean between rashness (an excess of confidence) and cowardice (a lack of confidence). The individual who chooses the mean is fulfilling their proper function (*telos*) as a human being, which for Aristotle is *eudaimonia*, or 'flourishing,' and on this basis is classed as virtuous.[1] Hence, we can define a virtue as 'a character trait a human being needs to flourish or live well' (Hursthouse, 1997, p. 219).

The use of consequentialist reasoning in political argument

Consequentialism encourages us to think about politics principally in terms of policy. This is because its maximization component provides a set of conditions for assessing the moral acceptability of policy programmes and political institutions. The quantity of welfare these policies and institutions produce can thus be calculated, and their moral worth evaluated, on the basis of whether they maximize the balance of welfare in society. In this way, the expediency that underpins consequentialism makes it appear 'conducive to the "worldly" aspect of political judgement' (Buckler, 1993, p. 59). However, the theory has a number of limitations, which make it unsuitable for promoting initiatives in *all* areas of policy. These difficulties are discussed in the following two sections, but first it is necessary to examine how consequentialist strategies may be employed in political argument.

As Williams observes, a central feature of consequentialist reasoning 'lies in maximising *expectation*, the product of the size of the pay-off and its probability' (1981, p. 61). Given that the pay-offs in the political arena are – or can easily be believed to be – very substantial, the probability that a specific pay-off will actually materialize can be relatively minimal. As a result, a state may infringe the rights of its citizens for the sake of a hypothetical situation that is unlikely ever to arise. Underlying Williams's claim is the suggestion that a mismatch can – and indeed does – occur between a politician's rhetoric and the outcome of a particular policy. This in turn reveals the close connection between the 'context of argumentation' and the requirements of hegemonic competition. After all, politicians need to convince the public that their policy programmes will have a larger pay-off than those of their rivals *and* that this pay-off is likely to materialize. To this end, they reinforce their chosen consequentialist argument with a number of rhetorical strategies, which typically include forms of coercion, representation and misrepresentation.

The increased emphasis on outcomes in public morality stems from the weakening of particular action-centred restrictions which, in other circumstances, would act as constraints. According to Thomas Nagel, this increased latitude concerning means entails that it is legitimate for governments to 'design institutions whose aim is to produce certain desirable results on a large scale, and to define roles in those institutions whose responsibility is mainly to further those results' (1991, p. 84). So, decisions made in the public arena will be more heavily consequentialist than those made by private individuals, given that political actors have to weigh up consequences of a far greater magnitude than those demanded by private morality. This is due primarily to the increased number of people who have a stake in the outcome of a politician's decisions, and for whom an ill-considered act could have devastating effects. The need to secure hegemonic advantage is once more of relevance here, on the ground that a wrong decision could lead to a politician's competence being called into question. Depending on its gravity, such an error could create a lack of confidence in their party, and even result in electoral defeat. It is therefore imperative that political actors should, as far as possible, consider the consequences of their judgements and actions for their party and the public alike.

Brian Barry offers an influential account of the use of consequentialist reasoning in political argument, which centres on the distinction between ideal-regarding and want-regarding principles. This distinction is founded on the ways in which people's wants are dealt with in the context of social evaluation, and not on the specific content of those wants. Hence, the 'wants' discussed here may be of any type, including the highest spiritual or personal ideals (Barry, 1973, p. 136). According to Barry, ideal-regarding principles 'rank the satisfaction of some wants higher than the satisfaction of others even if the preferences of the person whose wants are in question are different' (1990, p. 287). More specifically, they comprise both those principles which assign all value to the satisfaction of wants while simultaneously excluding some wants as lacking a claim to satisfaction,[2] and those which assign value to something wholly independent of wants, such as people's characters, beliefs, or tastes. It is important to note, however, that the ideals Barry refers to are those of the person who is carrying out the evaluation of people's wants, and not of the people involved (1990, p. xliv). So, an evaluator may assign a high value to a particular want, even if the majority of the people considered have given it a low value. A practical illustration of this point is the mismatch that can occur between the issue that a politician identifies as their party's top priority, and that which is chosen by the voters themselves.

Meanwhile, Barry defines want-regarding principles as those which:

> Take as given the wants which people happen to have and concentrate attention entirely on the extent to which a certain policy will alter the overall amount of want-satisfaction or the way in which the policy will affect the distribution among people of opportunities for satisfying wants. (1990, p. 38)

In assessing the degree of want-satisfaction, all satisfied wants are assigned equal weight, with no distinction made between an individual's higher social or personal ideals and their more vulgar desires. Bentham's version of utilitarianism, which propounds the notion that 'pushpin is as good as poetry, the quantities of pleasure being the same,' supplies an example of Barry's want-regarding theory in action (quoted in Barry, 1990, p. 39).

The distinction between want- and ideal-regarding principles can be illustrated by reference to the Conservative policy of extending private ownership of housing through the 'Right to Buy' scheme. Under this scheme, council tenants were given the opportunity to buy their homes from their local authority at a reduced price. In Barry's terms, we can say that the argument to sell this policy was based on the want-regarding principle expressed in the Conservatives' belief that the majority of citizens wished to own their own homes; and on the ideal-regarding principle that:

> A property-owning democracy with a stake in the country is in various respects better (i.e. more stable, more politically independent and so forth) than a society in which all or most of the housing is owned by the State or by the municipalities. (Day, 1968, p. 595)

A further example can be found in Margaret Thatcher's case for the Falklands war of 1982, which was founded on the want-regarding principle that the islanders wished to remain under British rule, and the ideal-regarding principle that it is better for a nation to defend its sovereign territory against aggression than to allow such action to go unchallenged.

Want-regarding principles can be further classified into aggregative and distributive principles. As Barry explains,

> An aggregative principle is one which mentions only the total amount of want-satisfaction among the members of a reference

group, whereas a distributive principle requires for its statement a mention of the way in which want-satisfaction is to be divided among the members of a reference group. (1990, p. 43)[3]

On Barry's view, the core principle of consequentialism, according to which the total welfare of a particular society should be maximized, is an aggregative principle, as are the principles of the common good and the public interest. Distributive principles, meanwhile, include goods such as freedom, equality, justice and equity (1990, p. 287), as well as resources like food, money and healthcare. A distributive principle may state, for instance, that all members of a particular group should receive an equal amount of want-satisfaction, or that no group member should fall below a specified minimum level of want-satisfaction. These principles are often invoked in politicians' efforts to promote policy initiatives; indeed, the former was present in the case for the free nursery education entitlement for all three- and four-year olds in Britain, while the latter was clearly evident in the arguments for the minimum income guarantee for pensioners. Finally, distributive principles may stipulate that some of the group members will have their wants satisfied only if they fulfil certain criteria. A principle of this kind is at work in the university admissions system, which demands that prospective students achieve the requisite grades if they are to secure a place on their chosen degree programme.

It is important to note that although Barry intends his theory to provide a general account of political argumentation, I use it to illustrate a particular mode of argument. Indeed, the two other forms of moral argument considered here cannot be reduced to Barry's framework, and I examine their role in political justification in the remainder of this chapter.

How deontological arguments are employed in politics

At the core of deontology lies the Kantian conception of the person as a rational being, whose inherent dignity is based on the autonomy that enables them to be both the originator and the subject of universal law. This conception of the self has been adopted and developed by such thinkers as John Rawls and plays a key role in deontological arguments in contemporary politics. Rawls envisages the person as 'both free and equal, as capable of acting both reasonably and rationally, and therefore as capable of taking part in social co-operation among persons so conceived' (1980, p. 518). This moral being possesses two moral powers, namely the capacity for a sense of justice and the capacity to form, modify and rationally pursue their own conception of the good.[4] Correspondingly, such persons are motivated by highest-order interests in the realization and exercise of these powers. As we will see below, this Kantian conception of the person is used to ground human rights, as well as certain freedoms, and to justify social institutions.

Deontologists claim that all human beings possess moral powers, regardless of such contingent factors as their gender, religion, or nationality. Consequently, the Kantian conception of the person provides a solid basis for universal human rights, which include the right to life, the right to a fair trial, and the right to respect for private and family life. The Kantian position also lends strong support to arguments in favour of intervention in those states that violate the human rights of their citizens. In such situations, the rights of individual citizens can override the right of the state to freedom from outside interference, and intervention is therefore justifiable on humanitarian grounds.[5] These issues are beyond the scope of the present discussion, but I return to them in Chapter 9. In the meantime, I consider Ronald Dworkin's formal definition of rights, according to which individual rights are political trumps that individuals possess.

On Dworkin's view, individuals have rights when, for whatever reason, a collective goal either cannot supply sufficient justification for denying them the opportunity to pursue their own particular conception of the good, or does not constitute a satisfactory justification for causing them to suffer a loss or injury (2005, p. xi). These rights can be absolute; for example, a political theory, which views as absolute the right to freedom of speech, will deny that there is any reason for failing to secure the requisite liberty for every individual, unless it is impossible for it to do so. Rights can also be less than absolute. After all, situations can arise in which one principle might be defeated by another, or even by an urgent political policy with which it disagrees on particular facts. Likewise, collective rights may be, but are not necessarily, absolute. This is because a community may simultaneously pursue a number of different goals, and it may need to compromise one of those goals for the sake of another (Dworkin, 2005, pp. 91–2).

Dworkin claims we can define the weight of a non-absolute right as its capacity to hold up against competition from other rights and goals; indeed, the definition of a right entails that it cannot be defeated by all social objectives. For the sake of simplicity, Dworkin claims, we may decide not to refer to a political aim as a right unless it possesses a specific threshold weight against collective goals more generally;

unless, for instance, it can be outweighed only by a goal of exceptional urgency, and not by appeal to any of the routine objectives of political administration (2005, p. 92). A case in point is the British government's policy of internment without trial for suspected members of the Irish Republican Army (IRA) in Northern Ireland between 1971 and 1975.[6] In the words of the then Home Secretary, Reginald Maudling, speaking in September 1971, this policy was intended to:

> Hold in safety, where they can do no further harm, active members of the IRA and, secondly, to obtain more information about their activities, their conspiracy and organisation, to help the security forces in their job of protecting the public as a whole. (quoted in Spjut, 1986, p. 715)

Although members of the IRA were apprehended under this legislation, many people who did not belong to that organization were arrested and imprisoned without trial. Nonetheless, the British government believed these arrests were justified, on the ground that the need to protect the innocent population against terrorist acts overrode the rights of the individuals concerned.

The Kantian conception of the person can be invoked to justify certain basic freedoms. Among these liberties, which are enshrined in many human rights instruments, are freedom of thought and liberty of conscience; political liberty – that is, the right to hold public office and the right to vote – and freedom of speech and association; and freedom from 'arbitrary arrest and seizure as defined by the concept of the rule of law' (Rawls, 1999, p. 53). These basic liberties, Rawls believes, enable persons to realize and exercise the powers that typify them as moral beings, and to advance their chosen ends under free social conditions. Political liberty, for example, is necessary because it enables a person to express their capacities for self-government and social interaction (Rawls, 1980, p. 526), and thus to be a rational, autonomous moral being who is capable of cooperation with other such beings.

For deontologists, social institutions can also be justified by the Kantian account of the self. These arguments are founded on the premise that social institutions can have important long-term effects and play a vital role in shaping the character and objectives of the members of that society, the types of persons they are and aspire to be. It follows that citizens will support those institutions that reflect their beliefs and aspirations, so the relationship between citizens and social institutions can be described as mutually supporting. On this basis, Rawls claims, the citizens of a well-ordered society uphold their existing institutions 'in part because they reasonably believe them to satisfy their public and effective conception of justice' (1980, p. 536), and thus enable them to exercise the powers they, as moral beings, possess. Conversely, those social institutions which distort the character and goals of its members, or do not allow them to express their Kantian capacities, are unjustifiable and are in need of reform.

Dworkin distinguishes between two types of political rights, which he terms background rights and institutional rights. He defines the former as rights that justify political decisions taken by society in the abstract, while the latter justify a decision made by a specific political institution. To illustrate, Dworkin asks us to imagine a political theory which states that every individual has the right to take possession of another's property if his or her need of it is greater than that of its owner. One may concede, Dworkin says, that this individual has no legal right to do so; in other words, that he or she 'has no institutional right that the present legislature enact legislation that would violate the Constitution, as such a statute probably would' (2005, p. 93). One might also concede that he or she has no institutional right to a legal decision that turned a blind eye to theft. Even if one granted these concessions, however, the initial background claim could be preserved by arguing that all the citizens of the society concerned would be justified in revising the Constitution to abolish private property, or perhaps in staging a revolution and bringing down the government. Indeed, one could assert, Dworkin continues, that each person has a residual background right that would necessitate or justify these courses of action, even though he or she lacks the right to 'specific institutional decisions as these institutions are now constituted' (2005, p. 93).

Dworkin also differentiates between abstract and concrete rights, and thus between abstract and concrete principles. An abstract right is a broad political aim, whose statement provides no indication of how that aim is to be compromised or weighed against other political aims in actual situations. For example, the grand rights that feature in political rhetoric are abstract, on the ground that politicians talk about a right to equality or dignity or free speech 'with no suggestion that these rights are absolute, but with no attempt to suggest their impact on particular complex social situations' (Dworkin, 2005, p. 93). Concrete rights, meanwhile, are political aims whose definitions are more clear-cut, and thereby give more precise expression to the weight they have against other political aims in specific circumstances. Suppose, for instance, that we endorse the right to freedom of speech and at the same time claim that the press had a right to publish details about Prince Harry's service as a front-line combat soldier in Afghanistan in 2007–8. The principle operating here demands a resolution of the conflict that it recognizes between the abstract right of freedom of speech, and the competing rights of Prince Harry to security and privacy while carrying out his duties. So, although abstract rights supply arguments in support of concrete rights, the claim of a concrete right is more authoritative than that of the abstract right on which it is based (Dworkin, 2005, pp. 93–4). Implicit in this discussion is the idea that rights need to be exercised *responsibly*. So, although free speech is regarded as an important right in a democratic society, it should nonetheless be curbed if its expression could place lives in danger.

Dworkin makes two further distinctions, the first of which is between rights against the state, which justify a political decision that demands action from some government agency, and rights against fellow citizens, which justify the coercion of specific individuals. The rights to free education up to the age of 18 and free healthcare for all are, if accepted, examples of rights that British citizens have against the state, while the right to recoup damages if a breach of contract has occurred is a right against fellow citizens. As a rule, the right to free speech falls under both categories. While Dworkin concedes that it seems odd to describe the rights that citizens have against one another as political rights, he points out that, for his purposes, we are interested in such rights only to the extent that they are used to justify political decisions of varying kinds. He also notes that the present distinction 'cuts across the distinction between background and institutional rights; the latter distinguishes among persons or institutions that must make a political decision, the former between persons or institutions whom that decision directs to act or to forbear' (2005, p. 94 n.1).

Dworkin's second distinction is between universal rights and special rights. Universal rights extend to all individuals who belong to a community, with exceptions made only for punishment, for instance, or incapacity. An example of a universal right is the right to vote; indeed, for the purposes of discussion, Dworkin assumes that political rights are, without exception, universal. Meanwhile, special rights are those that are provided for one particular group within the community, or possibly even for a single member. The exemption of turban-wearing followers of the Sikh religion from UK legislation that enforces the wearing of crash helmets by motorcyclists is a right of this kind.

Many deontologists object that consequentialism sacrifices the rights of individuals to the interests of the majority. Williams, for instance, discusses the moral disagreeableness that frequently arises in cases where an action is justified in terms of consequences or maximization, at the expense of a right. In these situations, he claims, there is a 'larger moral cost attached to letting a right be overridden by consequences, than to letting one consequence be overridden by another, since it is part of the point of rights that they cannot just be overridden by consequences (1981, p. 61). This argument is made from the standpoint of moral philosophy but, as we have seen, rights can be overridden by consequentialist concerns in the realm of politics. Such occurrences are fairly commonplace, due to the importance politicians attach to both outcomes and the need to attain hegemonic advantage over their opponents. This is not to say that consequentialist reasoning should always take precedence over rights, as there will be situations in which it would be undesirable – if not downright dangerous – for it to do so. Rather, this discussion reveals the limits of deontological strategies in political argument, particularly in policy areas concerned with the greater good of society.

How virtue theory is used in the justification of policy

For moral philosophers, virtue theory assigns a central role to notions of virtue and the virtuous individual, as opposed to statements about actions or rules. From a political standpoint, however, this emphasis on individual character has a broader application and focuses on the good of the community as a whole. As Shlomo Avineri and Avner de-Shalit explain, the community is defined as a 'body with some common values, norms, and goals, in which each member regards the common goals as her own' and, moreover, is viewed as being a good in itself (1992, pp. 6–7). This approach is often referred to as 'communitarianism' and contrasts with those versions of liberalism that emphasize the rights of individuals. The theories of Rawls and Dworkin provide two paradigmatic examples of the latter position, while Alasdair MacIntyre's version of the former is examined below.

MacIntyre asks us to consider what would be involved in establishing a community to create a good that all those involved in the project recognize as their shared good. He claims that the participants in such a project would need first to value the character traits that would help them to realize their common goals. In other words, they would need to identify a particular set of qualities as being virtues and the corresponding set of flaws as being vices. However, the participants would also need to recognize some actions as being so harmful that they damage the community by making it impossible for people to do or achieve good in some way and for a period of time. Such offences would typically include the murder of innocent persons, perjury, and theft (MacIntyre, 1985, p. 151).

In this community, the set of virtues that is propagated would teach people what kinds of actions would be rewarded with praise and merit, while the list of legal offences would teach them which actions would be classed as intolerable. If someone commits an offence of this kind, he or she is understood to have excluded himself from the community by acting in this way, and also to have invited punishment. After all, the community must recognize this breach of its bonds for what it is, and act accordingly. Consequently, the offender can be excluded from the community either permanently – in the form of irrevocable exile or execution – or temporarily – in the form of exile for a given period of time or imprisonment – depending upon the seriousness of his or her offence. 'A broad measure of agreement on a scale of gravity of offences would be partially constitutive of such a community', MacIntyre writes, 'as would a similar broad measure of agreement on the nature and importances of the various virtues' (1985, p. 151). So, an account of a community's moral life must include a both a table of the virtues and a catalogue of those actions which are absolutely forbidden if it is to be complete. We can also say that, for MacIntyre, membership of a community is dependent on whether a person acts to promote the good of that community, and is, therefore, virtuous.

A central feature of MacIntyre's account of the virtues is the concept of a practice, which he defines as

> Any coherent and complex form of socially established cooperative human activity through which goods internal to that form of activity are realised in the course of trying to achieve those standards of excellence which are appropriate to, and partially definitive of, that form of activity. (1985, p. 187)

Participation in a practice increases an individual's capacity to attain excellence, while broadening our conceptions of the goods and ends involved. Music, architecture and football are all classed as practices, while the virtues can be viewed as the 'skills' an individual needs in order to flourish within a given practice. It is important to note that all practices have a history and, to the extent that the virtues sustain the social bonds inherent in practices, they must maintain relationships to the past, as well as to the present and the future. The traditions through which specific practices are handed down and remodelled are themselves part of greater social traditions, which I discuss next.

According to MacIntyre, a living tradition is in part an argument about the particular goods that comprise it. This argument takes place within society and has often continued for several generations. Thus, an agent's pursuit of his or her good typically occurs within the framework of the specific traditions to which he or she belongs, and this is the case for the goods that are intrinsic to practices as well as the goods of a person's life. Traditions are sustained or destroyed by the exercise – or the failure to exercise – the relevant virtues. So, the purpose of the virtues is to maintain the relationships necessary for the attainment of the range of goods that are inherent in practices; to sustain the structure of an agent's life, in which they can search for their good as the good of their entire life; and to sustain the traditions that supply the historical context for both practices and the lives of individuals. The acknowledgment that a lack of the relevant virtues damages practices and the traditions from which they come brings with it the recognition of a further virtue, which MacIntyre identifies as the virtue of 'having an adequate sense of the traditions to which one belongs or which confront one' (1985, p. 223).

On MacIntyre's view, the liberal individualism propounded by Enlightenment thinkers precludes the embeddedness of an individual in both a community and a tradition (1985, p. 222). Because virtue is no longer founded on the teleological notion of universal human nature, the moral consensus that characterizes a community has broken down, and moral discourse has fragmented. It therefore follows that the modern nation state, which is not structured around a common conception of the good, 'systematically excludes and politically marginalises the kind of moral community necessary for the acquisition and development of the virtues' (D'Andrea, 2006, p. 283). On this basis, MacIntyre argues, anyone who is truly committed to the tradition of the virtues must reject modern politics (1985, p. 255).

The preceding discussion reveals that the application of MacIntyre's account to investigate the use of virtue theoretic arguments in politics is problematic, not least because his idea of a community defined by a single coherent tradition is increasingly difficult to defend in multicultural societies. These problems stem primarily from the fact that MacIntyre adopts the standpoint of moral philosophy, whereas this book is written from a political perspective. To overcome this difficulty, I take the parts of MacIntyre's theory that help to explicate some of the forms of moral arguments that are used in contemporary politics, and abandon the rest.[7] Therefore, in the remainder of this chapter I draw on MacIntyre's description of the establishment of a community to achieve a common venture, and his notions of a practice and desert, but reject his concept of a tradition.

MacIntyre's account of the instigation of a project to achieve a common goal can be applied to political parties, all of which have a particular conception of the good community, a catalogue of the virtues that would promote that community, and a table of the vices that would hinder its development. These notions are located within a party's ideology and are given public expression in such sources as its election manifesto and the speeches of its representatives. A new government is unlikely to bring about a drastic moral change in society, on the ground that a community's catalogue of the virtues and the vices will be fairly stable. Nonetheless, different political parties will seek, through such means as policy initiatives and the construction of discourses, to promote some virtues over others and to discourage particular vices. In this way, reference to the virtues becomes a means of justifying the policies concerned.

The use of policy programmes to discourage undesirable conduct can be illustrated by the Thatcher government's approach to lone-parent families. The Thatcherites' disapproval of these families was based on an ideological commitment to 'Victorian values', and the associated view that the best type of family comprises two parents – preferably married – one of whom acts as the bread-winner while the other is primarily concerned with care and nurture (MacLean, 1994, p. 512). From this stemmed the argument that 'lone parenthood *per se* is bad for both the families themselves and for society in general and the state, therefore, should seek to discourage the formation of such families or, at the very least, not encourage them' (Millar, 1994, p. 28).

Thatcher and her supporters also believed that the failure of absent parents to assume responsibility for their children was an important contributing factor to the growing 'culture of dependency,' in which people relied on the state to fulfil their needs and made no effort to help themselves. As Jane Millar explains, the principal offenders were identified as the father who abandoned his family responsibilities and expected the state to pick up the financial burden, and the lone mother who was increasingly reliant on the state for an income. Indeed, the Thatcherites came to define the receipt of benefits as an issue of individual choice, and claimants as epitomizing the abdication of personal responsibility (1994, pp. 28–9). For a party that envisioned the good community as one characterized by decency, self-sufficiency and respect for the rule of law, it can be said that such behaviour was regarded as a vice. This is clear when we recall that the Thatcherites blamed welfare dependency for a range of social ills, including sexual promiscuity and drug abuse.

According to MacIntyre, the fundamental question in politics is that of what resources each individual and group requires to enable it to contribute to the common good. Indeed, to the extent that a community is well-ordered, it is in the interests of all of its members that each person or group *should* be able to make its own particular contribution (1999, p. 144). By implication, the state should assist those who cannot contribute by giving them the opportunity and the means to secure the resources that will enable them to do so. Such assistance can take a number of forms and be targeted at a range of social groups, depending upon both the conception of a good community, and the catalogue of virtues and vices, endorsed by the party concerned. In the case of lone parents, the Conservative government passed the Child Support Act of 1991, which aimed to increase parental responsibility by compelling the absent parent (usually the father) to pay maintenance for his child(ren) through the Child Support Agency. This extra income saved public expenditure, enabled thousands of lone mothers to return to work (MacLean, 1994, pp. 512–17), and thus made it possible for them to contribute to the good of their community.

Alongside the common good, the concept of desert plays a key role in the promotion of policy. Joel Feinberg explains that if an individual is 'deserving of some sort of treatment, he must, necessarily, be so *in virtue of* some possessed characteristics or prior activity,' reasons which in turn form the basis of desert (1970, p. 58). Like the common good, desert is applicable only in the context of a community whose principal bond, MacIntyre says, is a 'shared understanding both of the good for man and of the good of that community and where individuals identify their primary interests with reference to those goods' (1985, p. 250). This is because a community like this will have a considerable understanding of what it is to contribute to the attainment of that good. As we have seen, MacIntyre believes the modern nation state is not a community of this type, and he is critical of politicians who present it as such in their rhetoric. However, these claims have an appeal in political argument, so assertions about community and the nation state are taken on their own terms despite MacIntyre's objections.

Politicians invoke the notion of desert in their efforts to sell a range of policies. These policies are often economic and are intended to reward people for acting virtuously. Pay increases for public sector workers such as nurses and fire-fighters are of this type, designed as they are to recognize both the contribution these individuals make to the greater good and the virtues they exhibit in doing so. These virtues could include selflessness, courage and dedication. The notion of desert is also evident in the honours system, which rewards exceptional members of society. Such rewards are not only given to individuals who possess 'conventional' virtues like courage or charity to an extraordinary degree, but also to those who exhibit excellence in a range of fields, including business, sport, and the arts. In MacIntyre's terms, these fields are practices, and the skills required for an individual to achieve the goods inherent in them, and therefore to flourish, are virtues. So, by recognizing outstanding individuals in this way, the state not only rewards them personally, but holds them up as exemplars of virtue for the rest of society to admire and imitate.

It is clear from this discussion that virtue theorists reject the deontologists' conception of the self as prior to its ends, whose identity is given independently of both its interests and its relationships with other people. They instead endorse the view that we are all members of a particular family, community or nation, and that these 'more or less enduring attachments and commitments...taken together, partly define the person I am' (Sandel, 1992, p. 23). On the basis of this account of the self, virtue theorists and communitarians condemn the individualism propounded by deontology as socially corrosive. Rosalind Hursthouse, for instance, argues that people do not live well when they think that 'getting what they have a right to is of pre-eminent importance; they harm others, and they harm themselves' (1997, p. 227). This is because such people, by focusing unduly on their own particular interests, overlook the responsibilities they owe to others. Thus, virtue theorists claim that arguments founded on rights have no place in their moral theory. From a political viewpoint, however, the objections of virtue theorists show only that the individualism propounded by deontology renders it unsuitable for promoting policies relating to community; indeed, we saw in the previous section that deontological arguments can be deployed effectively in the defence of individual rights and freedoms.

Virtue theorists also believe that consequentialist reasoning has no place in moral argument, on the ground that the virtues, by their very nature, should be exercised irrespective of the consequences of doing so. This will ensure, writes MacIntyre, that the virtue concerned will be 'effective in producing the internal goods which are the rewards of the virtues'. While the virtues are simply those qualities which can lead an agent to the attainment of a particular category of goods, MacIntyre continues, if we do not practise them irrespective of whether 'in any particular set of contingent circumstances they will produce those goods or not, we cannot possess them at all' (1985, p. 198). For this reason, virtue theory does not provide us with a means of judging the moral worth of political policies according to their outcomes. Moreover, by overlooking the inner life of the moral agent, consequentialism precludes the possibility of achieving the goods associated with the virtues. It also neglects the role of the community, which virtue theorists view as paramount because it instils in us the motives and traits we need in order to act morally. Nonetheless, consequentialism still has a vital role to play in political argument, particularly in efforts to persuade people to support policies concerned with welfare.

Conclusion

We have seen in this chapter that there is a role for all three moral theories in the promotion of policy. While moral philosophers may see each paradigm as offering an exhaustive account of moral justification, it is clear from a political standpoint that they all have currency, though in different policy areas, and therefore are useful resources. It is important to note, however, that a political actor may be limited in the moral arguments he can deploy at any given time. Indeed, the demands of ideological consistency or political expediency may rule out a particular moral argument – even if it is customarily deployed to promote the type of policy concerned – as I now demonstrate.

Although the principle of freedom of speech, for example, is usually defended as a right, it may be untenable for a politician to do so on occasions when an opponent is taking a libertarian position on the issue concerned. In such a situation, he or she may have recourse to John Stuart Mill's 'harm principle,' according to which 'the only purpose for which power can be rightfully exercised over any member of a civilised community, against his will, is to prevent harm to others. His own good, either physical or moral, is not a sufficient warrant' (1998, p. 14). In other words, it is acceptable to limit an individual's freedom if doing so prevents him or her from harming other people. A case in point is the furore over the cartoons of the Prophet Mohammed, which were published by the Danish newspaper *Jyllands-Posten* in September 2005 and caused offence to Muslims around the world. While those who supported the actions of the newspaper propounded the libertarian argument that freedom of speech cannot be undermined, even if it offends people, opponents contended that the right to free speech does not entail an obligation to be offensive (see Hensher and Younge, 2006). These contextual limitations on the range of moral arguments available indicate that the need to win rhetorical competitions may also influence the selection and modification of argumentative strategies, a consideration I examine in the next chapter.

3
The Context of Hegemonic Competition

This chapter examines the 'context of hegemonic competition,' in which the need to secure advantage in rhetorical competitions may further influence a political actor's choice of argumentative strategy. In the first section, I briefly define the key concepts of the discourse theory of Ernesto Laclau and Chantal Mouffe and, in so doing, highlight the similarities between this approach and Freeden's account of ideological morphology. Next, I examine the notions of an 'organic crisis,' which provides the backdrop for the dynamics of hegemonic competition, and 'wars of position.' In the following section, I consider the idea of a 'social imaginary' and explore the process by which it becomes institutionalized. The discussion in these sections is illustrated with examples from contemporary politics, which serve to demonstrate the practical relevance of hegemony theory. Finally, I explore the appeal of moral principles and arguments, and show that they are a key weapon in the struggle for hegemonic advantage.

The key concepts of discourse theory

As Steve Bastow and James Martin point out, 'discourse' refers to the 'structured pattern of meanings that frames our perception of, and organizes our activity in, the social and natural world' (2003, pp. 7–8). Its primary function is to establish a system of related signs, which include texts or speech systems as well as a wide range of non-verbal practices. By imposing frameworks that restrict the possibilities that people can experience, or the meaning that experience can incorporate, a discourse sets the parameters of what we can say and do, and thereby provides a medium for communication, thought and action.[1] However, it is important to note that the meanings of the signs contained within a discourse are only partially fixed. As a result, it is inevitable that something will escape from the apparently infinite process of signification that occurs within a discourse. This irreducible surplus of meaning is termed 'the discursive' or the 'field of discursivity' and comprises a field of undecidability which incessantly overflows and undermines any effort to create a fixed set of differential positions within any given discourse (Torfing, 1999, p. 92). The discursive is therefore the precondition for the articulation of a wealth of rival discourses.

'Articulation' refers to the linkage of at least two discursive elements within a discourse. This process typically takes place during periods of social upheaval, when opposing discourses compete to assign new meanings to both 'floating' and 'empty' signifiers, and thus to become the 'interpretative frameworks through which we live our structural positionings' (Smith, 1998, p. 78). 'Floating signifiers' assume novel meanings as they are joined with other signifiers in new ways. Thus, concepts such as 'equality' and 'liberty' may acquire one meaning if they are articulated in, for example, a liberal discourse, and another if they are articulated in a conservative discourse. In contrast, 'empty signifiers' like 'democracy' and 'order' have no intrinsic content and may be endowed with a wide range of meanings. Consequently, they may serve to unite disparate social movements behind a common cause (Townshend, 2004, p. 271).

There are a number of similarities between this account of the process of articulation and aspects of Freeden's theory of ideological morphology. The definition of a floating signifier in discourse theory corresponds to Freeden's notion of an effectively contested concept, while the similarities between the processes of articulation and decontestation in the assignation of meaning to disputed concepts are clear. As in Freeden's analysis, the meaning of floating signifiers is never fixed (or decontested) in perpetuity. So, every articulation is contingent, and thus can be challenged at a later time. Both perspectives also emphasize the importance of history in the process of assigning meaning to concepts, and Freeden would certainly concur with Anna Marie Smith's statement that 'even when the effects of past articulations are weakened, they are never totally lost; every signifier bears the traces of past articulations' (1998, p. 78). It is important to point out, however, that the presence of these non-determining traces means that a floating signifier is never wholly empty and, moreover, limits the range of possible meanings that can be assigned to it. Consequently, the remnants of past articulations within a signifier perform the same function as the ineliminable component of a concept in Freeden's theory.

The question arises of whether there are limits on the ways in which the elements within a particular discourse may be articulated. Laclau and Mouffe respond to this question by invoking the Althusserian concept of 'overdetermination,' which denotes the multiplicity of frequently opposing forces that are simultaneously at work in any given political situation (Althusser, 2005, p. 101). In so doing, however, Laclau and Mouffe appear to utilize this concept as a substitute for 'articulation', the result of which is that the problem of how to find the terms with which we can specify the limits that bring about the emergence of new discourses remains unresolved (Purvis and Hunt, 1993, p. 493). To overcome this problem, Trevor Purvis and Alan Hunt invoke Gramsci's idea of common sense, according to which 'every social stratum has its own "common sense" and its own "good sense", which are basically the most widespread conception of life and of man' (Gramsci, 1971, p. 326, n.5). If, as Stuart Hall argues, we sever the connection between common sense and social class, then common sense is effectively a hegemonic, or popular, discourse (1998a, p. 1057). Such a discourse both organizes social actions and constitutes the social relations they reproduce, and, as such, possesses almost structural properties. In this way, the structural aspect of common sense constrains the possible combinations of elements within a discursive formation; indeed, all discourse has 'conditions of existence' which cannot secure specific outcomes but nonetheless impose restrictions on the process of articulation itself (Hall, 1988, p. 10; Purvis and Hunt, 1993, p. 495).

Purvis and Hunt's question could also be addressed by invoking Freeden's notion of cultural adjacency. As elaborated in Chapter 1, cultural adjacency imposes limits upon the elements that a concept can possibly contain, and thus prevents it from overflowing. It also allows the presence of two contradictory elements within a concept if such a 'paradox' is culturally permissible. From the standpoint of discourse theory, we can say that cultural adjacency restricts the possible meanings of the signifiers that are articulated within a discourse, while the rejected meanings constitute the field of discursivity. If the discourse is to succeed in becoming hegemonic, the meanings of the signifiers articulated within it must be acceptable from a cultural perspective. In Laclau's words, the acceptance of a discourse 'depends on its credibility, and this will not be granted if its proposals clash with the basic principles informing the organisation of a group' (1990, p. 66). This last point raises the issue of plausibility. Smith explains that if a party adapts a discourse from another source in its efforts to win support for a particular policy, the adaptation must be plausible if it is to succeed. As the limits of the 'plausible' are invariably inflexible at any given time, new articulations can acquire plausibility only to the extent that they base themselves on traditions that have already been normalized. One example of this technique is the Thatcherites' equation of the autonomy of local authorities with the promotion of homosexuality, which was plausible because it borrowed heavily from the racist discourses that were prevalent at the time (Smith, 1998, p. 171).

The practice of articulation is also at work in the creation of nodal points,[2] which enjoy privileged status as the master signifiers within a discourse. This is because the meanings of other signifiers are defined through their relations with a nodal point and, as a result, become partially fixed. The incompleteness of this fixation is due to the openness of the social, which is itself a consequence of the perpetual overflow of meaning from the field of discursivity into every discourse. However, the nodal point is not 'an "essential" fixed point of reference, a point of supreme plenitude of meaning'; rather it has a structural function in the unification of a discursive field (Stavrakakis, 1997, p. 265). As we have seen, there is a proliferation of signifiers floating within the discursive as their conventional meaning has been lost. So, when a nodal point intervenes, it 'retroactively constitutes their identity by fixing the floating signifiers within a paradigmatic chain of equivalence', thereby bestowing a precise meaning on the other elements in the chain and unifying the discourse concerned (Torfing, 1999, p. 99). In some Green discourses, for instance, this unifying function is performed by the nodal point 'Nature', and such signifiers as 'democracy' and 'decentralization' acquire their distinctively 'Green' meanings by virtue of their articulation around it (Stavrakakis, 1997, p. 275). The notion of a 'nodal point' thus bears a close resemblance to the core cluster of an ideology in Freeden's theory, which also performs a structural role and is vital to the process of decontestation by virtue of its association with the other concepts that constitute an ideological configuration.

Hegemonic formations develop through the interaction of the logics of equivalence and difference. The logic of equivalence eliminates the differences between discursive elements by uniting them under a common identity, such as 'women' or 'the people'. A chain of equivalence is thus formed, and the single category that contains these various elements is situated in a relation of antagonism against that which it defines as its 'other'. Meanwhile, the logic of difference emphasizes the particularity of separate elements, examples of which are 'teacher' and 'pupil', and seeks to eliminate antagonism by articulating these differences within a single chain (Bastow and Martin, 2003, pp. 12–13). The effects produced by the logic of equivalence are constrained by the opposing effects generated by articulations created in accordance with the logic of difference. These limits ensure that neither of the two logics can provide a complete definition of the social; the effects of one representation are suppressed to the extent that it is displaced by the other. As Smith correctly points out, a great deal of hegemonic strategizing consists in 'the management of political representation – the deployment of the logic of difference and the logic of equivalence – according to the prevailing tactical conditions' (1998, p. 174). Thus, a politician might deploy one of the two logics in a setting where he or she is addressing supporters, such as the annual party conference, and utilize the other when he or she is speaking to the electorate as a whole.

Vincent Pecora defines an 'antagonism' as the 'articulated relation produced by a logic of equivalence defined against that which it excludes, yet implicitly accepts, as its other' (1991, p. 222). An articulation of this type is hegemonic and involves both the negation of alternative possibilities and meanings, and the negation of those individuals who identify themselves with these possibilities and meanings. This is achieved through the construction of the excluded identity as one of a succession of threatening obstructions to the complete realization of the meanings and possibilities propounded by the hegemonic articulation (Torfing, 1999, p. 120). In anti-globalization discourses, for instance, particular demands such as human rights, sustainable development and free trade are blurred together as united moments in a common opposition to global capitalism, thereby forming a chain of equivalence. At the same time, however, the logic of difference highlights the frontier that separates the anti-globalization movement from its other. The antagonist is represented by a sequence of differentiated demands that are articulated together to form a chain of equivalence, with the activities and commitments of multinational corporations and international financial institutions treated as symbolic of their shared goal of domination and exploitation. Thus, the antagonist 'is not just another differentiated identity: it stands as the limit of any rational order at all and is therefore conceived as almost unintelligible' (Bastow and Martin, 2003, p. 13). It is worth noting that there are numerous possible antagonisms in the social realm, many of which stand in opposition to each other. These antagonisms bring the existing order into question and, in so doing, provoke an identity crisis. In the next section, we will see how such a crisis provides the ground for the emergence of a new hegemonic discourse. First, however, it is necessary to define the concept of hegemony.

Hegemonic practice can take place only in an open society, where social classifications and boundaries are always available for redefinition. A discourse that offers such redefinitions is produced through the process of articulation and involves the formation of a social unity which is situated between the opposing poles of equivalence and difference. As a result, any discourse that achieves hegemonic status is grounded in a terrain characterized by conflict; indeed, as Smith puts it, the attainment of hegemony always involves the 'exercise of power: the brutal exclusion – concealed or explicit – of alternative frameworks' (1998, p. 172). A discourse can only become hegemonic if it can successfully construct a discursive formation that offers a 'surface of inscription' for a wide variety of attitudes, views and demands, and eventually becomes the framework of subject positions with which people and groups identify themselves. Thus, the concept of hegemony can be defined as the expansion of a discourse, or a collection of discourses, into a 'dominant horizon of social orientation and action by means of articulating unfixed elements into partially fixed moments in a context crisscrossed by antagonistic forces' (Torfing, 1999, p. 101).

The dynamics of hegemonic competition and 'wars of position'

An organic crisis reveals a multiplicity of spaces in which the recrystallization and redefinition of both identities and concepts can occur. At such a time, the contradictions present within different areas of society start to multiply, and various kinds of popular dissent and resistance start to resurface. Antonio Gramsci terms the field in which these conflicts take place the 'conjunctural', and this terrain is characterized by both the specific economic conditions and the unremitting efforts made by those who wish to uphold the status quo (1971, p. 178). To use Hall's example, the emergence of Thatcherism was preceded by the conjuncture of 1972–6, whose limits were overdetermined by Britain's rapid economic decline and the continuation of a political version of 'that exceptional state,' which had developed between 1968 and 1972. Hall identifies four key aspects that were present within this conjuncture, namely the ideological conflict between the Heath government and the Left; the economic crisis in the form of the recession that followed the Heath/Barber boom of 1972–3; the political struggle between the government and the organized working class; and the 'direct interpellation of the race issue into the crisis of British civil and political life' (1988, pp. 19–21).

In an organic crisis, Hall writes, the efforts made to defend the status quo must not be simply defensive – they must also be formative,

> Aiming at a new balance of forces, the emergence of new elements, the attempt to put together a new 'historic bloc', new political configurations and 'philosophies', a profound restructuring of the state and the ideological discourses which construct the crisis and represent it as it is 'lived' as a practical reality: new programmes and policies, pointing to a new result, a new sort of 'settlement' – 'within certain limits'. (1988, p. 43)

These new elements need to be constructed; they do not simply emerge. Hence, ideological and political efforts are needed to dismantle the established formations and to rearticulate their components into new ones. In Gramsci's terms, a struggle of this kind is a 'war of position,' which is a complex array of conflicts that occur at numerous strategic sites within civil society and state itself (1971, pp. 238–9).[3] Thus, a political party's struggle for hegemony takes place over many different fronts, where it competes with rival political formations to make itself both the principal focus of people's aspirations and the foremost popular force in politics (Hall, 1988, p. 207).

With regard to Thatcherism, the battle for hegemony took place within the dominant bloc, against both social democracy and the moderate faction of the Conservative Party. Indeed, it not only functioned within the same space, but operated directly on the contradictions contained within these opposing positions. As Hall observes, the strength of the radical right lay in part in its commitment to innovation, and not merely to rearticulating the elements that constituted the dominant 'philosophies'. Nonetheless, it disarticulated the elements of existing discourses and reworked them into a new and decisively right-wing logic. Hall identifies the two key themes of this new philosophy as anti-statism and anti-collectivism. At the level of ideology, anti-statism received a new lease of life as monetarism, with its ideals of free-market economics and possessive individualism, and came to replace Keynesianism as the dominant economic paradigm. This development took place gradually, and the Thatcherites translated monetarist principles into the language of moral imperative, common sense and experience. In so doing, they presented the discourse of 'social market values' as an alternative moral system to that of the 'caring society' (Hall, 1988, pp. 44–7).

Hall describes this transformation of a 'theoretical *ideology* into a populist *idiom*' as a 'major political achievement', on the basis of which the Thatcherites associated the idea of 'Britishness' with a return to competition, profitability and sound money, and drew an analogy between the national budget and the family budget. In Margaret Thatcher's words, 'We have a duty to make sure that every penny piece we raise in taxation is spent wisely and well. For it is our party which is dedicated to good housekeeping' (1983, p. 3). Thatcher and her followers identified the essential qualities of the British people as self-reliance and a sense of personal responsibility, and opposed them to the figure of the 'over-taxed individual, enervated by welfare state "coddling", his or her moral fibre irrevocably sapped by "state handouts"'. This attack on the fundamental principles of collective social welfare, Hall continues, was launched through the provocative image of the 'scrounger' (1988, p. 47). Indeed, as we will see below, the construction of Thatcherism as populist common sense was an important factor in the success of this doctrine as a hegemonic enterprise.

Turning now to the anti-collectivist strand of Thatcherism, this set of discourses targeted popular elements within the ideologies and philosophies of the dominated groups in society. According to Hall, these elements frequently manifested a contradiction between the power bloc and the interests of the classes it dominates. However, the class meaning of the terms in which this contradiction found expression was neither fixed nor necessary. Consequently, they could be rearticulated as elements within a wide range of discourses, in which the power bloc could be positioned in various ways relative to the popular classes. When the established configurations are disrupted during an organic crisis, it subsequently becomes possible, Hall says, to 'construct the people into a populist political subject: *with*, not against, the power bloc' (1988, p. 49). In Thatcherite discourses, the people were allied with new political forces in a national campaign to make Britain 'Great' again. This language of 'the people', united behind an effort to reverse the progress of 'creeping collectivism', to purge the state apparatus of Keynesian delusions, and to reinvigorate the power bloc, is highly compelling. After all, argues Hall, its radicalism linked up with radical-popular sentiments, but it turned them on their head, incorporated and defused their popular force, and created a populist unity in place of a popular rupture (1988, p. 49). This process, in which some elements of an ideological configuration are neutralized, absorbed and passively appropriated into a novel political formation, closely resembles the Gramscian notion of 'transformism' (see Gramsci, 1971, pp. 58–9).

In a time of organic crisis, popular identifications with political imaginaries and institutionalized subject positions collapse spectacularly, the result of which is that the dominant discursive formations become particularly susceptible to critique from a range of different perspectives. Smith explains that while an individual never identifies completely with their subject positions, it is likely that the crisis will heighten their awareness of the disparity between the explanations offered by their subject positions on the one hand, and the material consequences of their structural positionings on the other. During the Vietnam War, for instance, traditional US patriotism failed to garner popular support for military action, while increasing numbers of activists rejected the established political, racial and patriarchal discourses as morally bankrupt. In the language of discourse theory, we can say that the war provoked an identity crisis in an increasing number of subjects, the result of which was that their feelings of alienation became particularly unbearable and their desire to find new explanatory frameworks more intense (Smith, 1998, p. 164).

When the social order breaks down, it is important to note that it is not only those who are disempowered who experience an identity crisis, but also a considerable number of the members of the dominant groups in society. This experience brings with it a desire for order, and a concomitant susceptibility to those political discourses that pledge to restore social cohesion (Smith 1998: 164, 76). As Laclau observes, 'order' is present in an organic crisis only as 'that which is absent; it becomes an empty signifier,' which represents that absence (1996, p. 44). On this basis, opposing political forces vie to present their specific goals as those which alone can fill this lack. Thus, the act of hegemonizing something is precisely to perform this filling role. However, 'order' is not the only signifier whose meaning is available for new articulations. As we have seen, the meanings of other signifiers are also vulnerable to change, with any number of political forces competing to obtain maximum support for their definitions, and thus to secure hegemonic advantage over their rivals.

It is clear from the discussion so far that hegemonic strategies are at the height of their effectiveness during an organic crisis. At such a time, Smith says, an increasing number of subjects become unusually receptive to novel political discourses, and consequently start to experience the framework of social structures into which they have been flung as a hostile force that prevents them from developing into what they believe to be their real selves. This notion of a 'true self' has no foundation in reality and is itself in a permanent state of flux, on the ground that it will never become fixed. As subjects become increasingly conscious of this lack, rival political forces will try to 'hegemonize' the social. More specifically, they will endeavour to present their particular 'systems of narration' as a 'compensatory framework', and they will promote that framework as the only one that is able to bring the identity crisis to a satisfactory resolution (Smith, 1998, p. 165). To fulfil this objective, the rival discourses initially present themselves as 'myths', which seek to make sense of the crisis (cf. Charteris-Black, 2005, pp. 22–3). In so doing, they create a new objectivity by rearticulating the elements that were dislocated in the crisis to form new discursive configurations. However, it is worth noting that the myths are themselves incomplete and their content subject to change.

Eventually, one discourse begins to triumph over its rivals, on account of both its form and its connections with surviving and nascent institutions. While other discourses are inclined to maintain their 'single issue' focus, the demands that are given expression in the hegemonic discourse are 'metaphorized'. In other words, the discourse in question presents itself as a reading of the crisis – as a myth – and then as a 'surface of inscription', or 'space of representation', that undertakes to 'explain, to compensate for, and to suture over, the dislocation in the social structure' (Smith, 1998, p. 167), and thus bring the chaos to an end. By doing so, the hegemonic discourse appears to offer the fulfilment of all legitimate demands. It is important to point out that there is nothing in the crisis itself that guarantees that any particular discourse could assume this mythical role, and that the success of one discourse over its opponents is entirely contingent. Nonetheless, a discourse needs, Smith writes, to be more than the 'formal embodiment of order itself; it must [also] offer some compelling concrete alternative vision of the social' if it is to succeed in becoming hegemonic (1998, p. 81).

The dominance of a hegemonic discourse over its rivals is due only in part to its abstract form. Its achievement is also a consequence of its connections with social institutions that retain some level of authority for the duration of the organic crisis, its manifestation in nascent institutions that rapidly acquire authority, and its 'iterations of already normalized traditions' (Smith, 1998, p. 168). These relationships ensure that the disintegration of every institution and established discourse, and the collapse of every individual's identification with existing subject positions, is delayed in perpetuity. Thus, the authority of some institutions and traditions is preserved even as others crumble. The emerging hegemonic discourse must, Smith explains, rapidly secure strategic advantage by 'developing its appropriations from residual traditions, and by becoming embodied not only in the emerging institutions, but in the institutions that retain authority throughout the organic crisis as well'

(1998, p. 168). Hegemonic articulations are also more likely to operate efficiently if the preceding institutions and traditions are in decline, on the ground that the major political practices and values of the society concerned are more susceptible to reinterpretation. In contrast, those traditions which remained relatively intact throughout the crisis will be more effective in resisting redefinition.

The Thatcherites deployed these tactics in their bid to secure hegemonic advantage. Despite their attacks on the excessive statism of the Left, Hall claims, Thatcher and her followers sought to 'win' the state so as to reorganize it, and therefore to be within and against the state at the same time. With regard to the economy – most notably the state sector and the welfare state (which was bloated by the supposedly 'unrealistic' hopes of the British people) – the anti-statism endorsed by Thatcherism represented a radical project to overturn the Keynesian, welfare-corporatist consensus of the post-war period. This desire was manifested in the relentless drive towards deregulation and privatisation (Hall, 1988, p. 86). The Thatcherites were also strongly in favour of economic globalization, seeking to open Britain up to international capital and thus to 'prosperity'. Before attempting to attach to itself some of the new social forces, the proponents of Thatcherism needed to dismantle a number of old vested interests, which included the British Medical Association and the Confederation of British Industry. Although these organizations flourish in an enterprise culture, Hall writes, 'they [had] noticeably not availed themselves of the opportunity to rush into court provided by the anti-trade union legislation' and, in addition, they were unsettled by the extent of deregulation. These factors, continues Hall, provided an opening for what the Thatcherites viewed as the new forces of capitalism, among which were young brokers in the City, small businessmen, and those department stores prepared to sell optical goods at a price below that offered by the NHS (1988, p. 88).

On social issues, however, the Thatcher government was more interventionist than any other in the post-war period. This is evident in its concerns about law and order, family values and moral discipline. The discourses in which these anxieties found expression were central to Thatcherite ideology. Indeed, its attack on the 'permissive society' was a precursor to large-scale moral panics about such issues as drugs and homosexuality; followed by the mobilization around sex education and school libraries; and underpinned by the 'restoration of the family, the bulwark of respectable society and conventional sexualities with its fulcrum in the traditional roles for women' (Hall, 1988, p. 90). The moral agenda also included a revitalized cultural racism, which was organized around the nodal point of 'Englishness' and was manifested in the bitter controversy over Asian visas and visitors. Although there was a mismatch between these moral discourses and people's actual behaviour, the former were nonetheless important because a broad range of other languages had been incorporated within them. As Hall observes, they were the 'site for the mobilization of social identities and, by appropriating them, Thatcherism ... put down deep roots in the traditional, conventional social culture of English society' (1988, p. 91).

The social imaginary and its institutionalization

At the height of its authority, the hegemonic discourse becomes a social imaginary. Laclau explains that an imaginary 'is not one among other objects but an absolute limit which structures the field of intelligibility and is thus the condition of possibility for the emergence of any object' (1990, p. 64). The success of Thatcherism as a hegemonic enterprise stemmed primarily from its ability to construct its constituent political demands in such a way that they signified far more than their actual content. For example, the Thatcherites justified their assault on local government autonomy not simply as a necessary constitutional reform; rather, they repeatedly associated local authorities with profligate spending on projects that primarily benefited people from minority ethnic communities, gays and lesbians, and trades unions. In this case – and indeed in many others – the demands of the Thatcherites represented, Smith says, an 'authoritarian populist common sense that responded effectively to everyday concerns about the economy, the family, race, gender and sexuality' (1998, p. 171). Thatcherism thus became a defining discourse, an imaginary, in British politics, and provided a framework of identification for enough British voters – including many who rejected the literal content of Thatcher's views – to ensure Conservative victory in three successive general elections.

The hegemonic discourse becomes an imaginary when it gives full expression to its metaphorical aspect – its portrayal of itself as the principle of order – while suppressing its literal content, namely its particular demands and its beginnings as a single-issue movement (Smith, 1998, p. 167). It also represses the discourses it defeated in the struggle for hegemonic advantage, and thus its radically contingent nature. As Laclau observes, Edmund Husserl terms this forgetting and routinization of origins 'sedimentation,' a process which tends to culminate in both the disappearance of the array of potential alternatives and the fading of the residue of the initial contingency. So, when the discourse that is institutionalized as an imaginary adopts the appearance of an objective presence, we can say that sedimentation has occurred (1990, p. 34). From the preceding discussion, it is evident that the Thatcherites were able to represent their new, radical project as the only viable means of restoring order to Britain, at the expense of their opponents' positions. They also succeeded to an extent in linking their cultural, political, historical and sexual 'logics' to some of the strongest tendencies in the contemporary logics of the advancement of capitalism. In Hall's words, this achievement made Thatcher's Conservative party 'appear to "have history on its side", to be coterminous with the inevitable course of the future' (1988, p. 276) and to be the 'natural' party of government. It also enabled a degree of sedimentation to occur, though this state of affairs was by no means permanent.

When a hegemonic discourse becomes an imaginary, it must start to remake the dominant systems of subject positions. This is because the discourse concerned has its own range of approved subject positions which, to some degree, are unique. Initially, identifications with these novel subject positions may be rather unstable, given that their newness is clearly evident. Over time, these identifications may become increasingly routinized, the result of which is that the hegemonic formation is confronted with a range of new challenges within its own power centres. Such challenges may include, Smith says, 'unpredictable careerism, alienation, unintended acts of subversion as rules are applied in new contexts, [and] the exhaustion of popular demonizations' (1998, p. 168). As the authority of the imaginary grows, it becomes the framework through which an increasing number of identifications become possible, as a growing number of subject positions are recreated using its logic. Indeed, some identifications will become so widely accepted and so strongly supported by the institutional framework that the entire process of identification will, like the origins of the imaginary, completely vanish from sight. The reproductive cycle of the hegemonic regime is thus initiated, Smith writes, as the 'newly transformed subject positions tend to incite practices along the lines of "regulated improvisations"' (1998, p. 167). At the same time, Smith continues, people's awareness of the fact that the unity and coherence of the emergent hegemonic discourse derives from its negativity – that is, its antagonistic relation with those whom it defines as its enemy – diminishes. However, it is worth noting that although normalization has attained such a high degree of intensity, the possibility remains that alienation will reassert itself. If this occurs, then the hegemonic forces must continually deploy a range of tactics if they are to successfully manage the social, and thus maintain their authority. Hence, Smith argues, 'the work of a hegemonic discourse is never finished; it remains endlessly troubled by alienation...dysfunctional incitements, and resistances inspired by "outsider" discourse' (1998, p. 173).

The process of remaking the existing system of subject positions can be illustrated by reference to Hall's analysis of Thatcherism. According to Hall, the Thatcherites constructed an image of the 'new, share-owning working class', to which they harnessed a range of different social groups, and then proceeded to symbolically expand this social bloc around the notion of 'choice' in such areas as education and healthcare. Against this bloc, the Thatcherites constructed a narrative of Labour as the 'loony left', in which they fused political extremism and high rates with the powerful themes of sex and race. This delegitimization strategy was deployed to devastating effect in London, where the Conservatives were able to obliterate the legacy of the Greater London Council (GLC), and to bring the issues of race (in the form of the reaction against the anti-racism movement) and sex (through the hidden moral project of Thatcherism, namely the anti-feminist, anti-permissive, anti-gay, post-AIDS backlash) into the election without needing to raise them explicitly (Hall, 1988, pp. 262–3).

As the number of demands and symbols that a hegemonic project tries to articulate increases, it quickly becomes apparent that many of these elements stand in opposition to each other. In such a situation, Smith says, the hegemonic discourse must endeavour to neutralize these antagonisms by representing them as a bloc that is opposed to a common enemy, regardless of whether or not the social actors concerned have given their assent. To this end, it joins together its articulated elements in a chain of equivalence that stands in an antagonistic relation to another chain of signifiers, such as the opposition between 'the proletariat' and 'the bourgeoisie' in Marxist discourses. While each of the elements within the chain of equivalence maintains some specificity, the idea that they all stand united against the enemy bloc is, at that point in time, paramount (Smith, 1998, p. 174). To give a contemporary example, the Thatcherites represented trades unions, multicultural influences, feminist groups and a fictitious gay voting bloc as if they comprised an omnipotent apparatus that posed a direct threat to the rights of the general population (Smith, 1998, p. 177).

Alternatively, a single political discourse can effectively function as the 'horizon of intelligibility' for two opposing sides. As a result, struggles for hegemonic advantage do not always take place along party lines. Smith illustrates this point by reference to Bill Clinton's approach to welfare reform during the US presidential campaign of 1996, when Clinton deliberately depicted himself as a weak president who was compelled by a Republican-dominated Congress to act contrary to his wishes. In fact, Clinton had endorsed a neo-conservative stance on welfare prior to the election of 1992. When he came out of the pre-election session with the image of an 'embattled President and a reluctant compromiser', it was the Republican Congress who bore the political price of 'Contract with America' and not Clinton himself, even though the policy he had backed was only slightly more moderate than the one propounded by the Republicans. Thus, a neo-conservative political discourse functioned as the hegemonic horizon of intelligibility for both the Republicans and the Democrats, while Clinton himself simply engaged in limited tactical operations within an arena that had already been hegemonized (Smith, 1998, p. 176).

In the process of becoming an imaginary, the hegemonic discourse is incorporated into a range of major institutions. Consequently, the number of sites within the social realm, where identifications with the subject positions the discourse offers can be incited, is maximized. Institutionalization also entails the exclusion of alternative frameworks for identification as 'increasingly illegitimate, immoral, irrational and, finally, incoherent' (Smith, 1998, p. 172). This is achieved through a variety of tactics – including persuasion, violence, articulation and redefinition, and the general framing of the political landscape – that enable the hegemonic discourse to take advantage of the unique opportunities that are available in a specific historical configuration (Smith, 1998, p. 184). As such, institutionalization always involves the exercise of power. Although social structures and identities can become highly stabilized through the process of institutionalization, it is important to point out that no hegemonic configuration ever succeeds in becoming a wholly sutured totality in which every difference has been neutralized. This failure yields infinite possibilities and, when confronted with these developments, the imaginary that corresponds to the particular hegemonic discourse may change in unexpected ways (Smith, 1998, p. 65). Alternatively, the imaginary might enter into a full-blown organic crisis if it fails to incite identifications with the particular subject positions it offers.

A crisis can also develop as a result of counter-hegemonic activity. Smith explains that even though a political group may have monopolized a particular demand to the extent that its characterization of the demand in question seems to be the only possible definition, the logical possibility of alternative definitions always remains. Thus, political struggle entails both the assimilation of a wide variety of demands into a new historical bloc and strategic assaults on the discourse of the dominant bloc. The opponents of this dominant bloc must attack the principle of unity that holds it together if it is to loosen the control that the dominant bloc wields over the elements – values, symbols, campaigns and movements – that constitute it. If this attack is successful, then a growing number of these elements are transformed into floating signifiers, opening them up for redefinition and re-articulation by the counter-hegemonic movement (Smith, 1998, pp. 50–1).

As we have seen, Thatcherism incorporates two key discourses, namely its support for the enterprise culture and its endorsement of Victorian values. Hall observes that while these discourses appear contradictory, the Thatcherites nonetheless regarded them as the means to achieving a highly integrated 'British' society. This view stemmed from their belief that economic difficulties had their origins in politics and human nature, which in turn entailed that both the economic challenge, and the political and moral challenge, needed to be confronted and mastered together (1988, p. 85). In practice, however, the tension between the two discourses, together with the Thatcher government's failure either to halt or to reverse Britain's long-term economic decline, offered an opening for counter-hegemonic activity. Thatcherism's moral discourse was also vulnerable to critique, on the ground that it was moving in the opposite direction to the cultural attitudes of young people, which were heavily influenced by sexual politics, feminism and the cultural maturing of urban black youths (Hall, 1988, p. 91). Therefore, the possibility arose for young people to attack Thatcher's moral discourse and to redefine and rearticulate its constituent elements in their own terms.

The threat to Thatcherism was further compounded by the fact that it never won the support of the great majority of the dominated groups in British society. However, as Hall observes, 'elections are won or lost not just on so-called "real" majorities, but on (equally real) "symbolic majorities"'. The latter group included those people who shared the Thatcherite view that the creation of an enterprise culture was the way forward for Britain, and who envisioned themselves as likely to benefit from her government's policies in the future. In Hall's terms, these individuals formed an 'imaginary community' around the political project of Thatcherism. Nonetheless, support for Thatcherism was far from guaranteed, particularly as the number of people who benefited – or at least believed they could benefit – from its policies declined (Hall, 1988, p. 262).

Although a hegemonic formation creates numerous mechanisms to further its reproduction, which can include the absorption of potential opponents and the incitement of spurious counter-struggles, it will never succeed in becoming completely closed. This failure provides an opening for resistance, which may take the form of 'reactivation'. Laclau explains that reactivation involves rediscovery, through the emergence of novel antagonisms, that 'objectivity' is in fact contingent. This rediscovery can in turn 'reactivate the *historical* understanding of the original acts of institution insofar as stagnant forms that were simply considered as objectivity and taken for granted are now revealed as contingent and project that contingency to the "origins" themselves' (1990, p. 35). In short, reactivation is the opposite of sedimentation and can be achieved through re-politicization. This entails the creation of a new framework that enables us to appreciate that the identities and institutionalized social arrangements we previously viewed as necessary and timeless are in fact contingent and deeply political (Smith, 1998, p. 172).

Once a specific discourse has been successfully institutionalized, however, it becomes more difficult to effectively advance a radically different alternative. This difficulty is not due to any intrinsic property of the signifiers themselves, given the availability of numerous logically possible alternative articulations. Rather, in real historical circumstances, Smith writes, a particular articulation will only become effective in its role as a 'popular interpretative framework through which structural positionings are lived' to the extent that it is embedded in authoritative institutions. The success of the institutionalization of a discourse is in turn dependent upon the configuration of power relations that obtains within that particular historical context. On this basis, therefore, we can say that although other articulations are logically possible, the strategic efficacy of any given alternative is dependent on the prevailing historical conditions at the time (Smith, 1998, pp. 172–3). This point again echoes Freeden's account of the role of cultural factors in curbing the range of logically possible alternatives, and his belief in the importance of history in the attribution of meaning.

Moral argument and hegemonic politics

Moral prescriptions lend themselves readily to emotive appeal. As Hall explains, the language of popular morality is that which, 'without benefit of training, education, coherent philosophising, erudition or learning, touches the direct and immediate experience of the [popular] class' (1988, p. 143). It also has the power to describe and explain the complexities of the social realm in terms of clear and unequivocal moral polarities, such as good and evil, the result of which is that it resonates deeply with people's experiences. This is particularly important during periods of organic crisis, when popular morality supplies people with a framework to organize their experiences, and thus to make sense of them. In Hall's words, 'under the right conditions, "the people" in their traditionalist representation can be condensed as a set of interpellations in discourses which systematically displace political issues into conventional moral absolutes' (1988, p. 143). An example of this displacement can be found in Thatcherite discourses on crime, in which they created a relation of equivalence between notions of 'moral degeneration' and the breakdown of authority and social values, and thereby constructed criminality as a threat to people's possessions and way of life. By exploiting the moral panic over crime, the Thatcherites succeeded in capturing public attention and instilling in the silent majority a sense that 'ordinary people' needed to defend the social order against this threat (Hall, 1988, pp. 143–4). This in turn enabled Thatcherite discourses to prevail in the area of law and order, and thus to achieve rhetorical advantage over their rivals.

As Charteris-Black points out, politicians need to make 'bold rhetorical contrasts between right and wrong, between good and evil' if they are to 'create value in a marketplace of ethics' (2005, p. 148). One way of achieving this end is to use the logic of equivalence to create an antagonism between that which is constructed as 'good' and that which is represented as 'evil'. In this way, politicians whose party is in opposition will often contrast their vision of the future – of how good things can be under their leadership – with how bad the situation is under the government of the day. This technique is evident in Thatcher's speech to the 1975 Conservative Party conference, where she presented her vision of,

> A man's right to work as he will, to spend what he earns, to own property, to have the State as servant and not as master – these are the British inheritance. They are the essence of a free country and on that freedom all our other freedoms depend. (1975, p. 4)

These various rights were articulated together to form a chain of equivalence, while the policies of the Labour Party – the enemy bloc – were represented as its other, and therefore delegitimized.

According to Thatcher, the excess of state control under the Labour government had imposed limits on people's freedom, while its economic policies had led to record levels of peacetime taxation and public spending, rising prices, and excessive borrowing (1975, pp. 1–3). Thatcher represented these phenomena as equivalent signifiers and treated them as symptoms of 'the usual Socialist *disease*' (Thatcher, 1975, p. 2), which she subsequently placed in an antagonistic relation to remedy metaphors. In the peroration of her address, for example, she said, 'Let us resolve to *heal the wounds* of a divided nation, and let that *act of healing* be the prelude to a lasting victory' (1975, p. 7). Underlying these metaphors are the conceptualisations of LABOUR (= SOCIALIST) POLICIES ARE A DISEASE and CONSERVATIVE POLICIES ARE A MEDICINE, which associate the two parties with notions of 'good' and 'bad' respectively, and thus highlight the differences between them (Charteris-Black, 2005, pp. 100–2).

If a politician is to succeed in hegemonic competitions, he or she also needs to convey a compelling *ethos*. In classical rhetoric, *ethos* refers to the values or character of the speaker, which then form the basis of a persuasive appeal. Thatcher's defining *ethos* was her sense of moral conviction, which was evident in her response to calls for a reversal of her monetarist economic policies: 'To those waiting with bated breath for that favourite media catchphrase, the "U" turn, I have only one thing to say. "You turn if you want to. The lady's not for turning"' (1980, p. 6). The persuasive force of Thatcher's rhetoric stemmed largely from the high degree of consistency between her chosen words and her *ethos*. After all, a mismatch could create the impression that a speaker is attempting to mislead their audience, which in turn could diminish their credibility. And so, as Charteris-Black puts it, 'an important objective for political leadership is to create a perception that the speaker is to be trusted' (2005, p. 103).

Conclusion

The examination of the three components of the 'context of justification' is now complete. In Chapter 1, I considered Freeden's account of the morphological character of ideology, and the processes of conceptual decontestation and integration involved in the formation of an ideological position. Then, in Chapter 2, I described the three different modes of moral argument available to political actors and demonstrated their suitability for promoting initiatives in some policy areas over others. Finally, in the present chapter, I explored the 'context of hegemonic competition' and demonstrated that moral language plays an important role in the struggle for hegemonic advantage. In the following chapter, I introduce the analytical framework that will guide my examination of the process by which politicians select, modify and apply moral principles and arguments in order to win support for their policies.

4
Towards an Understanding of the Dynamics of Moral Argument in Politics

In the preceding chapters, we considered each of the three aspects of the 'context of justification': the 'context of ideology', the 'context of argumentation' and the 'context of hegemonic competition'. The present chapter brings these elements together, and in the first section I develop this account of the process of justification into a three-stage theoretical framework, which will guide the examination of the case of New Labour in Part II of the book. For analytical purposes, the framework reconstructs this process as one in which argumentative strategies are chosen, adapted and utilized in the light of the three contextual factors identified above. The framework suggests the use of qualitative research methods, and in the second section I outline the main features of this approach and examine its implications for the analysis of my chosen case study.

The theoretical framework

This section will introduce a framework that will enable us to disaggregate and reconstruct the process by which politicians select, modify and apply moral arguments to promote policy initiatives in different areas. First, however, it is necessary to consider how the three components of the 'context of justification' might influence a politician's choice of argumentative strategies. As we saw in Chapter 1, Freeden locates policy proposals on the perimeter of an ideology. These proposals are frequently justified – to both the members of the political party that initiated it and to the public – by reference to moral principles and arguments. This suggests that a politician's chosen argumentative strategy should be as consistent as possible not only with the policy in question, but also with the definitions of the concepts contained within their party's ideology. Such consistency is attainable through Freeden's notion of cultural adjacency, whose restrictions on the demands of logical adjacency permit ideologies to 'minimise the problems of internal inconsistency by creating acceptable connections between terms and arguments in order to escape logical criticism' (Freeden, 1996, p. 85). Equally, cultural adjacency can reduce any obvious inconsistencies between a party's chosen moral justifications and its ideological platform, a process that can be further refined through consideration of the requirements of argumentation. Indeed, these requirements may themselves provide additional reference points for decontestation.

The 'context of argumentation' encompasses consequentialist, deontological and virtue theoretic arguments, which tend to be deployed in distinct policy areas. Consequentialist arguments are typically used in the area of welfare, where politicians emphasize the increase in – though not necessarily the maximization of – well-being a policy will produce or, more broadly, its positive consequences. The ongoing government campaigns to encourage people to give up smoking to improve their own health and that of others are a case in point (see, for instance, Department of Health, 2007). Meanwhile, deontological reasoning frequently appears in politicians' arguments to promote constitutional reforms such as the Human Rights Act of 1998, a measure New Labour claimed would protect and uphold the human rights of every UK citizen (Labour Party, 2005, p. 111). Finally, virtue theoretic arguments are often employed to sell policies relating to community, an example being the introduction of citizenship education to the National Curriculum in 2002. For New Labour, the goal of this initiative was both to inculcate civic virtues in children and to promote the common good through the creation of a healthy political culture (Landrum, 2002, p. 221).

Within a hegemonic context, questions of securing advantage in moral and political wars of position and winning rhetorical competitions may further influence the selection and modification of argumentative strategies. Thus, a particular strategy may be chosen because it appeals to the commonsense intuitions of the electorate, for instance, or because it offers the best available means of undermining the arguments of a political opponent. A further important consideration in the 'context of hegemonic competition' is consistency, and there are two reasons why this is so. First, it is unlikely that an incoherent justificatory strategy will secure hegemonic advantage for a given policy. Hence, a policy and the strategy deployed to justify it should be consistent both internally and with each other. Second, a strategy that accords with the political party's ideological commitments is more likely to succeed in securing the moral high ground, and thus to be perceived as convincing, than one that contradicts them. This latter point ties in with the issue of integrity, given that people are more likely to view as honest a politician whose words are congruent with his or her *ethos*, or core values. Conversely, a party that acts contrary to its ideological commitments may be perceived as opportunistic and lacking in credibility, and consequently will be less likely to secure hegemonic advantage for its policy programmes. Politicians enhance the effectiveness of their argumentative strategies with a range of rhetorical devices, and an examination of these techniques will enable us to take into account the emotional as well as the intellectual and appeal of arguments.

It is important to point out that the three components of the 'context of justification' are not discrete entities; rather, there is interaction and overlap between them. For example, when Barry's account of political argument is applied in practice, we can say that ideal-regarding principles will be the same as – or related to but nonetheless consistent with – the conception of how society ought to be that is contained within the party's ideological platform. Meanwhile, want-regarding principles will be deployed in order to gain hegemonic advantage, and the want that is thought to be the most likely to achieve this end is selected over the other available wants. So, victory in hegemonic competitions may be secured through a well-chosen want-regarding principle, in conjunction with an ideal-regarding principle that is consistent with both the want-regarding principle and the party's ideological platform. If a conflict arises between a concept contained within the ideology and the party's chosen ideal-regarding principle, then the meaning of this concept may be modified through the process of decontestation.

We can also say that ideological morphology will influence the level of importance attached to various rights and freedoms. For instance, equality is a core concept for socialists, and the adherents of this ideology will emphasize the rights that are consistent with this concept. Similarly, liberals will focus on the rights and freedoms that promote their core concept of liberty. However, certain rights may have to be curtailed due to external factors, a case in point being a time of national emergency. As a result, the rights that a particular party favours will be subject to revision. These modifications are likely to have an effect on the meaning of the concepts that support the rights concerned, and in turn will trigger ideological change. Likewise, a party's catalogue of the virtues must be consistent with its ideological platform. This account is not fixed, and thus is susceptible to environmental influences. Any changes that occur may alter the meaning of one or more of the concepts that comprise the party's ideology, which will then initiate the decontestation of any affected neighbouring concepts.

This account of the 'context of justification' suggests the following analytical framework for investigating how politicians employ moral principles and arguments to promote policy initiatives:

1. An examination of how particular principles and arguments may be made answerable to an integrated ideological platform.
2. An examination of how particular modes of argument may be deployed compellingly with respect to specific types of policy.
3. An examination of how argumentative strategies may be formulated in ways that provide an opportunity to gain hegemonic advantage in the context of a competitive, rhetorical political situation.

Although there may be grounds for thinking that the 'context of ideology' is more fundamental than the other contexts, they may, in practice, rebound back on each other. Therefore, the process outlined above is neither linear nor hierarchical, and a comprehensive account of the justification of policy is possible only when all three stages have been considered. It is also worth noting that these stages do not represent the procedure by which real politicians select particular moral principles and arguments. Rather, they form analytical strands in a reconstruction of the process by which argumentative strategies are selected, modified and utilized in politics. Therefore, the framework will enable us to give a non-reductive account of this process, while remaining sensitive to the potentially conflicting considerations that enter into it.

The methodological implications of the framework

As we saw in Chapter 3, there are a number of strong similarities between discourse theory and Freeden's morphological approach to the analysis of ideologies. To recap briefly, both perspectives acknowledge the close relationship between language and the social world. Indeed, Freeden's methodology is, he says, 'based on permitting constant intercourse between political conceptualisation and the real world to which it relates and from which it springs' (1996, p. 39). The anti-essentialism of discourse theory is consistent with Freeden's endorsement of the effective contestability thesis (EFC), while the notion of a floating signifier espoused by the former corresponds to the latter's idea of an effectively contested concept. In addition, the process of conceptual decontesta-tion that Freeden describes accords with discourse theory's account of the process of articulation, through which signifiers are assigned a par-ticular meaning. Both perspectives recognize that the outcome of this process is contingent, and that concepts may be subject to redefinition at a later time. Finally, Freeden's notion of an ideological core closely resembles the nodal point in discourse theory, though it is worth high-lighting that the former consists of a cluster of concepts, while the latter is a single empty signifier that 'fixes the content of a range of floating signifiers by articulating them in a chain of equivalence' (Torfing, 1999, p. 303). The similarities between these two strands of the framework, and in particular the central role they accord to language, suggest that qualitative research methods are the most appropriate means of investi-gating the dynamics of moral justification in contemporary politics.

There is a variety of qualitative research techniques available to social scientists, ranging from semi-structured interviews to participant obser-vation. Nonetheless, as Jennifer Mason points out, these strategies share a number of common elements. First, they are rooted in a philosoph-ical paradigm which can, broadly speaking, be labelled as 'interpretiv-ist'. This paradigm is concerned with the question of how the social world is experienced, interpreted, constructed or constituted. While this question may be addressed in a number of different ways – for instance, by focusing on discourses, practices, processes, constructions, interpretations or meanings – all qualitative researchers will view at least some of them as meaningful features of a complex social world. Second, qualitative research employs methods of generating data that are, Mason writes, 'both flexible and sensitive to the social context in which the data are produced' (2002, p. 3). Third, qualitative research is based on methods of explanation, analysis and argumentation that acknowledge the importance of complexity, context and detail. This is necessary if it is to fulfil its objective of producing a comprehensive account of the social phenomena concerned.

The qualitative research technique to be used in this study is docu-mentary analysis. While documents are often employed to support the evidence gathered from interviews, Paul Atkinson and Amanda Coffey correctly argue that they should be treated as data in their own right and not simply regarded as secondary sources. This is because docu-ments frequently 'enshrine a distinctive documentary version of social reality. They have their own conventions that inform their production and circulation. They are associated with distinct social occasions and organised activities' (1997, pp. 47–8). This is not to say that there is a documentary level of reality existing independently of such other levels as that of social interaction; after all, the exchange and use of documents is a key feature of this activity. Nevertheless, it is imperative that the researcher treats documentary data seriously and gives them the analytic attention they deserve (Atkinson and Coffey, 1997, p. 48).

When undertaking an analysis of documentary sources, there are a number of factors that should be taken into consideration. In Mason's words, documents need to be ' "read" and interpreted in the context of, for example, how they are produced, used, what meanings they have, what they are seen to be or to represent culturally speaking' (2002, p. 108). This is because documents are 'social facts,' insofar as there are social conventions that govern the ways in which they are produced, distributed and utilized. However, it is important to note that they are not merely 'transparent representations of organisational routines, decision-making processes or professional diagnoses'; rather, they create specific types of representations in accordance with their own set of rules (Atkinson and Coffey, 1997, p. 47). Consequently, the researcher should approach documentary sources on their own terms and be mindful of the goals that they are intended to achieve.

The reconstructions of social reality that appear in documentary sources are often dependent upon specific ways of using language. As Atkinson and Coffey explain, 'certain document types constitute – to use a literary analogy – *genres*, with distinctive styles and conventions' (1997, p. 49). Thus, the different spheres of everyday life use language in their own particular ways. For instance, the language used in a children's book will differ from that which is used in a newspaper, while tabloid newspapers are written in a very different style from that which characterizes the broadsheet press. Likewise, such official texts as reports and documents use their own particular style of language, and this is itself one of a range of devices employed to create the unique mode of documentary representation. For this reason, it is advantageous to begin an analysis of documentary sources by adopting an interpretive perspective.

It is worth highlighting that documents do not exist in isolation and, as such, do not create specific realms or schemes of documentary reality as discrete activities. Instead, 'documents refer – however tangentially or at one remove – to other realities and domains. They also refer to *other* documents' (Atkinson and Coffey, 1997, p. 55). It thus follows that any analysis of documentary reality must not only examine individual texts, but consider how they are related to one another. The idea that documents are not free-standing and refer to other texts is termed 'intertextuality'. By recognizing these intertextual relationships, the social scientist is able to examine the similarities and differences between documents, as well as the way in which texts share conventional formats, and hence how they create a consistent style (Atkinson and Coffey, 1997, p. 57). The methodology expounded here is compatible with that of Freeden, who argues that the analyst of ideologies needs to concentrate on the 'patterns, continuities, and discontinuities political thinking displays, and the manner in which it shapes the politically possible', and not to seek to replace it with a normatively preferable standpoint that is detached from the realm in which political thinking actually takes place (1996, p. 39).

The analysis of documentary sources raises the twin issues of their authorship and their readership, whether actual or implied. These considerations are important because they allow the social scientist to gain an understanding of the system in which documents are produced, exchanged and utilized, and I now discuss them in turn. A characteristic feature of organizational and official documents is that their author is unidentified; indeed, this anonymity is a constituent part of the process by which such documents are produced. Moreover, the lack of an implied author is a rhetorical device that may enhance the official or authoritative status of a document by implying an objective reality that exists independently of any individual agent. However, this device alone cannot guarantee such status, which is also derived from the organizational contexts in which documents are created and consumed. Even if the author of a document is unidentifiable, its 'ownership' can nonetheless be implied by, for example, the government department from which it originates. Consequently, the social scientist is able to examine texts for evidence of their authorship – or the absence thereof – and to seek out the basis of any claim to authority they may make (Atkinson and Coffey, 1997, pp. 58–9).

The preceding discussion highlights the importance of the distinction between the 'author' as an individual – regardless of whether he or she is identified by name – and the 'implied author'. This point is particularly pertinent within a political context, where speeches are often written for a politician by a team of specialist speechwriters. In these situations, authorship is implied by the fact that the politician is delivering the speech in question, on the ground that he or she 'has the opportunity to edit the content of the speech and to improvise in its style of delivery', and so has ultimate responsibility for them (Charteris-Black, 2005, p. 8). It is, therefore, highly unlikely that a politician will publicly endorse any policies that he or she believes will fail, given that a subsequent retraction of these opinions may provoke accusations of insincerity or hypocrisy.

The construction of documentary reality also involves an implied readership. It is frequently the case that texts are directed at particular groups of reader, the reason being that only a restricted readership, which possesses specific abilities, will be able to comprehend them fully. Consequently, it is impossible for any text – irrespective of whether it is official or literary – to control exactly how it should be read. This is because reading is not the passive absorption of information, but is instead an active process to which the reader brings his or her own particular knowledge and experiences (Atkinson and Coffey, 1997, pp. 59–60). However, the purpose of some texts, such as political speeches, election manifestos and parliamentary debates, is to persuade their readers and listeners of a particular point of view, and to this end they employ a range of rhetorical techniques. In order to appreciate the appeal of these linguistic strategies, Freeden says, we need to 'readmit the role of the emotional as well as the intellectual attractiveness of arguments, and...to examine cultural as well as logical validations of political thinking'. Therefore, although consistency and logic are important criteria for the evaluation of political arguments, they are by no means the only standards we should use (Freeden, 1996, p. 37).

The investigation of how New Labour used moral principles and arguments to promote its policy initiatives will be carried out as follows:

1. An examination of the command papers, reports and dossiers that were either involved in or generated by the creation of the policy concerned. On this basis, they are deemed to be primary sources (Burnham et al., 2004, p. 165).
2. A study of a range of documentary sources, including speeches, parliamentary debates and election manifestos. These materials are classed as secondary sources because they are related to the policy documents and were produced soon after these proposals were presented in the public domain. Other texts to be considered include articles in academic journals, books, published memoirs, and biographies of the key players involved, all of which are classed as tertiary sources because they offer a reconstruction of the event after it took place (Burnham et al., 2004, p. 165).
3. A reconstruction of the reasons why New Labour chose the argumentative strategies it did, using the framework outlined above. First, the primary and secondary sources identified above will be examined in relation to the 'context of ideology,' in order to establish the degree to

which the policies and the arguments used to promote them express New Labour's core ideological commitments. Second, the three types of sources will be used to identify the argumentative strategies that New Labour employed in each policy area, and to assess the suitability of these arguments for promoting the initiative concerned. This investigation will supply the 'context of argumentation'. Third, the 'context of hegemonic competition' will be considered through an examination of the rhetorical techniques that New Labour deployed in support of its argumentative strategies. Here, I will compare New Labour's assertions about the effectiveness of its policies with the views of its critics and, where available, the social policy evidence about the effectiveness of these initiatives. I will also outline the Conservative Party response to New Labour's proposals, and highlight the main similarities and differences between them. This will enable me to assess the extent to which New Labour succeeded in setting the agenda in the four policy areas.

Conclusion

In sum, the use of documentary analysis in conjunction with the theoretical framework will yield a comprehensive account of the dynamics of moral argument in politics. It will thus reveal the mediations and modifications implicit in the process of justification, identify the emergence and resolution of tensions within and between argumentative strategies, and explicate any remaining inconsistencies or lacunae within New Labour's strategy as a whole. In Chapter 5, I will analyse the core concepts and principles that comprise the ideology of New Labour, and evaluate its success as a hegemonic project. The results of this investigation will supply the ideological component of the 'context of justification' and will enable us to assess the extent to which the moral principles and arguments that New Labour used to promote its policies were consistent with its ideology. I undertake this task in Chapters 6 to 9, where I examine the argumentative strategies that New Labour employed in the four policy areas in relation to its core ideological commitments, moral claims and terms of argument, and the demands of hegemonic competition.

Part II
The Case of New Labour

5
The Ideology of New Labour

The doctrine of the 'Third Way' featured heavily in early New Labour discourse. Its principal objective was to move beyond both the democratic socialism espoused by 'Old' Labour, which is often labelled the 'first way', and the neo-conservatism of the Thatcher and Major governments, which is frequently termed the 'second way'.[1] More specifically, the Third Way sought to temper free-market capitalism with social justice, while attempting to avoid an 'excessive domination of the state over social and economic life' (Giddens, 2000, p. 13). This chapter begins by outlining the assumptions that underpin the Third Way. Drawing on Freeden's morphological approach, I then consider how the meanings of the main concepts of New Labour's ideology were decontested in relation to one other, thereby forming an ideological 'core'. This account of New Labour's early commitments provides the basis of the 'context of ideology' and, in the following chapters, I highlight the changes in its core values that occurred during its time in office. Finally, I address the question of how New Labour was able to achieve hegemonic status. In so doing, I examine and reject Stuart Hall's contention that the New Labour project was not a hegemonic enterprise.

The underlying assumptions of the Third Way

Tony Blair's election to the leadership of the Labour party in 1994 consolidated the process of reform begun by Neil Kinnock in the 1980s and continued by John Smith in the mid-1990s. These reforms targeted both the organizational structure of the Party and its ideological platform, with the ultimate aim of making Labour electable again. The key structural changes were Kinnock's expulsion of Militant from the party; the replacement of the trade union block vote with the 'one member, one vote' system, which Smith accomplished in 1993; and the rewriting of Clause IV of the Party Constitution under Tony Blair.[2] In terms of ideology, Kinnock initiated a gradual shift from state socialism to a version of European social democracy, which purged Labour of its traditional socialist commitments to central economic planning and public ownership, and led to a reassessment of key revisionist ideas (Jones, 1996, p. 129). This process continued during Smith's leadership and gained momentum under Blair, culminating in the rebranding of the Party as 'New' Labour.

Alongside these internal changes, Labour had to come to terms with the economic and social legacy of Thatcherism. With regard to the economy, the Thatcher government had replaced Keynesianism with economic liberalism and the strong – though minimal – state, while its social policy was directed towards the creation of a society populated by self-reliant individuals and was underpinned by an authoritarian approach to law and order (Gamble, 1988). These developments fundamentally altered the political landscape and resulted in a deeply divided society, in which the wealth of the richest fifth of the UK's population had increased since 1979, while the underclass, consisting of people surviving on low incomes or state benefits, had mushroomed (Coates, 2005, p. 19). To confront these challenges, New Labour proposed its theory of the Third Way, an approach characterized by permanent revisionism and involving, Blair said, a 'continual search for better means to meet our goals, based on a clear view of the changes taking place in advanced industrialised societies' (1998a, p. 4). The main features of these changes, and New Labour's broad policy responses to them, are detailed next.

For Blair, the motivating force behind the theory of the Third Way was globalization, on the ground that no nation was immune from the profound economic and social changes it brings (1996a, p. 118). In economic terms, world financial markets had expanded significantly, with capital becoming more mobile and global trade competition more intense. Moreover, there was a growing global division of labour, the result of which was that many goods were no longer produced by a single firm, but by a network of different companies across the world (Driver and Martell, 2006, p. 22). Blair identified the cornerstones of this new global economy as knowledge, skills, services and small businesses. He explained that advances in technology, and the ascendance of information and skills as the motors of employment and new industries, had rendered obsolete the notion of a job for life and reduced the demand for unskilled manual labour. These developments made people less economically secure, the result of which was that the need for a high standard of education for all was greater than ever (Blair, 1998a, p. 6; 1996a, p. 120).

As regards British society, the most significant changes wrought by globalization were the transformation in the role of women and the erosion of the traditional class system. More women than ever before were entering the job market, while longstanding assumptions about the nature of family life and paid work were being overturned. These developments led to a loosening of cultural and family ties, with social relations becoming 'more fluid, more mobile and less bound by tradition, deference and patriarchal relations' (Driver and Martell, 2006, p. 22). As the influence of custom declined, a new individualism emerged, which fundamentally changed the nature of politics. People were no longer content to passively accept what public servants and professionals gave them, and instead wanted to make choices for themselves, to have a say in both the policies that affected them and in the services they used (Driver and Martell, 2006, p. 22). In turn, political institutions needed to adapt to these changes, and New Labour offered the Third Way as a new model of government that would meet this need.

According to Blair, the Third Way sought to meet four main policy objectives, the first of which was a 'dynamic knowledge-based economy founded on individual empowerment and opportunity' (1998a, p. 7). To this end, government should harness market forces to serve the interests of society as a whole, and should be enabling as opposed to commanding. Second the Third Way endorsed a strong civil society based on reciprocal rights and responsibilities, in which government and communities would act in partnership to promote the common good. Its third goal, meanwhile, was to promote a modern idea of government that was founded upon decentralization and partnership. This entailed a deeper notion of democracy and a greater degree of government accountability. Finally, the Third Way endorsed an approach to foreign policy that was founded on international cooperation, with states working together not only to fight or prevent wars, but also to tackle common problems such as drugs, terrorism and organised crime (Blair, 1998a, p. 7). These four objectives together gave expression to New Labour's commitment to modernization, and its desire to find new means of realizing the values of the centre-left.

The morphology of New Labour's ideological platform

Broadly speaking, the academic literature on the ideology of New Labour falls into two camps, though there is a degree of overlap between them.

The first seeks to position New Labour on the political spectrum, with Colin Hay, for instance, claiming that New Labour represented an accommodation to the legacy of Thatcherism (1999). While the proponents of this position are surely correct in saying that the Labour Party had to adapt to the changes made by the Thatcher governments, I believe it is an overstatement to describe it as 'Thatcherism Mark II'. After all, New Labour's ideology retained some key elements of democratic socialism, which were vital if the party was to remain recognizably 'Labour' and thus maintain its core support. Steve Buckler and David Dolowitz offer an alternative view, according to which New Labour occupied a 'social liberal' position that was consistent with the liberalism of John Rawls and emphasized procedural justice over patterns of distribution (2000, p. 301). Although they acknowledge the presence of centre-left ideas in New Labour's thinking, Buckler and Dolowitz do not address the influence of Thatcherism, and their characterization is incomplete as a result. Freeden, meanwhile, identifies concepts taken from conservatism, liberalism and socialism in New Labour's discourse. On this basis, he locates New Labour between these ideological traditions, though he quickly points out that it was 'not equidistant from them all' (1999, p. 48). As we will see below, concepts drawn from the three traditions were clearly present in New Labour's ideological core, so of the available accounts Freeden's is the most convincing.

The second body of literature seeks to identify the values that constitute New Labour's ideological platform. Julian Le Grand, for example, suggests community, opportunity, responsibility and accountability, or 'Cora' (1998), while Ruth Lister proposes 'RIO' – responsibility, inclusion and opportunity (2000). However, an examination of the texts in which key New Labour figures set out their party's guiding principles reveals that, *pace* Le Grand, accountability featured only rarely, while the concept of community, which is absent from Lister's definition, played a central role. A more comprehensive interpretation of New Labour is proposed by Freeden, who identifies community as a core concept, alongside equal worth, opportunity for all, responsibility, social justice and cohesion (1999, p. 48). These values all have a strong presence in New Labour's discourses, and Freeden's account forms the basis of my analysis of the 'context of ideology' for this reason. However, Freeden does not explain how these concepts fit together to form the core cluster of New Labour's ideological platform, and I undertake this task next.

New Labour's core concept of equal worth was decontested as the moral equality of all individuals, regardless of such contingent factors as their gender, age, ethnicity or sexuality. In Blair's words, 'common humanity demands that everyone be given a platform on which to stand' (1995a, p. 12). The principle of equal worth was given content by the liberal notion that people have a capacity for free self-development, and in turn supplied the moral basis of the concept of equality of opportunity. After all, if every individual matters the same, it follows that they should be offered the widest possible range of opportunities to fulfil their potential and increase their earning power (Brown, 1994, p. 3). Equal worth, and its concomitant notions of fairness and justice, also underpinned the core concept of responsibility, which New Labour viewed as a prerequisite for a strong, inclusive community.

According to Gordon Brown, 'the essence of equality is equality of opportunity,' and government has a fundamental responsibility to pursue this objective (1996, pp. 1–3). Brown's liberal conception of equality represented a departure from the ideology of Old Labour, in which the notion of equality was linked primarily to equality of outcome and to a 'determination to eradicate significant inequalities of income and wealth through redistributive measures' (Wickham-Jones, 2004, p. 32). Equality of opportunity thus played a secondary role. New Labour reversed this ordering and identified the root cause of inequality and poverty as a lack of opportunity and skills. To overcome this problem, New Labour enacted policies designed to increase the availability of educational and employment opportunities, which in turn were intended to promote human capital and enhance Britain's ability to compete in the global economy. However, it is important to note that New Labour's commitment to education was not based on ideas about its intrinsic value, or its potential to increase personal well-being. Rather, its purpose was to equip people to take advantage of the job opportunities they were offered, and thus to become active participants in the employment market. Consequently, the adjacent concept of full employment was decontested not as a job for all – as it was under 'Old' Labour[3] – but as 'the *opportunity* for all to work and prosper' (Blair, 1996a, p. 53).

However, critics on the Left of the party objected that this emphasis on equality of opportunity would have little or no effect on the distribution of resources between different groups in society. After all, in the words of Stephen Driver and Luke Martell, 'the distribution of wealth and income remains a major determinant of the opportunities an individual has in life (to attend university, for example),' so outcomes and opportunities are inextricably linked (2006, p. 207). In practice, New Labour offered people financial incentives, such as training grants and tax credits, to accept the opportunities offered to them, and thus enacted redistributive policies; indeed, Raymond Plant labels it 'the most directly redistributive Labour Government ever' (2004, p. 118). I assess the extent to which New Labour succeeded in reducing the gap between rich and poor in the next chapter. Nonetheless, the question remains of why New Labour prioritized the possession of marketable skills and qualifications over other activities, such as caring for children, which also benefit the community and yet are not sufficiently rewarded in a market economy (Hickson, 2004, p. 132).

Blair endorsed a constitutive notion of community, claiming that our relationships with other people 'are not add-ons to our personalities: they make us who we are' (1996a, p. 300). As such, the ideals of interdependence and mutuality (in terms of both obligation and interest) are not mere abstractions, but instead are facts of life. To support this point, Blair invoked the Third Way conception of human nature, according to which people are cooperative as well as competitive, and thus are interested in their own well-being as well as that of others. We cannot be independent without collective goods, Blair claimed, and the richness – or otherwise – of our lives is affected by the communities of which we are members (1998a, p. 4). Consequently, Blair believed that this notion of community permitted an idea of self-interest that was both more enlightened and more rational than other, narrower, definitions that focus solely on the individual (1996a, p. 218).

On Blair's view, the fundamental truths are that everyone is created equal; that people are interdependent, in the sense that every individual owes duty (or responsibility – New Labour tended to use these terms interchangeably) not just to themselves but to each other; and that 'the good society is one which works for the good of all and not just the few' (1996a, p. 300). Here, Blair linked community and responsibility to the concept of equal worth: if each individual matters equally, then nobody is excluded from their mutual obligations or from sharing in the goods that society provides. There was also a close relationship between the concepts of community and equality of opportunity. As Blair put it, the great strength of community – of what people can achieve together – is to 'make more equal our opportunity and ability to develop our talents to the full' (1996a, p. 156). The value of equality of opportunity was therefore dependent on community for its realization and, together with equal worth and responsibility, promoted the ideal of a cohesive community that lay at the heart of New Labour's ideology.

For New Labour, strong communities depended on the acceptance of the rights and responsibilities of citizenship, which included not only the obligation to obey the law and to pay taxes, but also the duty to teach children to be responsible, competent members of society, and to support teachers and others in this task (Blair, 1998a, p. 12). The process of inculcating society's values in children begins in the family. After all, Blair claimed, it is here that we learn to behave in a socially acceptable manner and to recognize that we owe responsibilities not only to ourselves, but to other people. Because we then 'build out from that family base to the community and beyond that to society as a whole', Blair believed the values that characterize a decent society are in many respects the same as family values, and that the restoration of good family and community life should therefore be a cornerstone of government policy (1994a). It was on this basis that he expressed support for the institution of marriage, saying: 'The Government's primary concern is with the stability of relationships where children are involved, and we recognise that this stability is most easily found within marriage' (Blair, 2001a, p. 3). This statement, together with Blair's belief that family breakdown was linked to the breaking of community bonds – which in turn was a significant factor in the breakdown of law and order (1994a) – brought his underlying moral agenda to the fore. It also revealed a tension between the social conservatism of the New Labour leadership and the neutral stance on non-traditional forms of family adopted by some sections of the party (Driver and Martell, 2006, p. 52).

New Labour's core concept of responsibility was given expression in the primary precept of Third Way politics, which stated 'no rights without responsibilities'. As Anthony Giddens puts it, those individuals or groups who benefit from social goods should 'use them responsibly, and give something back to the wider social community in return' (2000, p. 52). For Giddens, this principle applied to all citizens without exception, regardless of their position in society, and therefore appeared to be consistent with New Labour's core concept of equal worth. However, communitarian thinkers such as Amitai Etzioni argue that New Labour's contractual view of rights violates this commitment. This is because basic human rights are an affirmation of our equal dignity, and the state cannot simply take them away if we fail to recycle our household waste, for instance, or neglect some other social responsibility (Etzioni, 2000, pp. 29–30). In practice, the rights New Labour usually referred to in this context were welfare rights – namely benefits or services provided by the state – and the concomitant responsibilities were those of the recipients of these goods (Hale, 2005, p. 18). Even so, New Labour's emphasis on the conditionality of rights created a sense of moral unease among some on the Left of the party, who raised the question of on what basis the community would assist those who were unable to fulfil their obligations to the state (Driver and Martell, 1997, pp. 37–8).

The concept of responsibility was closely connected to New Labour's notion of community. As Blair explained, duty is a personal thing, but we also owe it to our society; indeed, the notion of responsibility to others is a cornerstone of a strong, active community. This view of mutual obligation, Blair argued, would enable New Labour to build a society that 'does not subsume our individuality but allows it to develop healthily' and, as such, embodied the broader conception of human nature that the Third Way endorsed (1996a, pp. 237–8). It also gave expression to the idea that the concepts of responsibility and community are interdependent. After all, a community from which responsibility is absent would rapidly fall apart, while responsibility without community is merely an idle dream (Blair, 1996a, p. 242).

The pairing of rights and responsibilities, together with the rejection of the dichotomy between personal and social responsibility, formed the basis of Blair's modern concept of citizenship. This new notion of citizenship had a coercive dimension, which is clearly expressed in Blair's statement that, in situations where duties are neglected, 'we should not hesitate to encourage and even enforce them' (1998a, p. 12). One example of New Labour's use of coercion is the home-school agreement, which it introduced in 1999 to promote a sense of responsibility for children's education by setting out the rights and obligations of both parents and schools. If parents fail to fulfil their duty to ensure their children attend school, Local Education Authorities (LEAs) have the power to take them to court. The implication of New Labour's modern conception of citizenship, therefore, was that an individual who failed to keep their side of the contract, either by refusing to act responsibly or by rejecting the opportunities offered to them, was deemed to have relinquished their stake in the community, and thus was described as 'socially excluded.'

As we have seen, Blair believed that a strong, cohesive society with a sense of mutual responsibility at its core provides the best environment for individuals to prosper. He tied this view to the concept of stakeholding, saying 'our relations with each other are not simply market-based: they require social and moral principles to underpin them...We have to balance the interests of all' (1996a, p. 223). As such, stakeholding meant treating people as being of equal worth, on the ground that everyone's interests are valid and deserve consideration. To this end, Blair argued, we need to accept a collective obligation to ensure that every citizen receives a stake in British society. He termed this view 'one-nation politics', which he defined as an 'active politics – the bringing of a country together, the sharing of the possibility of power, wealth and opportunity' (1996a, pp. 292–3).

If we take Blair's notion of stakeholding together with his claim that government has a duty to sustain a level of employment that is both high and stable if our society is to become one to which everyone feels they belong (1996a, p. 39), then it seems that the idea of every individual having a stake in society was decontested as full employment, which itself was effectively equality of opportunity for all. This interpretation is lent support by Blair's assertion that a failure to create a stakeholder economy would be not just a waste of people's talent and their potential to create wealth, but a denial of the 'basis of trust upon which a cohesive society – one nation – is built'. Moreover, he argued, if people feel as if they do not have a stake in their society, they have a limited sense of responsibility towards it and are unwilling to work for its success (1996a, p. 293). So, for New Labour, a stakeholder society, in which there is full employment and plentiful opportunities for education and training, is one that is strong, cohesive and populated by citizens who accept their responsibilities both to themselves and to other people. Despite the importance of stakeholding in early New Labour discourse, however, the term soon disappeared from its lexicon. Nonetheless, the assumption on which it was based – namely the need to 'mesh the impact of economic globalisation with the rights of social citizenship' – continued to flourish (Gould, 1999, p. 255).

New Labour's conception of community had implications for the relationship between the individual and the state. In Blair's words, his party wanted to 'give power back to the people, and in return [expected] them to take on greater responsibility for themselves' (1996a, p. 262). More specifically, it sought to go beyond the antagonism between the public and the private sector and to see them working together in partnership. To this end, Blair claimed that the state should be deployed as an 'enabling force, protecting effective communities and voluntary organisations and encouraging their growth to tackle new needs, in partnership as appropriate' (1998a, p. 4). In particular, these new needs related to the enhancement of people's economic opportunity and the reconstruction of society's economic base. The main idea was 'active community', which encompassed voluntary work and charitable donations and was itself founded on the view that community can be promoted by encouraging people to help others. As such, it gave New Labour's core values of equality and social justice practical force. Therefore, New Labour's goal was to create a society that is simultaneously diverse and inclusive, which promotes tolerance within accepted social boundaries and advances a civic activism that complements, but does not seek to replace, government (Blair, 1998a, p. 12).

New Labour also saw government as active, though its purpose was to guarantee – as opposed to deliver – in such areas as the provision of employment opportunities or certain public services (Martell, 2004, p. 5). A clear example of active government in practice was New Labour's policy of dealing with unemployment through the New Deals, rather than leaving it to market forces to solve. This policy programme is examined in the next chapter. The notion of active government also tied in with New Labour's commitment to social justice. In Blair's words, 'there is no progress unless every citizen has a real stake in it. Without a fair distribution of the benefits of progress, societies risk falling apart in division, rancour and distrust' (1998a, p. 20). Thus, the concept of social justice lay at the root of New Labour's commitment to community and social inclusion, which it saw as government's responsibility to facilitate.

Having examined to core concepts of New Labour's ideology, the relationship between them can be summarized as follows. The concept of equal worth supplied the moral basis of the value of equality of opportunity, which in turn grounded cohesion and social justice. If an individual accepted the educational or employment opportunities offered to them, he or she was said to have a stake in that society, and a society in which everyone had a stake was viewed as both just and cohesive. However, New Labour argued that equality of opportunity was possible only within the context of a strong, inclusive community, which gave its members the chance to reach their full potential on the condition that they accepted their responsibilities to both themselves and society in return. These responsibilities were founded on the notion of equal worth, the reason being that if all individuals are equally valuable and deserving of the opportunity to develop their talents, then by the same token nobody is exempt from the obligations they owe in return. If an individual refused the opportunities offered to them, and thus failed in their duty to society, they were said to be socially excluded. As such, the concepts of community and responsibility were mutually dependent. The combination of inclusion, a strong community and opportunities for all led to success, and therefore progress toward Blair's goal of 'one nation – tolerant, fair, enterprising, inclusive' (1995a, p. 12).

Although this summary suggests that New Labour's ideological platform exhibited a high degree of coherence on a theoretical level, the question arises of the extent to which this level of consistency was sustainable in practice. After all, politicians need to take into account such factors as structural constraints and the demands of political expediency when formulating new policy initiatives, which may create tensions between their proposals and their party's values. Such conflicts can in turn trigger conceptual decontestation and thus lead to ideological change. A further potential difficulty for New Labour lay in its rejection of the dichotomies between, for instance, social justice and economic efficiency, and the community and the individual. This move had implications for policy, on the ground that it inevitably led to 'trade-offs between the demands of different policy goals and competing interests' (Driver and Martell, 2006, p. 53). I return to these issues in the following four chapters. First, however, I examine the range of strategies that New Labour successfully employed in its quest to achieve hegemonic advantage over its opponents.

New Labour's success as a hegemonic project

As Freeden observes, New Labour was often described as a hegemonic enterprise (1999, p. 51). There are a number of reasons for this, which include Blair's strong, charismatic leadership style, his talk of a 'vision' for Britain, the party's attempt to create a new centre-ground consensus, and its highly developed skills in media management. Hall, however, argues that, unlike Thatcherism, New Labour was not a hegemonic project. This is because New Labour, in its 'overall analysis and key assumptions, [was] still essentially framed by and moving on terrain defined by Thatcherism'. Moreover, continues Hall, the Thatcherites had a clearly defined political programme; while Blair's true historic project was to adjust the British people to the legacy of Thatcherism (Hall, 1998b, p. 14). Although Michael Temple acknowledges that Hall's argument demonstrates the significance of Thatcherism, he argues *pace* Hall that Blair was important also, given that he had 'modernised and led his party in a more dynamic way than his predecessor, the late John Smith, could have done' (2000, p. 307). In this section, I contend that New Labour should be viewed as a hegemonic enterprise, and that while some elements of New Labour were continuous with Thatcherism, others were distinct.

The emergence of New Labour was preceded by the conjuncture of the early 1990s, the limits of which were overdetermined by the economic and social changes resulting from globalization and the creation of a culture of individualism during the Thatcher era. This conjuncture also had a political dimension, which consisted in the divisions within John

Major's government over such issues as Britain's place in Europe, and the widespread perception that the Conservatives were 'sleazy' after the tabloid press exposed the personal and financial indiscretions of several ministers. New Labour seized upon these difficulties and, in an effort to further delegitimize Major, it portrayed him as a weak leader who was 'incapable of stamping his authority on the government he nominally leads' (Blair, 1996b, p. 2). This strategy proved highly effective and, by the time of the 1997 general election, support for the Conservatives had collapsed to such an extent that 'competitive politics from 1997 to 2006 [was] a fairly one-sided affair' (Beech, 2009, p. 527).

Although this crisis consisted in numerous dislocations, New Labour – in common with other third ways – defined it in terms of the failure of the traditional politics of left versus right, and offered its own approach as the solution to it (Bastow and Martin, 2003, p. 18). Indeed, we have already seen that New Labour's primary objective was to move beyond the antagonism between 'Old' Labour, which it linked to the traditional state socialism of the past, and the New Right ideology of the Thatcher governments. The importance of the word 'new' in New Labour's discourse thus becomes clear, and it can be said to play a dual role. On the one hand, it distinguished the freshness and vitality of New Labour from the weary, tarnished Conservatives, who had held on to power for too long. On the other, it enabled the party to distance itself not only from the Thatcherites' representation of Labour as excessively statist and the party of the 'loony left', but also from the perceived failures of previous socialist governments. Indeed, on the latter point, Hay notes that one of New Labour's key objectives was to establish the 'competence of the party to assume once again the mantle of governmental power' (1997, p. 377).[4]

For Blair, the phrase 'New Labour, New Britain' was not merely a slogan; rather, it 'embodie[d] a concept of national renewal led by a renewed Labour party'. This rhetoric of novelty implied that there was no rational alternative to its programme of modernization; indeed, Blair's aim of forging a 'new and radical politics for a new and changing world' (1996a, p. 3) both promised a solution to the crisis and gave expression to the hegemonic ambitions of the New Labour project. For Temple, this exercise in rebranding was more effective than it first appeared. He explains that the addition of the word 'New' gave Blair a substantial degree of freedom, on the ground that it 'implies fundamental change but the old Labour brand name reassures voters that the new party has not forgotten its commitment to notions of fairness and social justice' (2000, p. 307). This enabled Blair to profess his commitment to

socialist values and offer an alternative vision of society to his supporters, while at the same time claiming that this vision must be achieved
in new ways that went beyond the old antagonism between left and
right (Blair, 1995a, p. 14).

Blair's freedom was augmented further by the fact that, in the 1997
campaign, 'policy was not the focus of much media attention, analysis
or scrutiny; and the principal parties seemed quite happy to accept this
silence' (Hay, 1997, p. 376). Indeed, the key pledges of the 1997 general election manifesto, which included the reduction in class sizes in
schools and the cutting of waiting times in the NHS (Labour Party, 1997,
p. 35), were uncontroversial, and thus were acceptable to the majority
of people. On this basis, we can say that in making these pledges, New
Labour appeared to promise the fulfilment of all legitimate demands.
After all, the rebranding of the Labour party, together with its emphasis
on ends over means, enabled individuals to project their own hopes
and meanings onto the New Labour project, which in turn broadened
its appeal beyond its traditional supporters.

As Alan Finlayson observes, the 'central image of New Labour's electoral marketing [was] Tony Blair himself' (2003, p. 51). This image was
carefully constructed and consisted of a number of elements, among
which was Blair's ability to come across as a 'normal person' who sought
to 'generate an identification of equivalence rather than of some greater
ideal to which we aspire' (Finlayson, 2003, p. 54). Blair achieved this primarily by peppering his speeches with phrases from everyday language,
such as 'you know' and 'I mean,' which gave them a more conversa-
tional style. He also articulated New Labour policies in a personal manner, as if they were his own beliefs and hopes for the future (Fairclough,
2000, pp. 97–110). This technique enabled Blair to cultivate an *ethos* of
honesty and openness, which New Labour contrasted with the 'sleazy'
Conservatives to devastating effect in its 1997 general election campaign. As Fairclough correctly points out, however, there was a tension between the figure of Blair the 'normal person' on the one hand,
and Blair the politician on the other. He explains that the relationship
between these two figures was central to Blair's appeal, which was itself
dependent upon a 'continuing sense of the authenticity of Blair the
"normal person," a continuing trust in Blair as a person' (2000, p. 118).
Indeed, we will see in Chapter 9 that the controversy surrounding the
2003 Iraq War damaged the public's trust in Blair to such a degree that
his popularity never recovered.

According to Stuart Hall, the inherent ambiguities within New
Labour's Third Way precluded it from being a clearly defined political

project. Further, its goal of going beyond such antagonisms as fairness or enterprise was so vague as to be useless. In Hall's words, this approach looked not like a solution to the problems facing Britain, but a 'soft-headed way around them. [The Third Way] speaks with forked, or at the very least garbled, tongue'. For Hall, New Labour's semantic imprecision stemmed primarily from its endeavours to be all-inclusive. More specifically, he continues, its proponents spoke as if there were no competing interests and demands that could not be brought together, and in so doing attempted to create a 'politics without adversaries' (1998b, p. 10).

However, I believe Hall overstates the importance of consistency in the assessment of an ideology, on the ground that no ideological formation is – and indeed cannot be expected to be – perfectly coherent. This raises the question of whether Hall is employing the criteria of logical or cultural consistency in his critique of New Labour. We saw in Chapter 1 that, for Freeden, an ideology is highly unlikely to fulfil the requirements of the former, while cultural adjacency permits the presence of two seemingly opposing concepts within an ideology if the 'contradiction' is culturally permissible. It thus follows that if Hall is judging New Labour by the standards of logic, then his criticism is unfair, whereas if he is using the criteria of cultural acceptability, then the charge of inconsistency is not as serious as it first appears. The notions of logical and cultural adjacency also enable us to reject the argument that the inherent vagueness of the Third Way gave New Labour 'almost unlimited ideological flexibility' (Temple, 2000, p. 310), due to the constraints they impose on the range of meanings available to the concepts present within an ideology.

At the same time, it is undeniable that New Labour sometimes used its ideological ambiguities to its own advantage. For instance, they enabled New Labour to successfully 'manage a broad coalition of interests unified around a programme of government' (Bastow and Martin, 2003, p. 64). These demands were often in conflict, so the use of coercion and skilful rhetorical manoeuvring was required to bring them together. In this way, New Labour was able to neutralize and absorb any resistance to its project, and thus to increase its dominance. New Labour also exploited its inherent ambiguities by deploying antagonistic discourses in different 'theatres of operation', perhaps emphasizing the economic benefits of a policy when trying to win the support of the business community, and focusing on the social justice aspect of that same policy in speeches addressed to members of voluntary organizations. This strategy afforded New Labour a means of concealing the contradiction between the two argumentative strategies, which in turn broadened its appeal and enabled it to portray itself as a coherent political enterprise.

On Hall's view, the 'populism' of the Thatcher project was an indicator of its ability to 'cut across and between the different divisions in society and to connect with certain aspects of popular experience' (1988, p. 6). This claim is equally true of New Labour, which employed the strategies described above to increase its popularity. As David Rubinstein explains, New Labour recognized that the working class was no longer the largest constituent of society, and that consequently 'the party's nominal appeal to the whole community would have to contain a specific appeal to the middle classes' (1997, p. 340). At the same time, however, New Labour could not risk alienating its core vote. So, to manage these competing demands, New Labour played on its ideological ambiguities to stress its novelty to the individuals and groups that hitherto had not voted for the Labour party, and to emphasize its commitment to social democratic values when addressing its traditional supporters. In this way, writes Matt Beech, New Labour succeeded in selling itself as the 'natural party of government; a party representative of much of Great Britain' (2009, p. 528).

In the process of becoming an imaginary, New Labour's discourses became embedded in a variety of social institutions. Mark Bevir and Rod Rhodes define institutions as the 'rules, procedures and formal organisations of government' (1999, p. 217), so it is clear that a discourse has a definite strategic advantage if it is institutionalized. New Labour formed connections with existing institutions and traditions in the following three ways. First, it developed some of its appropriations from Thatcherism, which had previously defined the terrain of British politics. Second, it became embedded in the new institutions that emerged from the organic crisis. One such institution was the Social Exclusion Unit (SEU), which was set up at the heart of government in 1997 and reported directly to the Prime Minister (Toynbee and Walker, 2001, p. 13). Although the SEU was closed down in 2006, its creation highlights the extent to which New Labour was prepared to make major changes in the system in order to perpetuate its power and influence. Third, New Labour's discourses became embedded in the institutions that retained their authority during the organic crisis, such as the CBI and regional Chambers of Commerce. Indeed, Blair assiduously courted these organizations in the run-up to the 1997 general election in an effort to convince them of New Labour's competence in economic matters (Blair, 1996a, p. 107). This strategy proved to be extremely successful. A final strategic benefit of institutionalization was that it maximized the number of sites within the social where subjects could be incited to identify with the subject positions New Labour offered. These subject positions, and New Labour's redefinitions of certain floating signifiers, are examined next.

When the New Labour project became an imaginary, it started to remake the prevailing subject positions in accordance with its own vision. As we saw in Chapter 3, Thatcherism carried out this process with great success, while New Labour expended 'enormous moral energy seeking to change "the culture" and produce new kinds of subjects' (Hall, 1998b, p. 12). They included the 'hardworking family', to which New Labour harnessed working parents from a variety of social groups, and the 'individual as customer as well as citizen', a subject position it constructed around the concept of choice in public services such as education and health. New Labour also assigned a new meaning to such floating signifiers as 'poverty', which it recast as 'exclusion'. This term was both less menacing and broader in meaning than poverty (Toynbee and Walker, 2005, p. 49); as Blair put it, exclusion is 'not just about poverty of income, but poverty of aspiration, of opportunity, of prospects of advancement', and encompasses such groups as teenage parents, looked-after children, and people with mental health issues (2006a, pp. 2–4). This redefinition gained widespread recognition, and we can therefore say that it achieved hegemonic status.

The question arises of how New Labour dealt with resistance from its opponents, and thus was able to maintain its dominance. Hall points out that, 'where a populist consensus cannot be won, it must be seduced into place', a claim he supports with the examples of the Thatcher government's massaging of statistics, intimidation of the media, and lying (1988, pp. 86–7). The legacy of these tactics was evident in New Labour's use of 'spin' and the high level of importance it attached to presentational matters. Hall criticizes New Labour's concern with style over substance and, moreover, objects that it failed to engage seriously with the arguments of its opponents. This failure was evidenced by the fact that its critics were 'systematically discredited through innuendo and spin-doctored at the back door as being trapped in a time warp, if not actually barking mad' (Hall, 1998b, p. 13). A case in point is that of the late Mo Mowlam, former Secretary of State for Northern Ireland, who was targeted by a whispering campaign which intimated that her fight against a brain tumour 'had left her "without the intellectual rigour" to hold a cabinet post' (White and Addley, 2000). Whether or not we agree with Hall that this unpleasant strategy was indicative of a flaw at the heart of the New Labour project, we cannot deny that it was a highly effective means of neutralizing dissent. After all, the fear of becoming the target of a smear campaign perhaps acted as a deterrent to New Labour's critics, making them think twice before speaking out against it.

Following its election victory in 1997, the New Labour came to dominate the British political landscape. Luke Martell observes that after the Conservatives were defeated for a second time by New Labour in 2001, the former 'changed strategy to move to the centre-ground and attempted to beat New Labour on what were its own issues, such as social exclusion and public services' (2004, p. 4). In so doing, the Conservatives defined themselves in relation to the Third Way and, as we will see in Part II of this book, often proposed policy programmes that bore a strong resemblance to those of New Labour. This suggests that New Labour's discourses had been successfully embedded in authoritative institutions, and that it had become increasingly difficult for its opponents to offer a radically different alternative to its ideas and policies. However, New Labour was unable to maintain its dominance because, as with any political project, it was vulnerable to counter-hegemonic manoeuvres, while the possibility that popular identifications with its subject positions would collapse was ever-present.

Conclusion

This chapter has examined the concepts that comprised the core cluster of New Labour's early ideology and showed how their meanings were decontested in relation to each other. The outcome of this process was a remarkably consistent ideological platform, though a number of conflicting concepts remained. These tensions stemmed largely from New Labour's desire to move beyond the traditional antagonisms of left and right – of economic efficiency or social justice, for example – and therefore to occupy the centre ground of British politics. Indeed, the question arises of how far New Labour succeeded in this aim, or whether in the end these conflicts proved irresolvable. In the assessments of the 'context of ideology' in the following chapters, I will seek to answer this question, as well as to identify the changes that occurred in New Labour's ideological platform during its three terms of office.

The present chapter also discussed some of the rhetorical and presentational strategies that New Labour employed to portray itself as the only viable solution to the crisis of the early 1990s, and ultimately to achieve hegemonic status in the wake of its 1997 general election victory. In the remainder of the book, I examine the moral arguments that New Labour used to promote four of its flagship initiatives, their relationship to its ideological platform, and the rhetorical techniques it employed in its efforts to achieve hegemonic advantage in these areas of policy. Here, I seek to explain why some of its argumentative and persuasive strategies were more effective than others, and consider their broader impact on the New Labour project itself.

6
New Labour's Welfare Reforms: The New Deals

In recent years, but notably during the Thatcher era, government spending on welfare benefits increased significantly, while at the same time the social insurance system was being progressively undermined.[1] As a result, questions of affordability and cost dominated public debate in the period leading up to the 1997 general election. In an effort to avoid a repeat performance of its defeat in 1992, Labour sought to cast off its image as the 'tax and spend' party and targeted its appeal at middle-class voters. After emphasizing the 'costs of economic failure and the limits of taxpayer tolerance', New Labour pledged to radically reform the welfare state and to move away from 'passive support for jobless claimants towards active efforts to improve their chances of securing employment within a more prudently managed and stable economy' (Purdy, 2000, p. 185). This approach was epitomized by the New Deals, which are the focus of the present chapter.

The chapter begins with a summary of New Labour's welfare-to-work policies. In the following three sections, I employ the framework elaborated in Chapter 4 to show how the different components of the 'context of justification' influenced New Labour's choice of justificatory strategy for the New Deals. Therefore, in the second section I examine the relationship between this policy programme, the arguments used to promote it and New Labour's ideological commitments, and reveal that there is a reasonable degree of consistency between them. Next, I analyse the moral arguments used to sell the New Deals and demonstrate that New Labour's choice of a primarily consequentialist justificatory strategy was appropriate to this policy programme. The fourth section then considers the tactics that New Labour deployed in its efforts to secure hegemonic advantage in the area of welfare policy. Here, I show that New Labour's chosen moral arguments, supported by a range of rhetorical techniques, enabled it to set the agenda on welfare policy. Indeed, the Conservatives' failure to offer an original alternative to the New Deals suggests that New Labour was able to force them onto its discursive terrain and was, therefore, successful in achieving hegemonic advantage over its opponents.

New Labour's welfare to work policies

According to HM Treasury, the primary objective of the New Deals was to enable unemployed people to 'compete effectively for the jobs that are continually being created in Britain's dynamic labour market' (2000, p. 10). The programme was funded by a one-off windfall tax on the privatized monopoly utilities[2] and based on a policy framework endorsed by the OECD. This framework consists of three elements, of which the first is active labour market policies. Such initiatives are intended to provide unemployed individuals with help and support that is tailored to meet their own particular needs, and so will enable them to reconnect with the job market. Meanwhile, the second element comprises policies designed to 'make work pay', which include the National Minimum Wage, changes to income tax and National Insurance contributions, and a range of Tax Credits.[3] Finally, the third element consists of initiatives to tackle the barriers that prevent people from returning to work. One such obstacle was the shortage of good-quality, affordable of child care facilities, which New Labour sought to rectify through its National Childcare Strategy. Other barriers include discrimination and poor basic skills, and in April 2002 New Labour introduced Jobcentre Plus to tackle them.[4] This agency provides a range of services, which include training and help with the cost of travelling to a job interview, and is intended to be flexible, work-focused and suited to the needs of each individual. The issues involved here are frequently multidimensional, so a 'partnership approach between a number of Government departments, other public sector bodies, employers and the community and voluntary sectors' was required (HM Treasury and DWP, 2003, p. 50).

New Labour launched the New Deal for Young People (NDYP) in April 1998. This scheme was targeted at young people aged between 18 and 24 who were receiving Jobseeker's Allowance (JSA). After six months of 'open' unemployment, participants entered a four-month 'gateway' period, in which they were assigned a personal adviser who helped them to acquire 'any needed basic skills (such as punctuality, how to compose a CV, and so forth) and engage in a serious job search' (Waltman, 2009, p. 126). If, at the end of this phase, they had not found unsubsidized employment, participants had to accept one of four options, the first of which was a subsidized job that included training and lasted for up to six months. To this was later added the opportunity to participate in self-employment test trading, during which the young person could 'experience the realities of self-employment while still receiving support and guidance from a provider' (Department for Social Development, 2006). The second option was a six-month work experience and training placement with a voluntary organization, while the third was six months of work experience with an environmental task force, including training. The fourth option was up to 12 months of full-time education for those lacking basic skills, during which JSA continued. After the Option stage, participants who had not found employment entered the 'follow through' period, which offered further guidance and support for up to six months. The programme was mandatory, so 'the receipt of benefit [was] conditional on willingness to accept offers of work or training. Failure to do so [was] penalised by loss of benefit' (Shaw, 2007, p. 47).

Meanwhile, the New Deal for the Long-term Unemployed (NDLTU) was introduced in July 1998. Initially, this scheme targeted people aged 25 or over who had been claiming JSA for two years or more, but from April 2001 it was renamed the New Deal 25 plus (ND25+) and extended to include individuals from this age group who had been out of work for 18 of the previous 21 months. Participants attended a compulsory interview with a personal adviser, after which they were required to accept either a subsidized job with an employer, self-employment test trading, a six-month training and work experience placement, or training in essential skills. At the end of this period, those who did not find work were entitled to follow-through support, during which they were encouraged to build on the experience they had gained in the Option phase and improve their prospects of finding work. As with the NDYP, participation in this scheme was mandatory, and those who failed to cooperate faced benefit sanctions.

According to New Labour, the NDYP was a great success, helping 280,000 young people to find work and reducing youth unemployment by 75 per cent. However, it claimed, 'too many people [were] still denied the opportunity to work', and to rectify this New Labour pledged to extend the New Deal to more people, specifically those who were classed as economically inactive (Labour Party, 2001, p. 26). Against the Conservatives, who had neglected this group during their time in government, New Labour argued that although people may be economically inactive due to caring responsibilities or disability, it does not follow that they are uninterested in, or incapable of, work. As a consequence, the benefit system needed to 'do more to help and encourage people on inactive benefits to return to work' (HM Treasury and DWP, 2003, p. 49). To this end, the NDYP was soon joined by a number of programmes designed to help New Labour to achieve this goal.

One such scheme was the New Deal for Lone Parents (NDLP), which was introduced on a national scale in April 1998. This programme was aimed at lone parents whose youngest child was under 16, and who were either unemployed or working for fewer than 16 hours a week. It was supported by the National Childcare Strategy, which was designed to provide good-quality, affordable childcare for lone parents, and thus to remove one of the major obstacles to employment. Although participation in the scheme was voluntary, lone parents were required to attend an interview, at which they received 'personal adviser support, help with childcare and training, and financial incentives' (DWP, 2007, p. 19). Benefit penalties applied if they failed to do so. In 2006, New Labour proposed to increase the frequency of these interviews to six-monthly for lone parents whose youngest child was under 11, and to quarterly for those whose youngest child was aged 11 or over (DWP, 2006a, p. 8). The government subsequently toughened its stance by ending the automatic entitlement to Income Support for lone parents with children aged 12 or over from November 2008, and reducing the qualifying age to seven in October 2010.

In April 1999, New Labour introduced the New Deal for Partners (NDP), which was a voluntary scheme that targeted the partners of unemployment benefit claimants. From April 2004, participants in this programme were offered the same support as that available under the NDLP, and attendance at a work-focused interview was made mandatory for the partners of all benefit claimants. For New Labour, the NDP was important because the benefit system had hitherto operated on the assumption that the partners of claimants – predominantly women – are 'adult dependents' who cannot, or do not wish to, work. However, New Labour recognized that either partner in a couple may enter the workforce, and argued that the state should give them the help and support they need to do so (HM Treasury and DWP, 2003, p. 27). New Labour's next initiative was the New Deal 50 plus (ND50+), which was launched nationally in April 2000. This voluntary programme was aimed at people aged 50 or over who had been in receipt of Jobseeker's Allowance/Income Support (JSA/IS) or incapacity benefits for at least six months. Participants were offered individually tailored support from a personal advisor and financial assistance, which included an In-work Training Grant and the Working Tax Credit for 50 plus. Finally, the New

Deal for Disabled People (NDDP) was introduced nationally from July 2001. This programme was also voluntary and was designed for people who were in receipt of incapacity benefits, namely Severe Disablement Allowance, Incapacity Benefit, and Income Support with a disability premium. Participants were assigned a personal advisor, whose role was to give them the information and advice they need to help them find suitable employment. A further goal of the programme, Millar notes, was to 'raise awareness of the employment needs of people with disabilities among employers and service providers' (2000, p. 5), and thus to tackle discrimination in the workplace.

The compatibility of the New Deals and their supporting arguments with New Labour's ideological commitments

After its defeat in the 1992 general election, the Labour party was faced with three choices regarding its welfare policy. The first was to continue with the market revolution that began under Thatcher and complete the changeover to a residual welfare state, while the second was to enact redistributive policies in order to protect the poorer members of society. Its third option was to remodel the welfare system along 'productivist' lines, supporting and – if required – compelling those it judged able to work to 'adapt to market forces, providing employers with a suitably skilled and motivated labour force and preserving social cohesion' (Purdy, 2000, p. 183). Labour resisted the first option on ideological grounds and, despite its instinctive leaning toward the second, finally settled on the third. To justify this move, Blair argued that British society had changed dramatically since the inception of the welfare state, with women playing an active role in the workforce, a growing number of elderly people requiring care as well as an income, and many people being unemployed for long periods of time (1995a, p. 14). On this basis, a new relationship between welfare and work was required.

As Driver correctly points out, New Labour's approach to welfare reform reflected a desire to bring together elements from Left and Right policy agendas, combining policies on 'incentives, prevention and rehabilitation, as well as a new paternalism'. With reference to incentives, New Labour adopted the Clinton Democrats' strategy of enacting policies to 'make work pay', while its initiatives to improve the human capital of both welfare claimants and those who are in work belonged to the categories of prevention and rehabilitation. These policies were consistent with a progressive social democratic approach to welfare reform and assigned to the state a substantial role in the provision of welfare

(Driver, 2004, p. 41). The influence of the Left was also evident in New Labour's emphasis on policies intended to invigorate citizens who wanted to work through the options of training, subsidized employment, or work experience with an environmental task force. Indeed, this aspect of the New Deals was evident in Labour policy thinking as far back as the 1980s, if not earlier (Taylor, 2007, p. 221). At the same time, however, the element of compulsion in the New Deals was reminiscent of New Right paternalism, which was made explicit in the requirement that participants in the programmes must act responsibly and accept the work and training opportunities they were offered, or face losing benefit.

The 'context of ideology' invites consideration of the extent to which the arguments New Labour deployed in support of its welfare reforms, as well as the policies themselves, were congruent with its ideological commitments. For Gordon Brown and Alistair Darling, the New Deals accorded primarily with New Labour's core value of equality of opportunity for all (2001, p. iii). This is because a key objective of the scheme was to ensure that the labour market functioned well for everyone in Britain, and that nobody was prevented from obtaining work because, for instance, they had a disability or had children to look after (HM Treasury and DWP, 2003, p. 3). New Labour linked this notion of opportunity for all to the values of equal worth and social inclusion, arguing that everyone who is able to work is entitled to have the opportunity to do so, and thus to have a stake in society, regardless of their circumstances (DWP, 2006b, p. vii). This combination of values was also evident in New Labour's policies to tackle workplace discrimination, and to remove the other barriers that prevent people from finding employment.

The New Deals and the arguments used to justify them also manifested New Labour's commitment to the goal of full employment, which was decontested as equality of opportunity for all (HM Treasury, 1997, p. 5). By putting 'work first', New Labour aimed to 'secure social justice for those who too often have been left behind, and to enable them to realise their full potential, to the economic and social benefit of the whole community' (Brown and Smith, 2003, p. i). As Driver points out, this strategy to boost the human capital of poorer people by giving them the skills they need to participate in the labour market constituted an attempt to manipulate the distribution of resources. 'In this way', he argues, 'opportunities [were] connected, in New Labour thinking, to outcomes' (2004, p. 32). By enacting policies to give people the opportunity to learn new skills and ultimately to find employment,

New Labour sought to realize its goal of a strong, cohesive society in which everyone has a stake. At the same time, however, the principles of social justice demanded that a civilized society should protect its most vulnerable members. On this basis, New Labour argued that those who were able to work should have the opportunity to enter the job market, while those who were unable to do so should receive the security they need.

Finlayson identifies a significant development of New Labour's welfare reforms as the 'emphasis on the individualisation of service delivery, and with it the encouragement of responsibility for gearing up for the new economy' (2003, p. 164). In other words, participants in the New Deals were expected to act responsibly and accept the opportunities offered to them, in return for the personalized programme of training and support they received. As Bevir explains, New Labour endorsed the communitarian notion that work is 'a leading tutor of responsibility', and shared the view of communitarians and new institutionalists that work is the solution to poverty (2005, p. 91). Consequently, New Labour believed that the best way to address social exclusion was to actively encourage people to enter the workforce, where they would learn the virtue of responsibility and ultimately become self-reliant. The core New Labour value of reciprocal rights and responsibilities therefore had a strong presence in the New Deals. Indeed, it was explicit in the argument that government had an obligation to provide participants with real opportunities for training and work, while those able to do so had a responsibility either to accept these offers or to stop claiming benefits.

Although the New Deals appear to be consistent with New Labour's ideological platform, a problem arises when we consider their practical implications. In this policy programme, as Kevin Hickson correctly points out, the burden of responsibility fell primarily on those at the bottom of society, who New Labour deemed to be socially excluded, 'with no corresponding duties, such as the responsibility to pay higher direct taxation, falling on those at the top' (2004, p. 133). This omission resulted in the exclusion of the rich, which violated New Labour's commitment to the values of social justice and community cohesion. It also undermined the value of equal worth, on the ground that if every individual matters equally, it follows that no one should be excluded from the reciprocal responsibilities that underpin a strong, cohesive community (Atkins, 2010, p. 52). There were further disparities between New Labour's arguments for its welfare reforms and their practical effects but, as we will see in the remainder of the chapter, they did not prevent it from achieving a consensus in this area of policy.

The moral arguments used to promote the New Deals

As elaborated in Chapter 2, politicians typically make the case for welfare reforms by reference to the amount of well-being or the positive consequences they will produce. The congruence between consequentialist reasoning (broadly conceived) and the area of welfare policy makes this mode of moral argument particularly suitable for selling such initiatives, and it is therefore unsurprising that a tripartite consequentialist argument constituted the primary case for the New Deals. The first strand of this argument focused on the benefits for participants in the schemes. According to the DWP, exclusion from the labour market can produce a range of negative consequences for individuals, which include 'loss of a role, social contact, daily routine, feelings of participation, and self-esteem and self worth' (2002, p. 1). In contrast, New Labour argued that work is beneficial because it 'strengthens independence and dignity. It builds family aspirations...and can improve an individual's health and well-being' (DWP, 2006a, p. 2). Therefore, by moving unemployed people off benefits and into work, the New Deals were intended to make participants in the schemes independent and self-sustaining, and not reliant on the state for an income.

The second strand of New Labour's consequentialist argument emphasized the positive effects of the New Deals on society as a whole. In Richard Layard's words, it had 'the potential to make our society significantly more efficient and more fair' (2001, p. 6). New Labour identified areas of the country in which unemployment is higher than average, and claimed that people with disabilities, lone parents and people from minority ethnic groups are often disproportionately concentrated within these regions. Such individuals may experience multiple difficulties, including poor-quality public transport and rising crime, which ultimately lead to social exclusion. As Andrew Smith, the former Employment Minister, put it, the goal of the New Deals was to foster social inclusion by bringing 'employment, training and benefits to people in the right way, so that they have the standard and quality of life that we want in a civilised society' (Hansard, 19 December 1997, c.627). This would enable people to contribute to, and have a stake in, society, thus benefiting the wider community by breaking the cycle of exclusion, crime and deprivation that blights Britain's poorest neighbourhoods. However, despite their success in reducing unemployment – particularly among the under-25s – New Labour's policies had little impact on in-work poverty, a condition linked to such factors as part-time employment, low pay, and a lack of job retention or job progression

(Kenway, 2008, p. 8; Smith and Middleton, 2007, p. 13). Given that several studies have found that people who are in in-work poverty are more likely to experience reduced well-being and social exclusion (see Smith and Middleton, 2007, pp. 71–2), New Labour's claim that it could create a fairer, more inclusive society by increasing the number of people in paid employment appears dubious.

Finally, New Labour emphasized the positive consequences of the New Deals for Britain's economy. This argument proceeded from the premise that people's skills and education are key determinants of productivity growth and economic performance (HM Treasury, DWP and DfES, 2004, p. 7). Consequently, the New Deals, which were designed to give people the opportunity to acquire new skills, would allow businesses to flourish and so promote economic growth. They would also challenge the trade-off between equality and efficiency that prevailed in the 1980s by simultaneously creating economic prosperity and promoting social justice (Brown, 1994, p. 19). In practice, however, it was estimated that in 2006 'as many as a third of all adults of working age lacked any recognised skills at all, or were at best low-skilled' (Taylor, 2007, p. 234). These individuals are more likely to be unemployed or in low-paid jobs, and therefore to be socially excluded. If we take this point together with figures which show that UK productivity in 2007 (in terms of GDP per worker) was 7 per cent below that of France and 23 per cent less than that of the USA (Office for National Statistics, 2009, p. 1), then it seems New Labour was unsuccessful in its attempts to reconcile economic efficiency and social justice.

New Labour's consequentialist argument for the New Deals can be expressed in Brian Barry's language of want- and ideal-regarding principles, which was considered in Chapter 2. As we have seen, New Labour believed that long-term unemployment is harmful to individuals, families and the community alike. Its effects are widespread and include family breakdown, poverty, crime, and drug dependency. Policies such as the New Deals, which were intended to promote social justice and alleviate these ills, were therefore in the interests of all citizens because they would improve the quality of life of everyone, not just of the poorest individuals. In Barry's terms, then, we can say that the New Deals offered a means of fulfilling the desire of the majority of citizens for a solution to the social problems that result from long-term unemployment.

The economic argument for the New Deals is also expressible as a want-regarding principle. After all, most people would wish to share in the benefits of economic prosperity, which include low interest rates, low inflation, high employment and improved public services. With regard to ideal-regarding principles, meanwhile, the New Deals were based on the ideal that a society in which everyone has a stake is better – that is, it is fairer, more cohesive and is populated by responsible citizens – than a divided, unjust society, in which large numbers of people are unemployed and dependent on social security benefits. As elaborated in Chapter 5, this vision of how society ought to be is present within New Labour's ideological platform, which again demonstrates congruence between its core values and the moral arguments it used to persuade people to back its welfare reforms.

The consequentialist case for the New Deals was supported by a secondary deontological argument, which drew on New Labour's core concept of reciprocal rights and responsibilities. For New Labour, everyone who was able to do so had a responsibility to find a job and take care of their family. In return, government had an obligation to ensure that they received the help they needed to find suitable training or work. As Blair put it, 'a sharper focus on individual responsibility is going hand in hand with a great improvement in the support provided by government. Responsibility from all – security and opportunity for all' (2001b, p. 2). The coercive aspect of the New Deals was intended to ensure that all unemployed people of working age were made aware of their options, and thus would be in a position to take responsibility for themselves. After all, one of the main goals of New Labour's welfare reforms was to tackle the 'culture of dependency' and ensure that a life on benefit was no longer an option.

A further motivation for the compulsory aspect of the New Deals is evident in Darling's statement that New Labour's welfare policies were based on a:

> Moral case for reform which reflects the duty we owe to our children to build a welfare state fit for their future ... If we do nothing these children will not only be born poor, they will live poor, and die poor. (1999, p. 35)

Blair's pledge to eradicate child poverty within a generation gave this deontological claim additional force (1999a, p. 1), and in the same year his government set targets to reduce child poverty by 25 per cent by 2004–5, 50 per cent by 2010–11, and eventually to eradicate it by 2020. However, despite some initial progress towards these goals, New Labour failed to meet its first target and, at the end of its time in office, was still far from achieving its second. Given that at least 50 per cent of children living in poverty in 2008 were in working families, it seems that welfare-to-work schemes alone are not enough to alleviate child poverty, and that an overhaul of the taxation and benefit systems is therefore required (Kenway, 2008, pp. 7–8, 4).

Overall, the examination of the 'context of argumentation' in this section reveals that New Labour's use of a primarily consequentialist justificatory strategy was appropriate to the New Deals. We have seen that New Labour emphasized the benefits of work as a means of enabling individuals to fulfil their potential and become self-reliant. By giving every citizen a stake in a fair society and thus reducing social exclusion, the New Deals were also intended to have positive consequences for the wider community. In addition, New Labour claimed that the programmes would, by giving people the skills they need to find work, increase the welfare of the population by promoting economic growth and prosperity. The core concept of social justice, which is decontested as reciprocal rights and responsibilities, found expression in the deontological case for the New Deals. Here, New Labour argued that unemployed people had a duty to accept the opportunities offered to them, and should be compelled to do so if they refuse. For New Labour, such coercion was justified because it encouraged personal responsibility, which Blair identified as a key element of good citizenship and a prerequisite for a decent, inclusive society (1996a, p. 218). Although there were some disparities between New Labour's claims for the New Deals and their practical outcomes, both its moral arguments and the policies themselves were nonetheless broadly compatible with its ideological commitments. Such coherence creates an impression of integrity and competence that can be advantageous in rhetorical competitions, and constituted one of New Labour's strategies for securing hegemonic advantage in the area of welfare policy. A discussion of the 'context of hegemonic competition' forms the next section of this chapter.

New Labour's tactics for securing hegemonic advantage

The key premise of New Labour's case for the New Deals was that the Conservatives' approach to welfare was seriously flawed. David Purdy explains that a residual welfare state began to emerge during the Thatcher and Major governments, which provided a 'low-level safety net for the poor, while encouraging the majority of citizens to take care of themselves' (2000, p. 183). In practice, this meant that people received little or no help to find work, and by the mid-1990s, the number claiming inactive benefits had trebled. For New Labour, the Conservatives' passive approach to welfare fostered benefit dependency, hindered opportunity and wasted talent, and as a result, trapped many people in long-term unemployment. This in turn contributed to a sharp increase in child poverty, which had reached 3.4 million by 1997 (DWP, 2008a, pp. 24–5).

However, the Conservatives were not wholly responsible for the growing culture of dependency, which in fact had been a problem since the early 1970s (Waltman, 2009, p. 123). Although the Thatcher government removed the requirement on benefit claimants to look for work in 1982, the introduction of Restart interviews in 1986 marked the beginning of a more active approach to welfare that would challenge the dependency culture (Freud, 2007, p. 12). The Major government consolidated this shift by introducing a Contract for Work, under which unemployed people were obliged to accept work if it was available, and by transforming unemployment benefit into JSA. This latter move both strengthened and formalized the connection between seeking work and claiming benefits and incorporated a number of programmes, such as 'restart' and 'job search plus', which were intended to help people find employment (Johnson, 2001, p. 65). Underpinning these developments was a desire to create a welfare system for a 'self-help society not a help-yourself society' that promoted independence by reconnecting more people with the job market (Major, 1996, p. 6). The similarities between this approach and New Labour's welfare reforms are striking, and it is therefore misleading to characterize the former as passive. Nonetheless, it proved strategically useful for New Labour to do so, as we will see below.

The consequentialist argument for the New Deals drew on a narrative of welfare under the Conservatives, in which New Labour established relations of equivalence between high unemployment, poverty, wasted potential, community breakdown and social injustice. Brown identifies the source of these difficulties as the New Right's belief that 'more inequality was essential to economic growth' (1994, p. 1), and thus creates a relation of equivalence between Thatcherite ideology, economic inefficiency and social problems. As Charteris-Black explains, such an association implies a causal relationship between these phenomena (2005, p. 97), which in turn enabled New Labour to hold the Conservatives directly responsible for Britain's ills. In so doing, New Labour deployed the strategy of delegitimization, which was intended to undermine and attack its opponent through the use of such techniques as marginalization, censure, and the presentation of the other in a negative light (Chilton, 2004, p. 47).

New Labour also used the technique of legitimization to make its case for the New Deals. Examples of this rhetorical strategy include 'positive self-presentation' as manifested in acts of self-justification, and 'self-identification as a source of authority, reason, vision and sanity' (Chilton, 2004, p. 47). New Labour deployed the latter approach to present its approach as the only viable solution to the problems created by the Conservative governments, with Blair claiming that 'we are the only people who can be trusted to change, reform and modernise the welfare state, because we are the people who believe in it' (1994b, p. 7). Here, Blair suggested that the Conservatives had seriously damaged the welfare state because they rejected the values on which it was built. In contrast, New Labour upheld these values, and therefore was uniquely qualified to undertake the necessary reforms. It was on this basis that Blair described the New Deals, which encouraged self-reliance and personal responsibility, as 'the only way forward as we break the old culture which left generations of families trapped in unemployment and poverty' (2001a, p. 2).

In making this argument, Blair made an appeal to *ethos* which, as we have seen, relies on 'the character of the speaker, on their honesty, for instance, or their authority' (Finlayson, 2007, p. 558) or, as in this case, on their fidelity to a particular ideological tradition. It was a Labour government that founded the welfare state so, by claiming that New Labour was the only party that believed in it, Blair perhaps sought to demonstrate that his character was in harmony with the *ethos* of the Labour movement. In so doing, he may have intended to alleviate the fear of many on the Left of the party that his plans to modernize the welfare state constituted a shift to the Right; his values were still Labour values, and any changes would be guided by them. This in turn could enhance his authority as party leader and strengthen his case for welfare reform.

The New Deals were one of several initiatives designed to make work pay and help people into employment. To this end, Brown claimed, an enabling state was required, which would offer unemployed individuals a means of escaping poverty by 'using the welfare state to foster responsibility and not to substitute for it'. Indeed, he continued, again drawing on the deontological argument, 'our guiding theme is not what the government can do for you but what the government can enable you to do for yourself' (1994, p. 5). The notion of enablement is significant, as it implies state intervention in accordance with Old Labour ideals but without the negative connotations that subsequently became attached to it. Thus, New Labour could again reassure those on the Left of the party that it was acting in accordance with traditional socialist values, while simultaneously avoiding the Thatcherite charge of excessive interference.

A key component of New Labour's enabling state was Jobcentre Plus, which delivers an 'active service to help people become independent and move from welfare into work' (HM Treasury and DWP, 2001, p. 32). Here, the word 'active' created a link between New Labour's approach and the activation strategies endorsed by the OECD and implemented by such nations as Finland and Norway. These strategies share several features with the New Deals, such as the 'regular reporting and monitoring of work availability and job-search actions', the focus on mutual responsibility and the use of sanctions to ensure compliance with the programme (OECD, 2007, p. 208). By establishing this connection and claiming that the New Deals 'incorporated lessons from ... successful labour markets in Europe, especially Scandinavia' (DWP, 2008b, p. 7), New Labour identified its approach with the success of other schemes and thus gave its policies greater legitimacy.

The use of the word 'active' also created an antagonism between the New Deals on the one hand, and the Conservatives' 'passive' approach, which New Labour blamed for encouraging welfare dependency, on the other. In Charteris-Black's terms, this is an example of antithesis, in which a combination of sequencing and comparison was utilized to contrast the Conservatives' 18 years in government with New Labour's time in office (2005, p. 7). Antithesis was a powerful tool in New Labour's rhetorical arsenal because it allowed the party to portray the policies of the Thatcher and Major governments as an abject failure, while presenting itself as offering tough measures to solve the problem. One such measure was the suspension of benefit payments for people who refused to participate in the New Deals, the purpose of which was to emphasize that the rights of benefit claimants are matched with responsibilities. These sanctions may also, Purdy suggests, have been intended to reassure taxpayers that public money was being spent appropriately (2000, p. 187). If this is so, they enabled New Labour to demonstrate the economic competence it emphasized during its first two terms of office, and thus enhanced its credibility.

New Labour also sought to strengthen its case for the New Deals by providing anecdotal evidence as proof of their effectiveness. One instance of this rhetorical technique can be found in Blair's speech to New Labour's 1998 conference, in which he told his audience of a recent encounter with an 'intelligent, confident' New Deal participant, who had been promoted by the firm that employed him under this scheme. He recounted their conversation as follows:

> I said to him, 'How could you ever have been without a job?' He said: 'You didn't know me six months ago. Six months ago you wouldn't have employed me, but I've discovered I'm better than I ever thought I was'. (1998b, p. 7)

By telling this young man's story, which exemplified the positive effects that the New Deal could have on the lives of participants, Blair gave his audience first-hand evidence of its success in helping people to find work. This in turn was intended to prove that his government's welfare reforms were fulfilling their stated aims, and thereby vindicated its approach. Of course, it would be easy for critics of the New Deals to find people for whom the schemes had been less successful and use their stories to contradict Blair's position. Nonetheless, anecdotes afford a powerful means of supporting a claim. They are, after all, about real people, and so will have a greater impact on an audience than facts or statistics.

In arguing for its welfare reforms, New Labour also invoked the dire consequences that would follow if the issue of restricted opportunity were ignored. Brown, for instance, asserted that unless this matter was addressed, Britain would 'continue to drift towards a low-wage, low investment, low skills economy... with all the economic and social ills that brings' (1994, p. 2). More specifically, argued New Labour, it would lead to more low pay, slow economic growth, unemployment and poverty, while Britain's communities would be at risk from the social problems associated with deprivation and exclusion (HM Treasury and DWP, 2003, p. 50). It was imperative, therefore, that urgent action be taken to stop the situation worsening, and it was to this end that New Labour's welfare policies were directed.

Here, New Labour perhaps sought to stir the emotions of its audience in its attempts to win support for the New Deals. More specifically, an effect of this argument may have been to induce fear by 'making truth claims, in the form of predictions, about [the] causal effects' (Chilton, 2004, p. 118) that would follow unless the New Deals – New Labour's programme to tackle social exclusion by increasing opportunities and helping people into work – were introduced. In practice, however, these schemes did not live up to New Labour's lofty rhetoric, a failure which to a large degree reflects the tendency among politicians to make exaggerated claims about the merits of their policy programmes when seeking to achieve hegemonic advantage over an opponent. In the remainder of the chapter, I will consider some of the Conservatives' objections against the New Deals, before outlining their alternative proposals for welfare reform.

A key Conservative argument against the NDYP was that it was failing to reduce youth unemployment, a charge they supported with figures from the Office for National Statistics to show that in 2006 there were '37,000 more unemployed people aged 16 to 24 than in May 1997, with the total rising from 665,000 to 702,000' (Browne, 2006a). These figures were seen as highly embarrassing for New Labour, given Gordon Brown's description of the high levels of youth unemployment he inherited from the Conservatives in 1997 as a 'human tragedy', 'sickening' and 'an economic disaster' (Browne, 2006a). They also flatly contradicted Blair's claim in September 2006 that New Labour had virtually eradicated long-term youth unemployment (2006b, p. 3).

New Labour responded by stating that although there were more unemployed young people in 2006 than there were in 1997, 'the *proportion* out of work has fallen' (Browne, 2006a, emphasis added). This is technically correct, as the unemployment rate for 18–24 year olds for this period decreased from 12.9 per cent to 12.2 per cent. However, the figure in fact started to rise again in 2004. Moreover, as a share of overall unemployment, youth unemployment had increased from 22.3 per cent in 1997 to 27.7 per cent in 2006. This rise is partially accounted for by the steady increase in the cohort of 16–24 year olds, from 6.4 million in 2000 (10.8 per cent of the total population) to 7.2 million in 2006 (11.9 per cent) (Bell and Blanchflower, 2010, pp. 9–10). Other contributing factors may have included a weakening of the labour market and the government's shift in focus from young JSA claimants to people on inactive benefits since 2004 (Petrongolo and Van Reenen, 2010, p. 8). As such, it is unfair to wholly attribute the rise in youth unemployment to a failure of New Labour's policies, but it is equally misleading to characterize the New Deals as an unqualified success.

Another Conservative objection against the NDYP was that it failed to help participants find long-term, stable employment. Phil Hammond, the Opposition's Work and Pensions Spokesman, described the scheme as a 'revolving door', on the ground that half of the participants who completed it were claiming benefits again within 12 months. Furthermore, the proportion who found work immediately after finishing the programme had almost halved since 1998, and in 2006 stood at 35 per cent (Jones, 2006). New Labour dismissed these claims as false, asserting that the scheme had helped over 1.6 million to find work, and that 'the true story is that more than 1.5 million 16 to 18-year-olds are in education and training – the highest number ever' (quoted in Browne, 2006b). This example demonstrates that, despite their critics' objections, New Labour continued to argue as if the New Deals had achieved their stated aims. However, the phenomenon of 'retreads' is well documented, with almost 25,000 young people entering and re-entering the NDYP on four or more occasions. This not only raises serious questions about the effectiveness of the programmes in giving participants the skills they need to keep a job, but also about the appropriateness of the 'keep taking the same medicine until it works' philosophy embedded in the New Deals (Field and White, 2007, p. 16).

It is clear from the preceding discussion that the Conservatives' criticisms of the New Deals were based primarily on statistics that revealed the failings of the schemes, and that New Labour retaliated by invoking another set of figures that demonstrated the exact opposite. It is likely that the real story lies somewhere between these two positions, as the New Deals were not the triumphant success New Labour claimed, but neither were they the unmitigated failure that the Conservatives portrayed. The question therefore arises of what the Conservatives offered as an alternative to the New Deals, and I briefly examine their plans next.

In January 2008, the Conservative party published its own proposals for welfare reform. Their plans proceeded from the assumption that the New Deals had failed to achieve a reduction in unemployment, while New Labour's excessive use of state control and bureaucracy within the welfare system had failed to tackle mass benefit dependency. Like New Labour, the Conservatives claimed this condition was intimately linked to poverty and social breakdown, and argued that work is beneficial because it reduces poverty and deprivation, and promotes individual well-being (Conservative Party, 2008, p. 10). On this basis, they adopted New Labour's commitment to support people who were unable to work, while helping those who can to find sustained employment. The Conservatives also endorsed New Labour's linkage of opportunity and responsibility, with David Cameron claiming that his party's welfare reforms would offer some of Britain's most deprived citizens 'the opportunity to live independent and fulfilling lives. Above all, they will help more people contribute to the responsible society I want to achieve' (2008a, p. 2). In policy terms, this association was evident in their pledge to apply benefit sanctions to those who refused to participate in their welfare-to-work programme.

A key difference between the New Deals and the Conservatives' proposals was that the latter contained a pledge to contract the delivery of the programmes to private and voluntary sector providers, who would then be paid by results. Those who failed to find work for people would not receive any payment (Conservative Party, 2008, p. 12). Underpinning this approach was the assumption that competition between providers for contracts and payment by results could improve the quality of service. These changes were recommended in David Freud's review of welfare-to-work policy (2007, p. 52) and were also incorporated within New Labour's Flexible New Deal (FND), which replaced the NDYP and the ND25+ in some areas from October 2009. These similarities indicate that despite their criticisms, the Conservatives accepted many of the basic assumptions of New Labour's policies, and that New Labour had therefore succeeded in setting the agenda on welfare.

Conclusion

This chapter has examined how New Labour used moral principles and arguments to make its case for the New Deals. The discussion of the 'context of ideology' shows that New Labour's chosen argumentative strategy and the New Deals themselves were broadly congruent with its core ideological commitments and, moreover, that this strategy remained remarkably consistent throughout its time in office. Meanwhile, an examination of the 'context of argumentation' reveals that New Labour's choice of a primarily consequentialist justificatory strategy was appropriate to a policy programme in the area of welfare. New Labour supported this strategy with a deontological argument, which drew on its core value of reciprocal rights and responsibilities. This argument enabled it to broaden its appeal beyond its traditional supporters and to win support on the Right, while challenging the passive approach that, for New Labour, characterized welfare policy under the Thatcher and Major governments.

An analysis of the 'context of hegemonic competition' indicates that New Labour supported these argumentative strategies with a wide range of rhetorical techniques, such as delegitimization, legitimization and antithesis, which it employed to create a negative portrait of welfare under the Conservatives, and to persuade its audience that it alone had the vision and the policies needed to solve the issues of restricted opportunity, poverty and social exclusion. New Labour also utilized emotive coercion to highlight the consequences of allowing these problems to continue unchecked, while Blair sought to reassure doubters on the Left of his party that although the New Deals contained elements of New Right thinking, his values were nonetheless consistent with those of the Labour movement.

Despite the objections of its critics and the growing body of social policy research that questioned the effectiveness of aspects of the New Deals, New Labour's rhetoric proceeded as if the programmes had achieved their original goals. However, the commissioning of Freud's review of welfare policy in December 2006 perhaps represents a tacit recognition that all was not as it should have been, and that reform was therefore required. The Freud report also influenced the development of Conservative welfare policy, which bore a striking resemblance to the New Deals. This failure to offer an original alternative to the New Deals suggests that although they found fault with their implementation, the Conservatives accepted the assumptions underlying the scheme, and that New Labour ultimately succeeded in securing hegemonic advantage in the area of welfare policy.

7
Rights and Constitutional Reform: The Human Rights Act of 1998

In 1950 the Council of Europe, of which Britain was a founder member, established the European Convention on Human Rights (ECHR). Although this agreement enshrines fundamental political and civil rights, its incorporation into UK law was the subject of debate for around 30 years. During this time, writes John Wadham, there was a 'gradual shift in establishment opinion from resistance or apathy towards any type of human rights legislation' to New Labour's enactment of the Human Rights Act (HRA) in 1998 (1999, p. 354). While the primary objective of the HRA was to ensure that legislation is compatible with the rights enshrined in the Convention, it also provides citizens with a clear statement of their fundamental rights and basic freedoms under the law.

This chapter begins by outlining the main features of the Human Rights Act of 1998. In the following section, I explore the relationship between the Act, the arguments used to promote it and New Labour's ideology. Here, I show that despite New Labour's claims, the HRA in fact emphasized individual rights at the expense of civic responsibilities, and thus failed to realize a core ideological commitment. Next, I consider New Labour's deontological argument for the incorporation of the ECHR into UK law. In so doing, I demonstrate that although it was suitable for this policy, it highlighted a number of practical obstacles to New Labour's goal of creating a culture of human rights. Finally, I discuss the persuasive strategies that New Labour employed in its efforts to secure hegemonic advantage, and I argue that problems with the content and implementation of the HRA meant that it failed to carry the public with it, though its underlying moral agenda was widely accepted.

The Human Rights Act of 1998

The European Convention on Human Rights of 1950 enshrines three types of basic rights. They are absolute rights, limited rights and qualified rights, and I will outline them in turn. Absolute rights include the right to protection from torture and from degrading or inhuman treatment or punishment (Article 3), the prohibition of slavery and forced labour (Article 4) and protection from retrospective criminal punishment (Article 7). As we saw in Chapter 2, these rights are also termed 'absolute rights' in Dworkin's theory, and they extend to all members of the community without limitation. Limited rights, meanwhile, include the right to a fair trial (Article 6) and the right to marry and found a family (Article 12). These rights apply to everyone unless specific and finite exceptions set out in the ECHR obtain. So, for example, Article 5 guarantees the liberty and security of person unless they have been convicted of a crime and sentenced to a term of imprisonment. Finally, qualified rights 'require a balance to be struck against the rights of others or the rights of society as a whole' (Goldsmith, 2006, p. 3). This category includes the right to respect for private and family life, home and correspondence (Article 8), freedom of thought, conscience and religion (Article 9) and freedom of expression (Article 10). Like limited rights, qualified rights are classed as non-absolute in Dworkin's model because, as we will see below, they can be outweighed by other rights or goals.

Qualified rights may be subject to interference from a public body only if three conditions are fulfilled. As the Home Office explained, any intervention must: (a) have a legal basis; (b) be undertaken in order to pursue a legitimate aim stated in the relevant Article, including the protection of public health, order or morals; the prevention of crime; or the protection of the freedoms and rights of other people; and (c) be 'necessary in a democratic society' (1997a, p. 25). In other words, the action must meet an urgent social need, pursue a legitimate objective, and be proportionate to that objective. Of the three tests, the proportionality requirement in condition (c) is the most important, because even if a policy that interferes with a Convention right secures a legitimate aim (such as the protection of public order), such interference is justified only if the means used to achieve the goal concerned are not excessive, unfair or arbitrary (Department for Constitutional Affairs, 2006, p. 13). The United Kingdom is also a signatory to the First Protocol to the Convention, which guarantees the right to protection of property (Article 1), the right to education (Article 2) and the right to free elections (Article 3). Dworkin refers to these rights as 'rights against the state,' and politicians typically invoke them to justify a decision that requires action from a specific government agency.

As Nigel Johnson observes, the majority of the rights guaranteed under the Convention are civil and political rights – as opposed to economic, social and cultural rights – though there is some overlap between them. For instance, the prohibition of degrading or inhuman treatment enshrined in Article 3 could be applied to conditions in a hospital or a residential care facility, or to treatment regimes for some mental health problems.[1] Similarly, Article 6, which guarantees the right to a fair hearing, is applicable not only to criminal trials but to such civil matters as housing benefit review boards, while the right to respect for private and family life (Article 8) could be invoked to secure the privacy of a resident of a nursing home (Johnson, 2004, p. 114). It is important to note, however, that situations may arise in which it is necessary to balance the rights guaranteed under the ECHR against each other. For example, a public figure's right to privacy (Article 8) may need to be weighed against a journalist's right to freedom of expression, which is guaranteed in Article 10 (Home Office, 1997a, p. 7).[2] In Dworkin's terms, we can say that this is a conflict between a concrete right (the right to privacy) and an abstract right (freedom of expression). These rights must be exercised responsibly, so although freedom of expression is an important right, it may nonetheless be limited if its exercise could cause harm.

Blair identified the Human Rights Act as a key component of New Labour's strategy for constitutional reform and the modernisation of British politics (1997a, p. 3). Before the Act came into effect in 2000, the UK was obliged under international law to observe the ECHR and was accountable for any contraventions. There were also limited situations in which the courts could take the requirements of the Convention into consideration in domestic proceedings. However, there was no requirement under domestic law for public authorities to act in accordance with the ECHR and, broadly speaking, there was no means of testing the application of the Convention rights in the UK court system. Indeed, UK citizens could enforce their rights under the Convention only by taking a case to the European Court of Human Rights in Strasbourg, a process that was costly in terms of both time and money. Given New Labour's commitment to maintaining fundamental human rights in the UK, it viewed these arrangements as inadequate, and therefore pledged to 'bring these rights home and allow our people access to them in our national courts'. This move, argued New Labour, would establish a 'floor, not a ceiling, for human rights' (Labour Party, 1997, p. 30) that could then be augmented through legislation such as the Freedom of Information Act, which was passed in 2000 but not implemented until 2005. The incorporation of the ECHR into UK law through the Human Rights Act would also, Blair claimed, complement the government's decision to place the advancement of human rights at the heart of its foreign policy, while raising public awareness of human rights (1997a, p. 3). The three main requirements of the Act are outlined next.

The first requirement of the Human Rights Act is that ministers should certify the compatibility of any proposed legislation with the ECHR. Although the HRA does not permit the courts to strike down Acts of Parliament, it demands that they 'interpret legislation as far as possible in accordance with the Convention' (Home Office, 1997a, p. 5). In situations where this is impossible, the higher courts can issue a formal declaration stating that the legislation concerned is incompatible with the rights enshrined in the ECHR. The onus then falls on the government and Parliament to rectify matters, and the HRA includes a 'fast-track' process that enables them to revise legislation in line with the Convention. This development is significant because it gives judges a more prominent role in the policy-making process, and thereby adds an important judicial element to the Constitution (Norton, 2007, p. 115). So, on this basis, we can concur with Driver and Martell that the HRA is '*de facto* a written bill of rights with a higher constitutional authority than all other laws passed by parliament' (2006, p. 151).

Meanwhile, the second requirement of the Act is that public authorities should behave in a way that is compatible with the Convention rights. On this basis, people can invoke their rights in any civil or criminal proceedings that a public body may bring against them, or in a case that they may bring against a public authority (Home Office, 1997a, p. 4). The courts and tribunals can then use their usual powers to award an appropriate remedy. Finally, the third requirement demands that UK tribunals and courts must take the Convention rights into consideration in all the cases they handle. In practical terms, this means they should both 'develop the common law compatibly with the Convention rights ... [and] take account of Strasbourg case law' when making judgements (Department for Constitutional Affairs, 2006, p. 7).

Overall, the incorporation of the ECHR into UK law had a number of important constitutional consequences. It changed the form of our civil liberties, which, in Vernon Bogdanor's words, are no longer 'specific inductive generalisations' based on particular cases, but are now derived from ' "principles of the constitution," principles of the

European Convention' (2001, p. 147). Moreover, the HRA enshrined the notion of human rights – as opposed to liberties – in UK law for the first time. These rights are positive rights, which range from the right to life to the right to freedom of peaceful assembly and association and, as such, mark a significant departure from the negative rights, or prohibitions, that had previously defined the tradition of common law in Britain (Burch and Holliday, 2000, pp. 87–90).

In its 2005 general election manifesto, New Labour, promised to consolidate these reforms by introducing a Single Equality Act to simplify and modernize existing legislation in this area, and by establishing the Commission on Equality and Human Rights. This body replaced the three existing equality Commissions – the Commission for Racial Equality, the Disability Rights Commission and the Equal Opportunities Commission – in October 2007 and, in addition, accommodated the three newer equality strands of age, sexual orientation, and religion and belief (Labour Party, 2005, pp. 111–12). The Commission was primarily responsible for advancing the agenda that underpins the Human Rights Act by promoting a culture of human rights in both the public services and in society as a whole. These measures, together with the Act itself, were intended to protect and uphold the human rights of every citizen. In the following section, I assess the extent to which the HRA, and the argumentative strategy used to support it, were consistent with New Labour's ideological commitments.

The compatibility of New Labour's arguments in favour of the Human Rights Act with its ideological platform

The incorporation of the ECHR into UK law and the arguments used to support it drew primarily on New Labour's core values of equal worth, equality of opportunity, and reciprocal rights and responsibilities. In the words of Lord Goldsmith, the Human Rights Act 'enshrines in our law the principle that all human beings should be treated with respect, equality and fairness' (2006, p. 3), and gives to each individual a number of fundamental rights and liberties. The concept of equal worth underpins the notion of equality of opportunity for all, which was present in both the core cluster of New Labour's ideology and in the HRA. Indeed, a central objective of the Act was to give people the opportunity to uphold their rights in UK courts, rather than having to take their case to Strasbourg. This measure was intended to make the legal system work better for everyone, not just the few who have the time and money to pursue a case in the European Court of Human Rights, and was consistent with New Labour's commitment to fairness and social justice. For New Labour, therefore, the incorporation of the ECHR into UK law was an important means to achieving its goal of a 'modern civic society based on the basic values of individual worth and equality of opportunity for all' (Scotland, 2001).

New Labour's core concept of equal worth was also present in the main goal of both the Human Rights Act and the ECHR, which is to ensure that the rights of *all* citizens are respected. In practice, this means that the rights of one individual will sometimes need to be balanced against those of another. For example, the right of someone who has been accused of a crime to question witnesses in court may have to be weighed against the rights of victims and vulnerable witnesses (Department for Constitutional Affairs, 2006, p. 6), or it may be necessary on occasions to balance the interests of the wider community against the personal rights of an individual. This second possibility is permitted by the qualified rights of the Convention, which weigh, for example, the right to freedom of expression against 'the right of others not to be defamed or to be the subject of racial hatred' (Goldsmith, 2006, p. 3). It also underlies the notion that rights and responsibilities go together; indeed, claimed the Department for Constitutional Affairs (DCA), the entire system of respecting rights 'works best when people recognise that and act responsibly towards others and the wider community'. The Human Rights Act made these ideas, together with the supporting judgments of the European Court of Human Rights, fully available to the UK courts. Moreover, continued the DCA, by giving the courts the power to declare legislation incompatible with the ECHR and offering Parliament the opportunity to amend it, the Act sought to balance the 'rights and responsibilities of the lawmaking and judicial parts of our Constitution, leaving the final word to the democratic process' (2006, p. 6).

According to David Lammy, former Parliamentary Under-Secretary in the DCA, the phrase 'bringing rights home' expressed New Labour's desire to promote a deeper understanding of what it means to respect human rights, and to 'build a new culture in which the language of rights and responsibilities become an integral part of the vocabulary of everyone' (2003, p. 3). If this goal was to be realized, New Labour needed to challenge the widespread assumption that the concept of human rights was a foreign innovation, and so was alien to the British way of life. To this end, Lammy argued that the significant part played by British lawyers in the drafting of the ECHR meant that it – and therefore the Human Rights Act itself – was imbued with many of our common values, which he identified as liberty, fairness, freedom of speech, and equality before the law. These values, he continued, are 'basic ethical principles, which underpin a decent society and inform the way the state treats its citizens' (2003, p. 4). In conjunction with reciprocal rights and responsibilities, they also supplied the foundations of New Labour's vision of a strong, cohesive community that enables each of its members to flourish. This ideal was central to New Labour's ideology, so the Human Rights Act and the arguments employed to promote it appeared to be consistent with New Labour's core values.

New Labour's human rights culture was based on a positive conception of human rights and had both an ethical and an institutional dimension. With reference to the former, New Labour believed people should understand that they are entitled to human rights as an 'affirmation of their equal dignity and worth, and not as a contingent gift of the state.' This understanding should, it continued, be tempered by a respect for the rights of other people and a sense of personal responsibility (Joint Committee on Human Rights, 2003, p. 1). Although this claim draws on New Labour's core concept of reciprocal rights and responsibilities, the reality was that both the Human Rights Act and the European Convention neglected the responsibility aspect of the human rights culture. This is because – unlike such human rights instruments as the American Convention on Human Rights (see Chapter 2) and the Universal Declaration of Human Rights (UDHR)[3] – the HRA does not include the provision that individual rights are accompanied by responsibilities owed to others. As a result, a person is able to claim rights against their community without having to accept any obligations in return.

This difficulty was also present in the institutional dimension of the Human Rights Act. Here, New Labour sought to create a culture in public life in which a respect for human rights was central to the design and implementation of legislation, policy and public services. The Commission for Equality and Human Rights was a vital component of New Labour's strategy for achieving this objective, given that its remit was to:

> Foster a culture of respect for human rights through raising awareness of the need to promote human rights in public authorities in the delivery of services, and through making individuals conscious of their rights and guiding them in asserting those rights. (Joint Committee on Human Rights, 2003, p. 4)

In practice, and despite New Labour's assertion that the ethical and institutional aspects of its human rights culture were together intended to create a 'more humane society, a more responsive government and better public services' (Joint Committee on Human Rights 2003, p. 2), the burden of responsibility fell squarely on the state, with no corresponding requirement that individuals should accept their obligations to society in exchange for their rights. The HRA thus failed to move beyond the antagonism of rights and responsibilities, and instead was weighted too heavily in favour of the former.

Until the 1990s, many in the Labour Party believed that human rights legislation would 'hand political power from a socialist parliament to a conservative judiciary' and, on this basis, viewed it unfavourably (Johnson, 2004, p. 113). More generally, claimed New Labour, post-war social democracy was too keen to broaden the range of individual rights 'without any corresponding concern with the responsibilities attached to rights and the duties individuals owe as members of families and communities' (Driver and Martell 1998, quoted in Johnson 2004, p. 116). Therefore, New Labour's decision to incorporate the ECHR into UK law, together with its insistence that rights should be accompanied by responsibilities, was viewed as a departure from Old Labour thinking. In accordance with its anti-statist commitments, New Labour sought to empower citizens as individuals, and so rejected the traditional socialist means of empowering people through group rights negotiated by the trades unions or the state. Consequently, Toynbee and Walker argue, 'the thrust of the human rights endeavour was against the state, and essentially anti-social democratic', and therefore ran the risk of transforming citizens into individualist consumers (2005, p. 273). This fear was well founded, given Lammy's assertion that human rights and New Labour's strategy for reforming the public services were both about 'focusing on individual need and moving away from block provision' (2003, p. 3), and led some critics to argue that the New Labour had moved too far to the Right on this issue. Despite these objections and its failure to fully realize its ideological commitment to reciprocal rights and responsibilities, New Labour continued to argue as if its values and policy were in harmony, as we will see below.

The moral arguments used to win support for the incorporation of the ECHR into UK law

As elaborated in Chapter 2, politicians typically use deontological arguments to promote policies in the area of rights and constitutional reform. This mode of argumentation was especially suitable for the Human Rights Act because it is founded on the concept of equal worth, which can be used to justify human rights and certain freedoms, as well as social institutions. New Labour's main argument in support of the HRA appealed to this value, with Lord Falconer asserting that human rights 'are for everyone. They apply to everyone... Regardless of age, race, sex or religion they are a constant on which we can all rely' (2007, p. 2). As Yvette Cooper, former Parliamentary Secretary at the Lord Chancellor's Department, explained, these rights are important because they embody the prerequisites for our existence as social beings, which include the right to freedom of peaceful assembly and association with others, the right to practise religious belief in community with others, and the right to respect for private and family life. By upholding these rights and freedoms, she argued, the Human Rights Act safeguards our ability to develop the fundamental relationships that bind our society together. If you 'deprive us of our families, our communities, and any capacity to build family or social relationships', she continued, 'you deprive us of much of what it is to be human' (2003, p. 3).

On Falconer's view, the freedoms enshrined in the Act are inseparable from the concept of democracy. This notion was consistent, he said, with New Labour's belief in a pluralist society in which every citizen is of equal worth, and where each individual is 'free to live and think as they wish, subject only to limitations required to protect the wider community' (2006a, p. 3). By safeguarding these freedoms, the Act sought to prevent governments and communities alike from trampling over the rights of individuals in the name of the majority opinion. As Cooper put it, the government needed to be careful not to allow the values that are associated with communities to 'blind us to their weaknesses, and lead to lower tolerance and lower priority being given to any form of protection for individuals at all' (2003, p. 4). To this end, a key feature of New Labour's vision of a culture of human rights was the balancing of the needs of communities against individual rights, in accordance with the framework supplied by the Human Rights Act.

However, it is important to note that Article 15 of the ECHR permits governments to derogate from their obligations under the Human Rights Act in times of national emergency, the result of which is that individual rights are not inviolable. New Labour declared the 'war on terror' to be such a time, and on this basis it opted out of Article 5 of the HRA, which guarantees the right to liberty. This allowed it to enact the Anti Terrorism, Crime and Security Act in 2001, which gave authorities the power to detain terror suspects without trial. Thirteen men were subsequently arrested under this legislation and held indefinitely in Belmarsh and Woodhill prisons, and Broadmoor high security hospital. Following appeals by nine of the detainees, the House of Lords ruled in December 2004 that their detention was incompatible with their Convention rights, on the grounds that it was disproportionate to the security threat and discriminated against foreign nationals (Verkaik, 2005).

Because the HRA 'preserves parliamentary sovereignty in the face of a declaration of incompatibility', writes Shami Chakrabarti, 'the House of Lords had no power to order the release of the detainees' (2005). In consequence, the then Home Secretary, Charles Clarke, initially declared the men must remain in prison, a position Blair supported. Even so, New Labour subsequently revised its 2001 legislation, and the Prevention of Terrorism Act became law on 11 March 2005. The Belmarsh detainees were released under control orders on the same day after three years in prison (BBC, 2005a). Although the HRA was utilized to secure the release of the detainees, their case highlights both the vulnerability of human rights and the ease with which governments can set aside their core values. In the case of New Labour, these values were fairness, equal worth (on the ground that the 2001 Act did not apply to British terror suspects), and rights and responsibilities (given its failure both to uphold the rights of the detainees and to fulfil its obligation to ensure that its legislation was compatible with the HRA). At the same time, the Belmarsh case shows how quickly governmental support for human rights can turn to frustration when they become inconvenient, and thus makes clear the importance of human rights as a limit on state power.

For New Labour, government has a responsibility to protect the most vulnerable members of society, and it viewed the Human Rights Act as pivotal in enabling it to fulfil this obligation. Through its framework of fundamental rights, the Act enshrined in UK law the idea that all individuals are of equal worth and thus should be treated fairly, equally and with respect. In Falconer's words, these principles 'protect vulnerable people: the elderly, disabled people and children. They give a voice and redress to those who need it most' (2004a, p. 2). One way in which they do so is by enabling people to bring human rights cases before the UK courts, when previously they would have had to travel to Strasbourg. More generally, they are central to the culture of human rights and responsibilities that New Labour sought to promote across both the public sector and society as a whole. So, for instance, if a local authority fails to respect the dignity of an elderly person in one of its residential care homes, then this failure should now be viewed as a violation of that individual's human rights and action taken through the courts if required. In this way, Cooper claimed, 'it is possible to change the climate of the debate' (2003, p. 6), and to create a culture in which the human rights of every citizen are upheld in accordance with the government's obligations under the Act.

The Human Rights Act was also designed to safeguard the rights of vulnerable people in cases where the rights of one individual are weighed against those of another, or against the interests of the wider community. As we have seen, New Labour held that all persons are of equal worth, and on this basis no individual's entitlement to human rights is greater than that of another. Consequently, the criteria for adjudicating between competing rights claims must be founded purely on fairness and principle; the outcome should not be determined by the relative strength or popularity of the parties involved. Indeed, Falconer argued, to make a person's entitlement to human rights dependent upon other qualifications is tantamount to claiming that one individual is somehow more human than another, 'something that is akin to the evils we fought in World War Two and fight against today' (2004a, p. 2). Thus, the Human Rights Act provided the government and the courts with a reference point and, as such, did not offer rigid prescriptions for every conceivable circumstance. For New Labour, this meant that the Act could accommodate the possibility of divergent opinions on the merits of particular cases, while at the same time guaranteeing that its core principles of fairness and balance are accepted and adhered to. However, we will see in the next section that the lack of guidance or training for decision makers on the HRA proved problematic, as it led to some controversial rulings that critics claim undermined both the Act and the notion of human rights itself.

In addition to the deontological case for the incorporation of the ECHR into UK law, New Labour deployed a secondary virtue theoretic argument in support of this policy. According to Baroness Scotland, the growing diversity of British society provides one of the most compelling arguments for the incorporation of fundamental values into statute law. This is because common values cannot be taken for granted in diverse societies, and instead 'need to be stated and affirmed so that everybody understands what they are, and so that we can all learn to interpret them in a similar way' (2001). In the terms of virtue theory, we can say that Scotland identified a need for a catalogue of basic virtues that was broadly acceptable to all British citizens. For New Labour, the first step towards meeting this need was the introduction of the Human Rights

Act and its attendant culture of human rights. As Lord Falconer put it, the government needed to show the country 'how fairness and respect matters to each and every one of us – and how respect for basic rights is the key to true equality'. This would enable New Labour to realise its vision of a 'thriving society, based on opportunity and fairness for all' (2004b, pp. 1–2), in which every citizen can flourish.

If we accept New Labour's argument that shared values are a prerequisite for a strong, cohesive community, its failure to balance the rights of the individual against responsibilities owed to the rest of society is all the more surprising. After all, we saw in Chapter 5 that Blair believed the two values go together, and that rights without responsibilities are socially corrosive. However, despite New Labour's intention to create a culture of human rights in which both values were present, the Conservative MP Nick Herbert argued that the neglect of responsibilities in the HRA had in fact created a culture in which rights had been 'devalued and misapplied', and that had 'distorted priorities in public bodies and undermined public safety' (2008, p. 7). I return to this issue in my examination of the 'context of hegemonic competition'.

New Labour's strategy for achieving hegemonic advantage

In its efforts to win support for the Human Rights Act, New Labour emphasized the novelty of its approach. As Baroness Scotland put it, 'the new act is about a new citizenship for a new society and a new economy' (2001). This statement placed the Act squarely within New Labour's broader strategy of modernization, which, in the words of the former Home Secretary Jack Straw, was intended to 'bring about a better balance between rights and responsibilities, between the powers of the state and the freedom of the individual' (Hansard, 16 February 1998a, c.781). New Labour also believed these developments would help to create a new culture of human rights, though it acknowledged that this process would require 'profound, systematic and gradual change' (Lammy, 2004, p. 2).

For New Labour, these reforms were necessary if Britain was to succeed in meeting the needs of its increasingly diverse population. As we have seen, New Labour argued that the Human Rights Act would promote community cohesion and social justice by supplying a framework of basic values that everyone can accept, upholding the rights of all citizens, and providing greater protection against discrimination. In so doing, it claimed to understand the challenges facing Britain and to offer a real solution to them. Here, New Labour used a strategy of legitimization to portray itself as the only party with the vision and courage to implement the radical changes required to modernize society. It then used this representation to create an antagonism between itself and Old Labour, which it claimed had been unwilling to enact human rights legislation, and sought to promote group rights as opposed to individual rights. As Peter Mandelson and Roger Liddle argue, the incorporation of the ECHR into UK law heralded the beginning of the 'modern age of citizenship', and meant that 'no one will ever be able to accuse Labour of being prepared to sacrifice individual rights on the altar of collectivist ideology' (1996, p. 196). In practice, however, the Human Rights Act went too far the other way and prioritized rights over civic responsibility. As we have seen, this imbalance also permeated New Labour's argumentative strategies, the result of which was that it failed to convey the responsibility aspect of its human rights culture to the public.

Although Cooper described the passing of the Human Rights Act as 'an immensely significant constitutional change' (2003, p. 1), Straw did not present the Bill that preceded it as such. He instead told Parliament that the Bill had the 'limited function of bringing the British people's rights home', and therefore was not intended to challenge 'constitutional arrangements that have evolved in this country to make us one of the world's most stable democracies' (Hansard, 16 February 1998b, c.770). In so doing, Straw portrayed the Bill merely a 'tidying-up exercise', which enshrined in UK law the rights that citizens already possessed under the European Convention, though he did acknowledge that it made these rights more accessible (Hansard, 16 February 1998b, c.768). In the terms of discourse theory, we can say that Straw created a relation of equivalence between human rights and British values, which he utilized to argue that the Convention rights belong in UK law, and to imply that their incorporation was therefore inevitable.

There is a potential instability here, and the question arises of why New Labour used these seemingly opposing arguments to win support for the Human Rights Act. One response is that it deployed them in an attempt to appeal to a number of different audiences. As we have already seen, Cooper and Scotland argued that the incorporation of the ECHR into UK law would have a significant effect on British society. Both speakers were addressing audiences with an interest in citizenship – the human rights organization Liberty and the Roscoe Foundation for Citizenship, whose remit is to promote active citizenship, respectively – and may have emphasized the social impact of the Act for this reason. Straw, meanwhile, delivered his speech in Parliament, with the principal aim of winning the backing of MPs for the Bill. On this basis, he perhaps downplayed some of its more contentious features, presenting it instead as a straightforward means of refining current legislation. If this analysis is correct, then New Labour's two arguments for the Human Rights Act were not flatly contradictory, on the ground that they focused on different aspects of the legislation, namely the social and the legal. Nonetheless, the uneasy relationship between the two arguments reveals a tension within in New Labour's justificatory strategy, which in turn damaged its credibility on this issue and helped to fuel public cynicism towards the HRA.

Straw's legal case for the incorporation of the ECHR into UK law proved successful, as the passage of the Human Rights Bill through Parliament was for the most part uncontroversial. An important factor in this success was the fact that the concept of basic human rights is acceptable to most people, and few would deny that it should be enshrined in law. Indeed, the Labour MP Terry Davis noted that in this debate, the former Shadow Home Secretary, Brian Mawhinney,

> Did not argue against human rights: he made it clear that he agreed with and supported the convention on human rights. He could do little else: even the modern Conservative party accepts the convention on human rights, as did its predecessors over the past 50 years. (Hansard, 16 February 1998c, c.794)[4]

Given the widespread acceptance of the notion of fundamental rights, New Labour may have felt it unnecessary to deploy an extensive array of tactics to secure hegemonic advantage for the Human Rights Act. Instead, it had to concentrate its efforts on challenging the arguments of its opponents and the various misconceptions about the Act, some of which I outline next.

As Cooper points out, some critics have objected that the Human Rights Act, and the ECHR on which it is based, are 'classical liberal documents designed always to champion the freedom and autonomy of the individual against the overbearing community and the oppressive state' (2003, p. 2). In so doing, they claim, these documents encourage people to believe they have an unconditional entitlement to human rights, and that they owe nothing to society in return. Human rights have thus degenerated into what Cherie Booth and Rabinder Singh describe as 'licence and selfishness' (2000, p. 3). Although Cooper agreed that too much discussion of rights without responsibilities was a cause for concern, she quickly claimed that New Labour's human rights legislation in fact contains a strong communitarian dimension. This was evident, she said, in its balancing of individual rights against the needs of the wider community and its recognition that rights are accompanied by responsibilities, which the new culture of human rights would promote. Indeed, Cooper continued, 'some on the libertarian right have criticised the Human Rights Act because it is not a purists' freedom charter in the classical liberal tradition'. The communitarian objection that the Act fosters selfish individualism is therefore misplaced, and arises because people focus solely on the 'rights' aspect of human rights at the expense of the 'human' aspect; they 'concentrate on the caricature, rather than the reality that lies behind it' (2003, pp. 2–3).

However, the absence of a provision in the Human Rights Act outlining the responsibilities individuals owe to society invalidates Cooper's claim that the Act has a significant communitarian aspect, while New Labour's emphasis on rights in its arguments to support this legislation meant that the idea of civic obligation was virtually absent from people's perceptions of the HRA. Herbert's claim that the Act has 'skewed regard for the rights of those who shout the loudest', while the rights of ordinary citizens receive little consideration, if any (2008, p. 7) is typical of this view. Falconer attributed the HRA's poor public image to the way in which its content and implementation were reported in the media, claiming that coverage tended to be 'dominated by a number of myths and misunderstandings, and by grey areas where matters of principle are at stake as much as matters of the law' (2007, p. 5).[5] I consider this defence below.

A notorious myth that received widespread media coverage was the so-called 'Kentucky Fried Chicken episode'. The story goes that a man in Gloucestershire, who was on the run from the police, took cover on the roof of a house and proceeded to demand cigarettes, drink and Kentucky Fried Chicken from his pursuers. A police spokesperson was claimed to have said, 'Although he's a nuisance, we still have to look after his wellbeing and human rights' (quoted in Falconer, 2007, p. 5). On this incident, Falconer noted that the Human Rights Act did not in fact entitle the man to have his demands met. Rather, it was a 'purely operational matter for the police to decide whether or not providing him with food would bring about a peaceful and swift resolution to the stand-off' (2007, p. 5). Nonetheless, said Falconer, the media reported that the man was given food because of his human rights.

Falconer also highlighted a grey area in the Human Rights Act. He described how a group of nine Afghan citizens hijacked a plane and subsequently sought asylum in Britain, claiming they would be tortured or killed if they were returned to Afghanistan. A tribunal accepted their application and ruled that, because of the judgment on the Chahal case by the European Court of Human Rights,[6] the hijackers could not be deported. This verdict sparked a storm of controversy, with the media condemning the Human Rights Act as a charter for terrorists and hijackers, and raising such questions as

> Why should they be allowed to stay? Why should they be free to potentially pose a threat to the public? Why are they being rewarded for a very serious crime? What will stop others like them? Why should their human rights outweigh mine? (Falconer, 2007, p. 6)

None of these questions has a straightforward answer.[7] While Blair described the outcome of the case as an 'assault on common sense' (quoted in Grayling, 2006), Falconer believed that, having made a commitment to human rights, society should uphold them, even if doing so proves difficult or unpopular (2007, p. 6).

On Falconer's view, these cases showed that the bulk of the media reports on the Act are devoted to the human rights of minority groups. Consequently, he claimed, the public hears only about the peripheral effects of the HRA, namely 'when the State is challenged in the courts, or in the grey areas where decisions are seen as going against the grain of popular opinion', or when it is wrongly applied. Such errors can produce results which are the opposite of those intended, and hence give rise to negative perceptions of the Human Rights Act. After all, continued Falconer, we rarely hear about the ways in which human rights legislation functions within, and for the benefit of, society as a whole on a daily basis (2007, p. 6). This prejudicial reporting, Falconer believed, ultimately made the Act a scapegoat for a variety of social ills, among which are the growth of a compensation culture and the early release of dangerous prisoners (2006b, p. 4).

However, it is an over-simplification to blame the media for the poor public perception of the Human Rights Act. After all, Mark Evans writes, 'there is evidence that a growing number of "special" groups benefit from the Act (such as asylum-seekers, foreign suspected international terrorists, and victims of violent crimes and their families)', whereas its impact on the general public is small by comparison (2008, p. 84). This point demonstrates that New Labour failed in its efforts to create a widespread 'culture of human rights', though Herbert goes further and argues that it shows the very concept of human rights is being undermined. He explains that the terrible violations of human rights in such countries as Burma and Zimbabwe are on a different scale of seriousness from the abuses that occur in Britain. So, to invoke the same rights and the same language in 'relatively trivial complaints in our own country, whether or not they are successful' is to devalue both the infringements taking place abroad and the concept of human rights itself (Herbert, 2008, p. 9). Although there have undoubtedly been complaints that have brought the HRA into disrepute, it is equally true that not all cases diminish human rights in this way. Nonetheless, there has been sufficient misuse of the notion of human rights to ensure that the Act lost support among MPs and the public alike.

So, how did the Conservatives respond to the Human Rights Act once it had been enshrined in UK law? On Cameron's view, this legislation had a number of positive effects, with some court rulings establishing important precedents that will greatly benefit society. For instance, the separation of an elderly married couple in different care homes was held to be unlawful under the Act, and families of the deceased now have the right to representation at coroner's inquests (2006a, p. 5). However, he argued that the Act had made it more difficult for the police to fight crime and was impeding the struggle against terrorism. To support his first point, Cameron cited the case of foreign ex-prisoners who had fled before they could be deported. Here, he claimed, the 'obvious thing to do would have been to issue "Wanted" posters', but police forces across the UK refused to do so because it would contravene Article 8 of the Human Rights Act, which guarantees the right to respect for family and private life. Indeed, Cameron continued, the Association of Chief Police Officers stated that photographs would be released only as a last resort, in those cases where public safety overrides the right to privacy of the individual concerned (2006a, p. 6).

With regard to terrorism, Cameron believed the Act and the Chahal case were serious obstacles to the government's efforts to protect the public. He argued that these developments had not only prevented the deportation of those foreign nationals who are deemed a serious security risk, but the 'lengths to which the authorities have to go even to detain them are [now] so great that many serious suspects are allowed to remain here at liberty'. This, Cameron continued, demonstrated that the Human Rights Act and the Chahal case restricted the powers of the Home Secretary to such an extent that the rights of terror suspects can no longer be properly balanced against the rights of the British people. Consequently, he claimed, public safety – together with public confidence in the notion of human rights – has been gravely undermined (2006a, p. 8). For the Conservatives, the solution to these problems lay in a new Bill of Rights for Britain, which would 'provide a hard-nosed defence of security and freedom' while at the same time achieving the balance between rights and responsibilities that was lacking in the HRA (Cameron, 2006a, p. 11).

According to Cameron, the Conservatives' modern British Bill of Rights would 'define the core values which give us our identity as a free nation' and guarantee our basic liberties, among which are civil rights, equality under the law and the right to trial by jury (2006a, p. 12). This, Cameron believed, would give people a sense of ownership over their rights. The Bill would also set out the basic obligations and responsibilities of every person who lives in Britain, whether they are a citizen or a foreign national, and provide guidance for the courts and the government in applying human rights legislation in cases where the irresponsible conduct of some individuals jeopardizes the rights of others. Finally, the Bill would defend our Convention rights in terms that are clearer and more precise than they are at present, thereby facilitating the enforcement of these rights in cases where they should be protected, while making it more difficult to extend them inappropriately. After all, Cameron stated, 'greater clarity and precision in the law, as opposed to vague general principles...is more in accordance with this country's legal tradition' (2006a, p. 12). In sum, the Conservatives believed their Bill of Rights would provide a clear statement of people's rights, facilitate the protection of these rights in the British courts, and make it easier for the government to fight crime and terrorism.

There are some strong similarities between the British Bill of Rights and the Human Rights Act, which indicates that the Conservatives accepted the principles underlying the latter but found fault with its content and implementation. Indeed, by drawing on the claims that the Act is hindering the struggle against terrorism and crime, Cameron's criticisms tapped into the growing public scepticism about human rights. This move can be seen as part of a wider strategy to increase support for the Conservatives' alternative policy, in which Cameron 'play[ed] to the tabloids by pledging to repeal the Human Rights Act while pleasing *Guardian* readers who support a bill of rights'. His proposals were also intended to 'unite both the authoritarian and libertarian wings of the Tory party by promising security and freedom' and, at the same time, to appeal to the two sides of the debate on European integration by expressing a commitment to the ECHR while promising a 'British solution' to the problem (Klug, 2006). In this way, the Conservatives sought to unify a range of conflicting demands around their proposals, and thus to win hegemonic advantage over New Labour in the area of rights and constitutional reform.

Cameron's announcement received a mixed reception, with the Liberal Democrats welcoming his proposals and Labour condemning them as 'wrong, muddled and dangerous' (quoted in Carlin, 2006).[8] Francesca Klug, meanwhile, claims the Conservatives would not need to abolish the Human Rights Act in order to introduce a Bill of Rights, on the ground that many of the European states who have incorporated the ECHR into their law have an additional Bill of Rights. Indeed, she writes, New Labour policy was at one time to bring in the Human Rights Act as a ' "first stage," to be followed by a bill of rights that would add flesh to its bones'. It may be the case, Klug continues, that Cameron wanted a Bill of Rights that would cause less trouble for a future Conservative government than the HRA did for Blair, but in practice this is unattainable (2006). After all, Britain would still be bound by the ECHR and, as Lord Tebbit put it, 'European law would override [the Bill] and we would be back where we are now, but in a bigger muddle perhaps' (quoted in Woodward, 2006). Given this latter point, Cameron's modern British Bill of Rights should perhaps be seen more as an attempt to destabilize New Labour and win public support than as a serious alternative to the HRA.

Conclusion

This chapter utilized the framework provided in Chapter 4 to analyse New Labour's case for the Human Rights Act of 1998. An examination of the 'context of ideology' indicates that although its chosen justificatory strategy and the HRA itself appeared consistent with New Labour's core values, both the argument and the policy prioritized rights over civic responsibility, and thus breached its commitment to reciprocal rights and responsibilities. As regards the 'context of argumentation', my assessment reveals that New Labour's deontological argument was appropriate for the Human Rights Act, but it again highlights the mismatch between its discourse and the legislation itself. The discussion of the 'context of hegemonic competition' shows that New Labour used relatively few strategies in its efforts to win support for the HRA, perhaps because the concept of human rights is so widely accepted. This proved to be a mistake, however, as New Labour's use of two distinct arguments to appeal to different audiences created confusion about the HRA and suspicion of the government's intentions. More seriously, in its efforts to distance itself from the collectivism of 'Old' Labour, New

Labour over-emphasized rights to such an extent that it created a culture in which they are rapidly becoming devalued.

The Conservatives took advantage of the negative public perception of the HRA, which was fuelled to a degree by a hostile tabloid press, and presented their British Bill of Rights as an alternative. This proposal contained many of the same ideas as the Human Rights Act, such as a set of core values for Britain and the balancing of rights with responsibilities. However, the Conservatives claimed that their Bill would improve on the HRA by tightening it up and reducing the number of grey areas it contains. This suggests that although the Conservatives accepted the moral agenda underlying the Human Rights Act, they found fault with both its content and its implementation. As such, the aim of the British Bill of Rights was to rectify the flaws in the HRA, and ultimately to win back the support of the public for the concept of human rights.

8
Community: New Labour's Policies on Anti-Social Behaviour

When New Labour came to power in 1997, it inherited from the Conservatives an increasingly divided society in which an underclass of people was 'cut off from [the] mainstream, without any sense of shared purpose' (Blair, 1997b). These individuals, and the areas where they lived, often suffered from a range of difficulties associated with high levels of social deprivation, such as unemployment, poor basic skills, bad housing and anti-social behaviour. New Labour introduced the New Deals in an effort to address the first two problems, while the latter was the target of a number of measures, including the Crime and Disorder Act (1998), the Anti-Social Behaviour Act (2003), and the 'Together' campaign, which was launched in 2003. These initiatives formed the basis of New Labour's 'Respect Agenda' (2005), which aimed to tackle anti-social behaviour by teaching respect for society's values. As Blair put it, 'the only way to rebuild social order and stability is through strong values, socially shared, inculcated through individuals, family, government and the institutions of civil society' (1996c, p. 148).

I begin this chapter by outlining the measures New Labour took to instil respect in individuals who behaved anti-socially. Next, I consider the relationship between these initiatives, the arguments employed to support them and New Labour's ideological platform. In so doing, I demonstrate that although New Labour's approach was based on the values of community and reciprocal rights and responsibilities, some of its policies for dealing with anti-social behaviour were contrary to these commitments. In the following section, I discuss the moral arguments that New Labour used to promote its anti-social behaviour agenda. Here I show that its virtue theoretic argument was appropriate for a policy programme in the area of community, but that its neglect of the social causes of anti-social behaviour in its rhetoric and policies was problematic. Finally, I assess New Labour's tactics for achieving hegemonic advantage, and I argue that although its discourses on anti-social behaviour were quickly accepted as 'common sense', its subsequent emphasis on punishment over prevention was to cost it the centre ground in this area of policy.

New Labour's strategy for tackling anti-social behaviour

The 1998 Crime and Disorder Act states that an individual is behaving anti-socially if he or she is 'acting in a manner that caused or was likely to cause harassment, alarm or distress to one or more persons not of the same household' (quoted in Home Office, 2004, p. 2). Specific examples of anti-social behaviour include nuisance neighbours, graffiti and litter, begging, inappropriate use of fireworks, and young people threatening or intimidating others. New Labour argued that these problems can be found anywhere – in town centres, housing estates, rural areas, and people's homes – and create a climate in which more serious crime takes root. In turn, the high visibility of the effects of anti-social behaviour in public places engenders not only the fear of crime, but also the perception that levels of crime are high (Home Office, 2003a, pp. 6–13), while severe anti-social behaviour can be detrimental to the health and family life of its victims.

The Home Office identified several factors that can contribute to anti-social behaviour, among which are failure at school, substance abuse and family problems. For Blair, the complexity of these problems necessitated a joined-up approach, with government working in a 'more coherent, integrated way, across departmental boundaries, and with all the agencies – public, private and voluntary – that can help turn things round' (1997c, pp. 3–4). To coordinate these efforts, and to further embed its discourses in social institutions, New Labour established the Anti-Social Behaviour Unit (ASBU) in January 2003.[1] It also introduced a raft of measures to address the problem of anti-social behaviour which, for reasons of space, cannot all be examined here. Instead, the chapter focuses on New Labour's policies to tackle the root cause of all anti-social behaviour, which it identified as a lack of consideration or respect for other people, and a failure to understand that our individual rights are founded on the responsibilities we owe to society (Home Office, 2003a, p. 17). These initiatives were intended to inculcate the values and behaviour that supply the foundations of respect through a combination of punishment and early intervention.

According to the Cabinet Office, 'early intervention' has two meanings: 'early in terms of age or early in terms of the onset of a problem – whatever the age of the individual' (2006, p. 19). One such intervention was parenting programmes, which encompassed a number of approaches (including family therapy and parenting advice) and were designed to give parents the skills they needed to manage their children's behaviour. These programmes were delivered by Youth Offending Teams (YOTs), who worked with families on a voluntary basis under a parenting contract or, if this approach failed, through a parenting order.[2] In brief, parenting contracts are non-statutory written agreements between the child's parent(s) and a YOT worker, while parenting orders are court orders with which non-compliance is a criminal offence. Both interventions were intended to be supportive rather than punitive, and can comprise parenting classes and a set of specific requirements designed to tackle the child's anti-social behaviour by, for instance, ensuring that he or she attends school or stays at home during certain hours (Ministry of Justice, Department for Children, Schools and Families and Youth Justice Board, 2007, p. 4).

While many parents wished they had been offered help at an earlier stage, claimed the Home Office, there were some who were unwilling or unable to accept this assistance. These families typically had complex problems, such as a parent in prison, domestic violence or serious difficulties in parenting, and needed intensive, long-term support that was tailored to their specific needs. Even with this support, however, some parents were unable to manage their children's behaviour, and New Labour developed intensive support schemes to help them. These programmes were targeted at families where a 'lack of parental capacity or ability contributes significantly to the child's behavioural problems' and provided an environment in which a child was helped to develop a sense of responsibility for their actions. The intensive fostering scheme, for example, was introduced as an alternative to custody and involved professionals from different agencies working together to address the needs of the young person concerned. At the same time, parents were helped to improve their parenting skills in preparation for their child's return home (Home Office, 2003a, p. 27).

While it was important to address the family problems that underlie a child's anti-social behaviour, argued the Home Office, 'we should be in no doubt that communities cannot be expected to suffer nuisance, disorder, damage and harassment for month after month.' Consequently, the support given to families needed to be tied to an understanding – by the perpetrators and professional agencies alike – that the protection of communities was paramount (2003a, p. 29). To this end, the agencies involved had to make it clear to families that they were prepared to use a range of civil and criminal sanctions to secure their compliance. In addition to injunctions, parenting contracts and parenting orders, these sanctions included Anti-Social Behaviour Orders (ASBOs), which I discuss next.

ASBOs came into force in 1999 and were civil orders imposed on individuals who had committed minor anti-social acts. The primary purpose of an ASBO was to restrict the recipient's behaviour by, for instance, prohibiting them from entering areas where they had previously caused trouble, or from drinking alcohol in public. Although they were introduced with a 'positive aim of referring young people at risk to appropriate support before they fall into crime', ASBOs were used mainly as a punishment and, because a breach constituted a criminal offence, hastened the recipient's entry into the criminal justice system (Margo and Stevens, 2008, p. 13). The misapplication of ASBOs perhaps stemmed from the fact that the courts did not have the power to compel a young person to address – and hopefully to resolve – the underlying causes of their anti-social behaviour, and New Labour sought to rectify this fault by introducing Individual Support Orders (ISOs) in 2003. In an echo of the individualized service delivery offered under the New Deals, ISOs required young people with ASBOs to participate in activities that were tailored to their particular needs (Home Office, 2003b, p. 35), which could form part of a 'contract' between the offender and the youth court alongside such other requirements as an apology to their victim or voluntary work in the community. For New Labour, these reparations were a 'valuable way of making young offenders face the consequences of their actions and see the harm they have caused', and could therefore act as a catalyst for reform (Home Office, 1997b, p. 19).

From the discussion so far, it is evident that the main aims of New Labour's anti-social behaviour agenda were to promote civic virtues and social inclusion, and to uphold the interests of the community. These goals suggest the use of a virtue theoretic argumentative strategy, which I examine in the third section. First, however, I assess the extent to which they were consistent with New Labour's core values.

The compatibility of New Labour's case for its anti-social behaviour agenda with its ideological commitments

Throughout the 1980s, the Conservative Party dominated the debate on law and order. Its uncompromising approach resonated with public concerns over crime, while its policies of harsher sentences for criminals and increased powers for the police won widespread support. In contrast, Labour was perceived as being 'soft on crime', a weakness that was reflected in its consistently poor performance in opinion polls (Parmar, 2000, p. 207). By the early 1990s, however, an unprecedented increase in recorded crime raised serious questions about the efficacy of the Conservatives' policies, to which Blair's pledge to be 'tough on crime, tough on the causes of crime' (1993) delivered the final blow. As Tim Newburn and Robert Reiner explain, this formula appeared to balance the 'populist desire for punitiveness with...the traditional social democratic idea that crime had deep social root causes' (2007, p. 319), and thus to offer a new approach to law and order that went beyond the old antagonism of left and right.[3]

According to the then Home Secretary, David Blunkett, New Labour's initiatives for tackling anti-social behaviour were founded primarily on the values of community and reciprocal rights and responsibilities (2003a, p. 1). These values also played a prominent role in New Labour's argument for its policy programme, central to which was the belief that 'every citizen has the right to live their life free from fear and distress and...they in turn have a responsibility not to cause fear or distress to others' (Home Office, 2003b, p. 5). To realize this goal, New Labour sought to create a 'web of rights and responsibilities that involves the whole of society; every individual and every community'. As such, each individual is responsible for their own conduct, and parents have an obligation to set standards of behaviour for their children and ensure they are adhered to. Meanwhile, the community has a duty to take action against the minority of people who behave anti-socially and cause misery to others, and the public services have a responsibility to do everything in their power to ensure the peace, safety and prosperity of Britain's communities. In return, central government has an obligation to 'set out the framework and provide leadership, tools and resources to ensure that local agencies and communities can deliver the new approach' (Home Office, 2003a, pp. 17–18). The ASBU was charged with coordinating this joined-up strategy, which manifested New Labour's ideological commitments to active community and active government.

According to the Home Office, a central aim of New Labour's policies on anti-social behaviour was to effect

> A cultural shift from a society where too many people are living with the consequences of anti-social behaviour, to a society where we respect each other...a society where we have an understanding

that the rights we all enjoy are based in turn on the respect and responsibilities we have to other people and to our community. (2003a, p. 6)

As Peter Squires correctly points out, these measures were intended to implement New Labour's 'model of active social democratic citizenship', where rights were paired with responsibilities in a 'something for something' society (2008, p. 314). We have already seen that New Labour viewed this pairing as a prerequisite for a strong, cohesive community in which every citizen can flourish and, because of its commitment to the value of equal worth, held that no one should be prevented from sharing in the benefits of community membership. For this reason, it believed government had a responsibility to enact policies to bring excluded individuals back into society, and to take action against those who refused the help offered to them.

The starting-point in New Labour's drive to eradicate anti-social behaviour was the family. As elaborated in Chapter 5, New Labour believed that the family is the best environment for raising children and – together with marriage – forms the basis of a stable society. This is because strong families 'teach values, provide stability, offer the support that children need, and protect them physically and emotionally' (Home Office, 2003a, p. 21). However, in dysfunctional families where children experience poor parenting, respect and personal responsibility are absent. As a result, claimed New Labour, there is an increased risk that these children will engage in anti-social behaviour,[4] and face social exclusion and a lack of economic opportunities as adults. Because the authorities had become more adept at spotting these risk factors, any problems could be identified and acted on at a very early stage (Blair, 2006a, p. 5). This intervention was intended to make parents aware of their responsibilities and help them to manage their children's behaviour, which in turn would prevent potential difficulties from becoming more serious.

As Karen Clarke observes, 'there is an ambiguity in the term parental responsibility between parents' responsibilities *to* their children (meeting children's needs) and parental responsibility *for* children (parents' accountability to others, and in particular to the state, for their children's actions)' (2007, p. 168). Both of these definitions were present in New Labour's family policies, with the first exemplified by Sure Start and the second by parenting orders and contracts. However, she argues, New Labour failed to recognize that its conception of parents' responsibilities *to* their children, which it broadened to include paid work (in terms of providing a role model), may have been at odds with the requirement to supervise, control, and thus be responsible *for* children. This problem was particularly acute for lone parents, who had to balance caring for their children with paid work and who were the target of an increasingly tough regime under the New Deals. The time pressure involved in juggling these roles, together with the fact that most working lone parents are in low-paid jobs, limited their opportunities for participating in their communities, and thus increased their risk of social exclusion (Clarke, K., 2007, pp. 167–9). In this respect at least, it seems New Labour's policies for reducing exclusion exacerbated the problem they were intended to solve.

Despite New Labour's original pledge that ASBOs should be issued to under-18s only in exceptional circumstances, almost half of them were used to curb the 'problem behaviour' of children (Goodchild, 2006). This development was problematic because it failed to respect some of their fundamental rights, and therefore violated New Labour's commitment to the values of equal worth, reciprocal rights and responsibilities, and inclusion. As Phil Scraton argues, many of the conditions that ASBOs imposed on under-18s breached the UN Convention on the Rights of the Child – specifically 'Article 9 (separation from parents and the right to family life), Article 13 (freedom of expression), Article 15 (freedom of association) and Article 16 (protection of privacy)' (2005, p. 19). Moreover, the imprisonment of children who failed to comply with the terms of an ASBO contravened several of the principles enshrined in Article 40 of the UN Convention, including the child's right to be 'treated in a manner consistent with the promotion of [their] sense of dignity and worth' and to be 'dealt with in a manner appropriate to their well-being and proportionate both to their circumstances and the offence' (quoted in Scraton, 2005, p. 19).

While New Labour would perhaps have argued that rights are conditional on responsibilities, and that children who behave anti-socially (and thus fail to fulfil their responsibilities to the community) have forfeited these rights, the use of ASBOs against young people often proved counter-productive. Instead of achieving their stated aim of breaking the link between juvenile offending and adult criminality (see Straw, 1997, p. 2), ASBOs could in fact speed up a young person's entry into the criminal justice system, while the imprisonment of children who breached the terms of their orders stigmatized them and risked entrenching their offending behaviour (Scraton, 2005, p. 19). This in turn heightened their sense of alienation and exclusion, and indeed was hardly conducive to the creation of a culture of respect.

New Labour's moral arguments in support of its anti-social behaviour policies

Although the concept of reciprocal rights and responsibilities lay at the heart of New Labour's policies for tackling anti-social behaviour, it does not follow that deontological principles afforded the best means of promoting them. This is because deontology focuses on the rights and freedoms of the individual, and so marginalises our constitutive commitments. Virtue theory, in contrast, is based on the idea of a community that inculcates in its members the values and traits that will enable them to act morally and to promote the common good. Since this notion accorded with New Labour's goal of creating a strong, cohesive community populated by responsible citizens, it follows that an argument that resonated with virtue theoretic reasoning was the most appropriate strategy for promoting its anti-social behaviour agenda.

As stated in Chapter 2, the members of a community need to recognize as virtues those qualities which would promote the common good, and to condemn as vices the flaws which would harm it. These catalogues of the virtues and vices together provide citizens with a guide to action and supply a comprehensive account of the moral life of that community. For New Labour, the virtues included good manners, civility, a respect for other people, their privacy and their property, and an awareness that the rights of all citizens come with responsibilities. Given that 'the behaviour which expresses these values includes thinking about how our own actions affect others, acting unselfishly and helping others' (Respect Task Force, 2006, p. 5), New Labour believed a common commitment to society's virtues and the conduct that embodies them was the precondition for respect.

For the majority of people, claimed New Labour, the values and conduct that support respect are intuitively understood and form an integral part of their everyday routine, finding expression in successful parenting and high standards of teaching in schools. However, there was a widespread public anxiety that the virtues underpinning respect were in decline, and that anti-social behaviour had increased as a result (Respect Task Force, 2006, p. 5). New Labour attributed this development primarily to the socioeconomic changes that had occurred since the start of the twentieth century, on the grounds that they had altered the structure of the family and fractured communities. While the latter was sometimes due to 'desirable objectives like social mobility or diversity', failed economic policies and mass unemployment also contributed (Blair, 2005a). Moreover, the influence of civil institutions such as the Church and community organizations decreased and, by 1997, the common framework of respect and rules that united communities at the beginning of the twentieth century had weakened considerably (Respect Task Force, 2006, p. 5).

The same period also saw the growth of an 'underclass' of people, who were 'cut off from society's mainstream, living often in poverty, the black economy, crime and family instability' (Blair, 1996c, p. 293). For Blair, this development was very costly to the community in terms of increased welfare payments, higher levels of crime and environmental damage, and wasted talent. Moreover, he continued, the existence of the underclass 'destroys the sense of common purpose and effort essential to sustain a country as a working society and economy', and was therefore a social and economic evil (1996a, p. 116). If we recast this argument in the language of virtue theory, we can say that Blair believed the changes that occurred in the twentieth century caused the broad consensus about the nature of the virtues to break down. The resultant lack of a common standard of conduct led some people to believe they could act in any way they wished, regardless of whether their behaviour promoted the good of the wider community. This belief undermined the ideal that citizens should cooperate to achieve a common goal, while the failure of some parents to inculcate the virtues in their children was a key factor in the growth in crime and anti-social behaviour.

By explaining these social ills primarily in terms of the emergence of an immoral underclass, Blair played down the role of structural factors. While he perhaps intended to distance New Labour from the traditional Left by bringing the idea of personal responsibility back into the account (see Blair, 2005a), some critics argue that Blair's neglect of social circumstances rendered his explanation inadequate. Squires, for instance, identifies several elements that combined to create an 'anti-social urban environment', among which were inequality of income and opportunity, discrimination, a 'growth in criminogenic opportunities associated with drugs...and a burgeoning night-time economy'. These problems are concentrated mainly in deprived council estates and inner city areas, he continues, so it is perhaps unsurprising that anti-social behaviour first emerged as a problem of social housing management in the 1970s (2008, p. 307). If we accept the claim that people's behaviour is influenced – though not wholly determined – by their environment, then we can concur with Squires that anti-social behaviour may in fact be a 'fairly predictable outcome of anti-social circumstances, or a "normal" response to exceptional circumstances' (2008, p. 304). It thus follows that the causes of anti-social behaviour are myriad and complex, and that this phenomenon cannot be reduced simply to a lack of 'respect'.

A key component of New Labour's strategy to address anti-social behaviour was prevention. Blair believed that intervention in chaotic families was necessary 'not just where there has been a criminal offence committed, or the child has been say excluded from school, as is currently the case, but if they are showing the propensity to get involved in antisocial behaviour' (2005b, p. 5). The idea of early intervention has sinister connotations, a point Blair acknowledged when he explained that, in the majority of cases, it simply meant that families could be given extra support in the form of, for instance, parenting classes (2006a, p. 5). By doing so, New Labour aimed to help parents recognize and fulfil their responsibility to teach their children society's values and standards of behaviour, which in turn would 'create the conditions in which families can flourish and all children have the chance to succeed' (Home Office, 1997b, p. 12). These conditions were identified as the prerequisites for a strong, stable community, so for New Labour, early intervention and – if necessary – the coercion of families to accept the help on offer were justifiable by reference to the virtue theoretic ideal of the common good.

New Labour's early intervention strategies achieved a measure of success in helping families to lead less chaotic lives. As Toynbee and Walker point out, parenting orders reduced the re-offending rates of young people in the target families by a third, despite the fact that roughly half of these families did not complete them. Indeed, they continue, many of the parents who were initially reluctant to comply with parenting orders came to believe they had a positive effect on their family (2005, p. 227). However, the long-term efficacy of the parenting courses that often formed part of these orders was less clear. After all, they tended to be short in duration, lasting around eight weeks, and were typically offered when the family's difficulties were already entrenched. Moreover, the schemes rarely involved the young people themselves, which raised the question of how far their anti-social behaviour could be addressed by interventions directed at their parents (Ghate and Ramella, 2002, pp. 51, 75–9). They also failed to address the 'structural inequalities that contribute to depression, low levels of parental supervision and other indicators of inadequate parenting' (Margo and Stevens, 2008, p. 15), which again highlights the centrality of notions of individual failure or weakness in New Labour's account of the causes of anti-social behaviour, as well as in its strategy for dealing with it.

In common with MacIntyre, New Labour held that 'punishment is necessary to signal society's disapproval when any person...breaks the law' (Home Office, 1997b, p. 20). Any punishment should be both quick and proportionate to the crime, thereby ensuring that the offender repays his or her debt to the community in full. Although it was originally introduced as a preventative measure, the ASBO was one of the most widely used punishments for anti-social behaviour.[5] Indeed, Margo and Stevens note that 4,274 ASBOs were issued between 1 October 2004 and 30 September 2005, up from 2,874 the previous year. In spite of this, they continue, the number of incidents of anti-social behaviour did not fall, while 'the breach rate for ASBOs imposed on under-18s [was] around 55 per cent, of which 46 per cent resulted in a custodial sentence in 2004' (2008, p. 67). These figures suggest that punitive measures alone are ineffective in preventing anti-social behaviour, and that ASBOs needed to be accompanied by other interventions to address the young person's problems. Although New Labour introduced ISOs to perform this role, the Labour MP Ann Coffey observed that they were issued in only five per cent of cases (Hansard, 18 January 2007, c.947). It therefore appears that, despite New Labour's claims, its anti-social behaviour agenda was geared more towards punishment than prevention; the first half of its 'tough on crime, tough on the causes of crime' mantra took priority over the second. I return to this point in the next section, where I examine New Labour's strategies for achieving hegemonic advantage on law and order.

New Labour's tactics for securing hegemonic advantage

According to Blair, the social changes that took place in Britain during the twentieth century fundamentally altered the nature of crime. In particular, they brought about a growth in violent offences fuelled by drug abuse and the wider availability of guns, as well as a range of new problems that included people trafficking, mobile phone theft and computer fraud. However, the criminal justice system was increasingly unable to meet these new challenges and by 1997 it had become unfit for purpose: 'trials were ineffective, witness protection was poor and the courts were very inefficient. There were huge delays, for example, between young criminals being charged and coming to court' (Blair, 2005a). Furthermore, high levels of bureaucracy prevented the authorities from dealing effectively with the growing problem of anti-social behaviour. Blair explained that although the police could prosecute people for behaving anti-socially, the reality was that the process took 'many police hours, much resource and if all of that is overcome, the outcome [was] a fine' (2005b, p. 6). As a result, the police did not believe prosecution was worth the effort, so anti-social behaviour continued unchecked, bringing misery to communities across Britain (Blair, 2006b, p. 1). The choice facing New Labour, therefore, was either to accept that nothing could be done to improve the situation, or to give the police and local authorities new powers to deal with it (Blair, 2005a).

New Labour used this narrative to delegitimize the Thatcher and Major governments, blaming them for the crisis in the criminal justice system and the rise in anti-social behaviour. More specifically, Blair argued that their inability to deal with these problems was indicative of a failure not just of their policies but of their entire philosophy, which he summed up by quoting Mrs Thatcher's famous remark that 'there [is] no such thing as society' (1998b, p. 7). For many on the Left, this comment epitomized the crude individualism of the Conservatives' approach, which had contributed significantly to the decline of the family and accelerated social breakdown. However, Thatcher's words are often taken out of context, the result of which is that their meaning has become grossly distorted. She was in fact attacking 'the confusion of society with the state as the helper of first resort' (Thatcher, 1993, p. 626), as the rest of her argument clearly shows:

> I think we've been through a period where too many people have been given to understand that if they have a problem, it's the government's job to cope with it...They're casting their problem on society. And, you know, there is no such thing as society. There are individual men and women, and there are families. And no government can do anything except through people, and people must look to themselves first. It's our duty to look after ourselves and then, also to look after our neighbour. People have got the entitlements too much in mind, without the obligations. There's no such thing as entitlement, unless someone has first met an obligation. (1987)

The desire to encourage people to act responsibly in exchange for the entitlements they receive is, of course, entirely consistent with New Labour's core values. Nonetheless, the caricature of Thatcher's views is so well known that Blair was able to contrast it with his own party's commitment to the values of community and cooperation, and thus to undermine the Conservatives' position.

Blair also deployed a strategy of legitimization, claiming that New Labour alone had the moral authority to rebuild social order in Britain.

As we have seen, New Labour held that a strong, stable community was founded on reciprocal responsibilities and a respect for others. For Blair, the inculcation of these values in all citizens was a matter of fairness, on the ground that 'those who lose most through the absence of rules are the weak and the vulnerable' (1995b, p. 126). Because of its belief in mutual respect and social justice, Blair continued, the Left was uniquely positioned to 'fashion a new moral purpose for [the] nation' that combined personal and social responsibility and upheld social rules and order. These rules were embedded within a strong, active community, which in turn gave the Left the moral authority to enforce them (Blair, 1995b, p. 127). Here, Blair sought to cultivate an *ethos* of fidelity to Labour's ideological tradition by linking his commitment to restoring social order to his party's core values. This association was perhaps designed to reassure his audience that he was not proposing a 'lurch into authoritarianism' or attempting to impose a 'regressive personal morality' (1995b, p. 126), both of which are associated with the New Right. It also conferred legitimacy on Blair's approach, and thus strengthened his position as leader.

In his speech to the Labour Party conference in 2000, Blair combined these two strategies to offer his listeners a number of 'decisions of destiny' (2000, p. 4). One such choice was between 'a government with the strength to build strong communities, or a government that believes there is no such thing in society', and for Blair the effects of the latter's philosophy were clear to see:

> Crime, anti-social behaviour, racial intolerance, drug abuse, destroy families and communities. They destroy the very respect for others on which society is founded. They blight the life chances of thousands of young people and the quality of life of millions more. Fail to confront this evil and we will never build a Britain where everyone can succeed. (2000, p. 10)

Here, Blair created a relation of equivalence between various social ills and reified them into a force for evil that destroys respect and hampers opportunity. As I have previously noted, New Labour believed these problems disproportionately affected – and indeed were caused by – the underclass, whose emergence was also linked to the decline in respect. For this reason, it is unsurprising that Blair described the existence of the underclass as a 'moral and economic evil' that most Western economies 'suffer from' (1996a, p. 293). In so doing, he communicated a strong negative evaluation, which then provided the ethical legitimization for his commitment to tackling anti-social behaviour.

Blair's ability to describe these social problems as 'evil' implied moral authority on his part and, moreover, gave his actions an epic dimension (Charteris-Black, 2005, p. 151). In representing himself as an agent of good, Blair invoked the myth of the battle between good and evil, which in turn activated the conceptual metaphors POLITICS IS ETHICS and MORALITY IS CONFLICT that were central to his Conviction Rhetoric. Also important were the metaphors BAD GOVERNING IS DESTROYING and GOOD GOVERNING IS CREATING, the first of which underlies the destruction metaphors 'destroy' and 'blight' that Blair used to depict the problems of the underclass as a force of evil. As Charteris-Black explains, these reifications for destruction 'imply a mental schema in which various social processes that erode social cohesion are negatively evaluated because they entail serious material damage' (2005, p. 125). Given that this damage occurred during the Conservatives' time in office, Blair was able to delegitimize his opponents by associating them with bad governing.

Having made this association, Blair established a relation of antagonism between the failings of the Conservatives and his own party's commitment to 'build strong communities'. The word 'build' implies creativity, which activates the GOOD GOVERNING IS CREATING conceptual metaphor and thereby conveys a positive evaluation. So, by inviting his audience to view New Labour as a creative force, Blair sought to legitimize his government's approach as well as his own leadership. Although this combination of metaphor and contrast enabled Blair to heighten rhetorical tension, and thus to maximize the emotional impact of his argument, there is a danger that this strategy can 'lead to an irreversible commitment to certain political positions' (Charteris-Black, 2005, p. 161). This proved to be so for Blair, as I demonstrate below.

In making the case for its anti-social behaviour agenda, New Labour also employed the technique of emotive coercion, perhaps with the intention of inducing fear in its audience. The starting-point of this argument was Blunkett's statement that 'the anti-social behaviour of a few, damages the lives of many' (2003b, p. 3), on the basis of which New Labour made predictions about the consequences that would follow if anti-social behaviour continued unchecked. Hence the Respect Task Force claimed that the problem behaviour of parents can put their children at risk of harm and – more seriously – that bad behaviour and a lack of respect can be passed from one generation to the next. In the community, meanwhile, the effects of anti-social behaviour – abandoned cars, graffiti, and broken windows – intensify the fear of crime and cause people to withdraw from public places. This leads to a 'spiral of decline, which makes people feel less able to confront and deal with anti-social behaviour' and thus makes the problem worse. Given the severity of these consequences, therefore, the Respect Task Force believed urgent action was required to prevent the anti-social behaviour epidemic from spreading further (2006, p. 6).

New Labour's use of emotive coercion proved too successful, however, as many people perceived that crime levels were high despite a drop in the number of offences committed (Squires, 2008, p. 315).[6] This was due in part to the breadth and flexibility of the concept of anti-social behaviour itself, which encompassed a range of disparate problems from begging to nuisance neighbours and indeed became widely accepted as unchallenged 'common sense'. While the creation of this equivalential chain enabled New Labour to attribute a common cause to all forms of anti-social behaviour, namely a lack of respect, the remarkable fluidity of the term brought a growing number of 'problem' behaviours within its ambit, and public concern increased accordingly. New Labour's assertion that anti-social behaviour could occur anywhere from inner cities to rural areas did not help matters, as it conveyed the impression that communities across Britain were under siege (Garrett, 2007, p. 844). This claim was clearly an exaggeration, given that anti-social behaviour was primarily a problem affecting Britain's most deprived communities. Nonetheless, it contributed to the growing public anxiety about crime and disorder, and was thus 'a significant own goal' for New Labour (Squires, 2008, p. 315).

The perceived prevalence of anti-social behaviour, together with its wide definition, contributed to a moral panic about youth crime. Erich Goode and Nachman Ben Yehuda explain that moral panics combine 'heightened emotion, fear, dread, anxiety and a strong sense of righteousness'(1994, p. 31), and can be diagnosed by the presence of 'folk devils' and a 'disaster mentality'. The 'folk devil' is a deviant individual whose behaviour is damaging to society and whose actions must be 'neutralised' (1994, pp. 28–9). In the panic surrounding anti-social behaviour, this role was played by 'feral youths', who had 'no parental control or respect for anybody' and rampaged around Britain's cities in gangs, leaving a trail of misery in their wake (BBC, 2005b). The 'disaster mentality', meanwhile, comprises a number of elements, which include rumour, overreaction and 'predictions of impending doom' (Goode and Ben Yehuda, 1994, p. 29). Instrumental in the creation of this mentality was the media, which regularly reported on Britain's violent 'yob culture' and condemned the government for its failure to respond effectively. A typical example can be found in the *Daily Mail*, which describes an 'epidemic of lawlessness' that stemmed from the 'relentless growth of a lethal sub-culture of fatherless children and disorderly homes' and, if left unchecked, would ultimately lead to the 'collapse of social order' (Phillips, 2005). These stories fuelled public concern about anti-social behaviour, which in turn prompted calls from certain sections of the community for tough measures to tackle the problem – such as the restoration of discipline in schools and harsher punishments for 'yobs' – and led to an escalation in public hostility towards young people.

Blair and Blunkett went along with this moral panic and, in so doing, 'became their own worst enemies, their dramatic announcements themselves stoking up fear' (Toynbee and Walker, 2005, p. 231). Instead of publicizing the progress made by the YOTs in addressing the underlying causes of anti-social behaviour, New Labour responded by introducing a range of seemingly knee-jerk measures, such as fixed penalty notices ('on-the-spot fines') for offences ranging from throwing fireworks to making hoax emergency calls (BBC, 2002). Although these tough-sounding initiatives were intended to reassure the public that it was taking their concerns seriously, they also indicate that New Labour had become trapped in its own rhetoric, as I argue next.

By representing anti-social behaviour as part of a force of evil that needed to be confronted head on, Blair committed his party to a tough, punishment-centred approach to dealing with the problem. Anything less could be perceived as 'soft' on crime, which risked undermining his self-representation as an agent of good, and ultimately his authority as leader. This perception would also leave 'New' Labour vulnerable to accusations that it had gone back to its 'old' ways and, moreover, that it was failing to match its strong words with action. The balance thus shifted in favour of punishment and away from prevention, despite a growing body of evidence to show that punitive measures are ineffective in diverting young people from crime (Farrington-Douglas with Durante, 2009, p. 14; Margo and Stevens, 2008, p. 48). Ironically, researchers have also found significant public support for programmes to improve parenting skills and intensive interventions for children at risk of offending, while the criminal justice approach to reducing crime is viewed as effective by only a third of people (Home Office, 2008, p. 6; Margo and Stevens, 2008, p. 18).[7]

Following New Labour's shift towards punitive populism, the Conservatives attempted to win back the advantage on law and order with their 'Real Respect' agenda. Like New Labour, Cameron identified 'family breakdown, drugs, children in care [and] educational underachievement' as risk factors for criminality, and endorsed the view that anti-social behaviour was the result of a 'collapse in social responsibility' (2006b; BBC, 2005b). The consequences of this breakdown were clear to see, with city centres turned into 'war zones' on Friday and Saturday nights, and neighbourhoods wrecked by graffiti, vandalism and a 'less tangible, but perhaps more damaging, sense of menace in the air'. For Cameron, the only way to address the problem of anti-social behaviour was not through such short-term measures as curfews and ASBOs, but by creating a 'pro-social society' in which its underlying causes are confronted and dealt with directly (2006b).

According to Cameron, the failure of New Labour's approach was symbolized by the figure of the 'hoodie',[8] who he described as

> A response to a problem, not a problem in itself. We – the people in suits – often see hoodies as aggressive, the uniform of a rebel army of young gangsters. But, for young people, hoodies are often more defensive than offensive... In a dangerous environment the best thing to do is keep your head down, blend in, don't stand out. For some, the hoodie represents all that's wrong about youth culture in Britain today. For me, adult society's response to the hoodie shows how far we are from finding the long-term answers to put things right. (2006b)

While punishment still had an important role to play in dealing with those who breached the boundaries of good behaviour, continued Cameron, it was imperative that 'inside those boundaries we... show a lot more love' and give these young people the emotional support and understanding they desperately need (2006b).

Although the Conservatives accepted New Labour's narrative of the causes and consequences of anti-social behaviour, their proposed solution to the problem differed in a number of important ways. In a rejection of New Labour's criminal justice-based approach, Cameron claimed it was not the responsibility of the police to mend the 'broken society', and instead promised to give individuals, businesses and the voluntary sector the opportunity to work together to help restore respect (quoted in Conservative Party, 2006). He also acknowledged that anti-social behaviour has structural as well as individual causes, and indeed described it as a natural response to difficult circumstances. On this basis, Cameron argued that 'no child is ever really feral. No child is beyond recovery, beyond civilisation' (2006b). This optimistic view of young people came in response to mounting concerns that the government and the media alike were 'demonising [them] as "thugs" and "yobs" in their efforts to assert a tough approach to [anti-social behaviour]' (Squires, 2008, p. 318).[9] It also provided the starting-point for the Conservatives' efforts to build a new consensus on law and order based on a 'greater understanding both of the socio-economic circumstances in which crime seems to flourish, and of the individuals who engage in anti-social or criminal behaviour' (Dorey, 2007, p. 146).

Conclusion

In conclusion, this chapter has deployed the theoretical framework presented in Chapter 4 to examine New Labour's case for its anti-social behaviour agenda. An analysis of the 'context of ideology' reveals that New Labour's chosen argument and the policy programme itself were based on its core values of community, reciprocal rights and responsibilities and inclusion, and so appeared to be congruent with its ideological platform. In practice, the tension between New Labour's notion of parental responsibility *to* children and the requirement to be responsible *for* children risked exacerbating the exclusion of lone parents in particular. Moreover, the use of ASBOs to curb the 'problem behaviour' of children contravened some of their fundamental rights, which in turn breached New Labour's commitment to the values of equal worth, inclusion and reciprocal rights and responsibilities, and often proved counter-productive. An assessment of the 'context of argumentation', meanwhile, indicates that New Labour's virtue theoretic argument was well suited to its anti-social behaviour agenda, on the ground that both are based on notions of community, inclusion and civic virtue. However, by focusing primarily on individual weakness or failure, Blair's account of criminality downplayed the role of social factors: 'tough on crime' took precedence over 'tough on the causes of crime'.

An examination of the 'context of hegemonic competition' reveals that New Labour used strategies of delegitimization and legitimization to undermine the Conservatives and to portray itself as the only party able to rebuild social order. Also of importance was Blair's Conviction Rhetoric which, together with emotive coercion, fuelled public concern about anti-social behaviour even as crime rates fell. Instead of attempting to defuse the moral panic surrounding the issue, New Labour's fear of appearing 'soft on crime' led it to introduce a flurry of tough-sounding measures intended to reassure the public that it was taking the problem seriously. However, it was becoming increasingly apparent that New Labour's punitive policies were ineffective in preventing anti-social behaviour, and that it was necessary to bring the causes of crime back into the equation. To this end, the Conservatives introduced their 'Real Respect' agenda, which moved away from the hard-line rhetoric of their predecessors and sought to restore the balance between punishment and prevention that was the cornerstone of New Labour's early approach. This enabled the Conservatives to reclaim the centre ground from New Labour, and ultimately to seize hegemonic advantage on the issue of law and order.

9
Foreign Policy: The Iraq War of 2003

On 12 May 1997, ten days after New Labour's landslide general election victory, Robin Cook outlined a new, ethical foreign policy. This approach was based on the assumption that nation states are interdependent, and set out four main goals. Cook's first three objectives, which committed the government to the promotion of Britain's security and prosperity, and to the improvement of the quality of life of its citizens, were widely accepted. However, the fourth goal – to 'secure the respect of other nations for Britain's contribution to keeping the peace of the world and promoting democracy around the world' – was more contentious, founded as it was on the claim that Britain has a national interest in promoting 'our' values abroad. As Cook explained, 'the Labour Government does not accept that political values can be left behind when we check in our passports to travel on diplomatic business', and for this reason must act to 'support the demands of other peoples for the democratic rights on which we insist for ourselves' (1997, pp. 1–2).

On 18 March 2003, Tony Blair announced his decision to go to war against Iraq, a move some scholars regard as the defining moment in New Labour's foreign policy (e.g. Dunne, 2004). This war was deeply controversial, and questions over its moral and legal basis led many to believe that the government had abandoned its ethical approach to international affairs (e.g. O'Malley, 2007, p. 9). What cannot be disputed, however, is that Blair used explicitly moral language to argue for the invasion of Iraq, which suggests that a concern for ethical matters was at least present on a rhetorical level, if not on a practical one. I begin the chapter by summarizing the government's case for military action, which it presented in three official dossiers, before assessing the compatibility of this argument with New Labour's ideological platform.

Next, I examine the two moral arguments that Blair utilized in his efforts to win support for the Iraq war, which drew on consequentialist and deontological reasoning and emphasized the dangers of Iraqi weapons of mass destruction (WMD) and Saddam's human rights violations respectively. In the following section, I assess the extent to which these arguments achieved hegemonic status. Here, I show that although Blair was able to 'rhetorically coerce' MPs into supporting military action, his reliance on Conviction Rhetoric over solid evidence led to accusations that the government had misused intelligence in making the case for war. The ensuing controversy caused irreparable damage to Blair's *ethos* and, moreover, was a key factor in the decline of the New Labour project.

New Labour's case for the war on Iraq

On 24 September 2002, Blair presented to Parliament his case for going to war on Iraq. This argument centred on a dossier compiled by the Joint Intelligence Committee (JIC) which, Blair claimed, showed that Saddam Hussein possessed WMD and, as such, posed a serious threat that needed to be addressed.[1] On Blair's view, the intelligence gathered from within Iraq 'established beyond doubt' that, despite UN sanctions and the policy of containment that had been in place since the end of the first Gulf War in 1991, Saddam had 'continued to produce chemical and biological weapons, that he continues in his efforts to develop nuclear weapons, and that he has been able to extend the range of his ballistic missile programme' (2002a, p. 3). Among these weapons were growth media obtained for the production of biological agents (in sufficient quantities to manufacture over 25,000 litres of anthrax spores); more than 30,000 special munitions designed to deliver chemical and biological agents; and up to 360 tonnes of bulk chemical warfare agents. The UN inspectors had been unable to account for these weapons prior to their expulsion from Iraq in December 1998 (JIC, 2002, p. 16). Subsequent talks and a UN resolution passed in 1999 failed to gain readmission for the inspectors and, in July 2002, Kofi Annan, the then Secretary General of the UN, called a halt to the negotiations.

According to the dossier, recent intelligence supported the JIC's assessment that Iraq possessed WMD and showed that Saddam was determined to retain them. This determination was ascribed to Saddam's belief that these weapons were strategically important and that they augmented Iraq's power in the Middle East. Moreover, Saddam had 'learnt lessons from previous weapons inspections, [had] identified possible weak points in the inspections process', and was already exploiting these weaknesses through such measures as the concealment of sensitive documents and pieces of equipment, and the use of mobile facilities for the production of biological weapons (JIC, 2002, p. 19). The intelligence also indicated that Saddam was willing to use chemical and biological weapons, which could be deployed within 45 minutes of an order to do so, against a number of targets including the Shia population of Iraq. This last point was taken particularly seriously because Saddam had previously used chemical weapons in the Iran–Iraq war, and against the Kurds of Halabja in 1988 (Blair, 2002b, pp. 2–4).

The terrorist attacks of September 11 led Blair to recognize the threat that rogue states in possession of WMD and extreme terrorist organizations posed to global order and security. He described these threats as 'twins of chaos,' and argued that because they are 'answerable to no democratic mandate, [they] are unrestrained by the will of ordinary people'. Although their origins and motives are different, Blair continued, they nonetheless share a hatred of Western values and seek to destabilize us (2003a, p. 3). The connection between terrorist groups and rogue states with WMD was fairly loose, but Blair believed it was growing stronger, and that there was a real and present danger of terrorist groups acquiring these weapons (2003b, p. 6). While Iraq represented only one part of this threat, claimed Blair, it was 'the test of whether we treat the threat seriously' (2003b, p. 9). It was imperative, therefore, that the international community should unite behind the UN and confront this danger directly.

On 2 December 2002, the Foreign and Commonwealth Office (FCO) published a second dossier that focused exclusively on the human rights violations committed by Saddam's regime. This document was compiled from a range of sources – including intelligence material, evidence gathered by human rights organizations and eyewitness accounts from Iraqi exiles – and expanded on the findings presented in the September dossier.[2] According to the FCO, the abuse of human rights was a 'deliberate policy of the regime. Fear is Saddam's chosen method for staying in power' (2002, p. 4). To this end, Saddam endorsed, for example, the use of torture, which was described as 'endemic' in Iraq; the abuse of women, which was justified on the basis that women do not have the right to life; degrading and inhumane prison conditions; and the relentless persecution of the Shia and the Kurds (FCO, 2002, pp. 7–16). These violations continued over many years, despite the condemnation of the UN Commission on Human Rights and the UN Security Council. On 19 April 2002, the former organization passed a resolution highlighting

Saddam's 'systematic, widespread and extremely grave violations of human rights and of international humanitarian law', which, it said, had created an 'all-pervasive repression and oppression sustained by broad-based discrimination and widespread terror' (quoted in FCO, 2002, p. 4). On this basis, Blair claimed, the only real prospect of liberation for the Iraqi people lay in the removal of Saddam's regime and the democratization of their country. Although he never explicitly justified the invasion of Iraq in terms of regime change, Blair presented it as the reason 'why if we do act we should do so with a clear conscience and strong heart' (2003b, p. 11).

A third dossier, entitled *Iraq – Its Infrastructure of Concealment, Deception and Intimidation* and published by the Coalition Information Centre (CIC),[3] was presented to the media on 3 February 2003 in an attempt to persuade an increasingly sceptical public that the war was justified (Seldon, 2007, p. 150). This document, it was claimed, drew on a variety of sources, including material provided by the intelligence services, and showed 'how the Iraqi regime is constructed to have, and to keep, WMD, and is now engaged in a campaign of obstruction of the United Nations Weapons Inspectors' (CIC, 2003, p. 1). In so doing, it reiterated the need to take action to disarm Saddam. However, it soon emerged that large sections of the dossier were plagiarized from academic articles, some of which were several years old. This discovery was deeply embarrassing for the Blair government, but as Michael White and Brian Whitaker reported in the *Guardian*, government officials insisted it 'in no way undermines the underlying truth of the dossier, whose contents had been re-checked with British intelligence sources' (2003). In the words of one official, 'the important thing is that it is accurate' (quoted in White and Whitaker, 2003). Despite this assertion, the document subsequently became known as the 'dodgy dossier'.

For Blair, it was clear that the international community needed to address the issue of Iraq. The evidence published in the dossiers showed that Saddam's regime posed a 'serious and current' – though not imminent – danger (Blair, 2002a, p. 3), which was made more acute by the increasing interdependence of states. As Blair explained, 'a major regional conflict does not stay confined to the region in question', and so has the potential to destabilize the entire global order (2002a, p. 4). Consequently, he continued, the international community needed to show its united determination to deal with Saddam through a programme of disarmament overseen by the UN, and thus to ensure its authority was maintained. Blair believed that the case for disarmament was entirely reasonable, given that Saddam had rejected the demands of the international community for 11 years and, moreover, that the UN was justified in issuing him with an ultimatum to 'comply willingly or be forced to comply'. Military action should be taken only as a last resort, but if Saddam continued to resist the UN, Blair asserted, Britain should not 'shrink from doing what is necessary and right' (2002b, pp. 4–6).

By 16 March 2003, Saddam had failed to comply with UN Resolution 1441, which offered him a final opportunity to disarm, and Blair made a last-ditch appeal for a 'clear ultimatum to Saddam that authorises force if he continues to defy the will of the whole of the international community' (2003c, p. 2). Such an ultimatum was not forthcoming, and on 20 March Britain followed the USA into Iraq. This action, which bypassed the UN Security Council, had limited support from the international community and, moreover, breached one of New Labour's core ideological commitments, as I demonstrate in the next section.

The compatibility of New Labour's arguments for the Iraq War with its ideological platform

As we saw in Chapter 5, the Third Way approach to foreign policy was founded on the assumption that the world had changed dramatically as a result of globalization. For Blair, 'globalisation is not just economic. It is also a political and security phenomenon' (1999b, p. 3). Thus, isolationism was redundant, and an increasing number of problems, such as environmental degradation, terrorism and organized crime, could be solved only by working with other countries. To this end, Blair claimed, the Third Way endorsed a foreign policy that was founded on the principle of international cooperation, whose aim was not simply to 'fight or avoid wars but to tackle [these] common problems' (1998a, p. 7). According to Blair, the record of NATO, the WTO, and the EU showed that cooperation should be viewed not as a threat, but as an opportunity. Indeed, given the new dangers facing the world, he continued, we need to 'deepen and extend these initiatives, not reject them' (1998a, p. 18). This is the sum total of the account of foreign policy that Blair offered in his pamphlet *The Third Way*, so we will turn to his 'doctrine of the international community' for a fuller statement of his views on the subject.

Blair outlined his doctrine of the international community in a speech given in Chicago in April 1999, when the Kosovo war was at its height.[4] The basic premise of Blair's conception of international affairs was the increasing interdependence of states that resulted from globalization, from which it followed that 'national interest is to a significant extent governed by international collaboration'. The idea that self-interest can only be advanced through cooperation underpinned the constitutive notion of community that lay at the core of New Labour's ideological platform. As we have seen, Blair believed that as we come to recognize the responsibilities we owe to others as well as to ourselves, we will understand that our well-being is bound up with that of other people. In other words, human beings – like the states that comprise the international community – are mutually dependent. This ideal was coming into its own within domestic politics, claimed Blair, and so needed to 'find its own international echo' (1999b, p. 3).

The interdependence of individuals and states was only one aspect of New Labour's concept of community. For New Labour, shared values were a prerequisite for a strong national community, and Blair believed this was equally true of the international community. He explained that in the post-Cold War era, 'our actions are guided by a more subtle blend of mutual self interest and moral purpose in defending the values we cherish'. These values included human rights, an open society, liberty, and the rule of law and, Blair believed, it was in Britain's national interest to establish and spread these values. This is because shared values promote community cohesion, and therefore reduce conflict. So, in the same way as shared values are linked to self-interest in the context of the national community, values and interests are said to merge within the international order (Blair, 1999b, p. 7).[5] Although Blair did not directly discuss the role of reciprocal rights and responsibilities in building a strong international community, his position can accommodate them as follows.

According to Charles Beitz, the interdependence of states means that their claims to autonomy can no longer be taken for granted, and are dependent instead on whether their institutions conform to suitable principles of justice (1979, p. 83). As such, only those states whose institutions are just and those whose institutions are likely to become just, without the need for external interference, are protected by the principle of non-intervention (1979, p. 90). This argument can be reframed in New Labour's language of rights and responsibilities as follows. Like individuals in domestic society, each state has responsibilities as a member of the international community, which include the obligations to uphold the human rights of its citizens, to act in accordance with international law, and to respect the autonomy of other states. If a state fulfils these responsibilities, it receives in return the right of self-determination, and thus is protected under the principle of non-intervention. However, if the state concerned refuses to act responsibly, it can be compelled to do so through such measures as economic sanctions and military force.[6] By taking such action, it can be said that the members of the international community are actively cooperating to promote the goals of global justice and inclusion, and also to uphold the values of that community.

Conor Gearty argues that, from Blair's perspective, the terrorist attacks of 11 September 2001 vindicated the doctrine of the international community (2003, p. 2). Indeed, Blair claimed that these events led the international community to recognize that the world needs order, and that progress is possible only under conditions of stability and security. The values underpinning these conditions are democracy, justice and freedom and, in those nations where they are absent, argued Blair, 'regimes act unchecked by popular accountability and pose a threat; and the threat spreads'. Consequently, he continued, 'the promotion of these values becomes not just right in itself but part of our long-term security and prosperity'. Blair then explicitly linked the spreading of these values to intervention. Although he acknowledged that it is impossible to intervene in every situation, he claimed nonetheless that the relaxation of the non-intervention principle was justified in cases where disorder threatened to destabilize the international order (2002c, p. 2). As a result, writes Justin Rosenberg, 'the absolute nature of state sovereignty is becoming ... conditional upon the state concerned observing certain basic standards of human rights [and] democracy' (2000, p. 19) or, in Blair's terms, sharing 'our values'. It is clear, therefore, that Blair believed intervention was justified in non-democratic states that did not conform to these standards, and that values played an instrumental role in promoting his goal of a strong, stable international community.

In many respects, Blair's argument for the war on Iraq was congruent with his conception of international relations. His claims concerning Saddam's WMD programme and its potential to destabilize both the Middle East and the wider world invoked the assumption of interdependence that underpinned the 'Blair doctrine', which in turn echoed the enlightened notion of self-interest that underpinned New Labour's concept of community. Blair's case for military action also drew on the idea of an international community founded on shared values and reciprocal rights and responsibilities that I outlined above. As we have seen, Iraq's institutions were deeply unjust, and for this reason one could say that it had forfeited its right to protection under the non-intervention principle. Consequently, Britain had a responsibility as a member of the international community to oust Saddam and to 'help Iraq move towards democracy' (Blair, 2003d, p. 2). Not only would democratization benefit the Iraqi people by establishing human rights and the rule of law, Blair argued, but it would 'bring Iraq back into the international community where it belongs, not languishing as a pariah' (2002b, p. 5). This would enable Iraq to share in the goods of community membership, while advancing the interests of the international community through the promotion of global security. As Blair put it, 'a stable democratic Iraq, under the sovereign rule of the Iraqi people, is a mortal blow to [the terrorists'] fanaticism', hence 'the dangers of the threat we face will be diminished' (2004, p. 7).

From this discussion of the 'context of ideology', it seems that Blair's case for the war on Iraq was consistent with New Labour's ideological position. However, a serious problem arises when we recall the importance Blair attached to international cooperation, which was clearly undermined by his failure to secure UN support for military action against Iraq. Blair defended this move by claiming that it was in the long-term interests of the international community to uphold the will of the UN in the face of a ruthless dictator like Saddam. After all, he argued, a refusal to enforce Resolution 1441 would 'do the most deadly damage to the UN's future strength, confirming it as an instrument of diplomacy but not of action, forcing nations down the very unilateralist path we wish to avoid' (2003b, p. 9). I consider this argument and its implications in the following two sections.

New Labour's moral arguments in support of the Iraq War

As noted above, Blair offered two moral arguments for the invasion of Iraq, the first of which drew on consequentialist reasoning and formed the basis of the case he put before the UN Security Council. This argument was premised on the claim that Saddam possessed WMD, and thus posed a grave threat to international security. In Blair's words, the intelligence from Iraq showed that the situation had become 'more not less worrying', and that 'the threat is serious and current, that [Saddam] has made progress on WMD, and that he has to be stopped' (2002a, p. 3). For Blair, this issue was of particular concern for two reasons. First, Saddam had defied seventeen UN resolutions relating to his WMD programme since 1991. Indeed, the weapons inspectors published a report on 7 March 2003, which listed '29 different areas where they have been unable to obtain information' due to Saddam's refusal to cooperate (Blair, 2003b, p. 4). This non-compliance demonstrated that Saddam would go to great lengths to conceal his WMD and, moreover, constituted a material breach of Resolution 1441. It was imperative, therefore, that the UN should take decisive action against Saddam. As Blair put it,

> Let it be clear that he must be disarmed. Let it be clear that there can be no more conditions, no more games, no more prevaricating... And let it be clear that should the will of the UN be ignored, action will follow. (2002d, p. 3)

Blair believed this approach gave the UN both an exceptional opportunity and a serious responsibility. The opportunity, he claimed, was to demonstrate that the international community could unite and meet the threat of Saddam together, while the responsibility was to tackle it (2003a, p. 2).

Second, Saddam had previously used WMD against both his own people and his enemies, and he was prepared to use them again. As such, Blair argued, it was clear that Saddam posed a grave danger to the region and the wider world, so 'to allow him to use the weapons he has or get the weapons he wants would be an act of gross irresponsibility and we should not countenance it' (2002d, p. 2). The explication of the consequences of inaction for regional and global stability formed a major part of Blair's argument for military action against Iraq. In February 2003, for example, he posed this rhetorical question: 'Are we sure that if we let [Saddam] keep and develop [WMD], he would not use them again against his neighbours, against Israel perhaps?' and asserted in his *Foreword* to the September dossier that Iraq's WMD represented a 'current and serious threat to the UK national interest' (2003a, p. 2; 2002a, p. 3). Blair subsequently elaborated on this rather extraordinary claim by saying 'there is no way that [Saddam], in this region above all regions, could begin a conflict using such weapons and the consequences not engulf the whole world' (2002b, p. 5).

A failure to take action against Iraq would also have serious consequences for the UN, whose authority, Blair believed, would be fatally undermined. It was the UN that passed Resolution 1441, so the international community had to unite behind it to resolve the threat from Saddam, whether diplomatically or militarily (Blair, 2003b, p. 9). After all, Blair claimed, diplomacy is essential, but when confronting a dictator it 'has to be backed by the certain knowledge in the dictator's mind that behind the diplomacy is the possibility of force being used' (2002d,

p. 3). If instead the UN followed strong language with weak intentions, the outcome would be worse than if it had never spoken at all. Saddam would feel hugely strengthened, while other tyrannical regimes would perceive the will of the international community as 'decaying and feeble' (Blair, 2003b, p. 12). As a result, the UN would lose all credibility, and other dictators would feel free to act with impunity. In short, Blair said, 'weakness in the face of a threat from a tyrant is the surest way not to peace but to war' (2003b, p. 6).

Blair's consequentialist argument in favour of the Iraq war can be summarized as follows. Saddam had WMD and was continuing to develop his capability in defiance of the UN. He had refused to comply with seventeen resolutions and was unlikely to cooperate in the future. Given that Saddam had previously used WMD against his enemies and his own people and was prepared to do so again, he posed a grave threat to the stability of the Middle East and – as a result of interdependence – to the rest of the world. This threat was heightened by the growing possibility that Saddam might diffuse his WMD technology to terrorist organizations, which in turn would lead to widespread chaos and disorder. Moreover, if the UN failed to enforce its resolutions, its authority would be undermined and, should a similar situation arise in future, its will would be ignored and catastrophe would follow.

The deontological argument for war played a secondary role until the Labour Party Spring Conference in Glasgow, where it took centre stage. By this time, the credibility of the WMD claims had diminished significantly (Rangwala, 2003, p. 1), so it was perhaps no accident that this argument, which emphasized the suffering of the Iraqi people under Saddam's regime, was presented on the same day as the huge 'Stop the War' protest was taking place in London.[7] Blair's deontological argument consisted of two strands, the first of which was based on the assumption that 'the containment of Iraq through sanctions was becoming ineffective and was morally unacceptable because of its effects on the Iraqi population' (Bluth, 2004, p. 871), while the second centred on Saddam's appalling human rights record. Given that both strands of this argument drew on the notions of equal worth and rights and responsibilities, we can say that Blair's deontological strategy was appropriate in this instance.

According to Blair, the sanctions regime in Iraq was failing, as evidenced by Saddam's income of approximately $3 billion a year from illicit trading. This money was unaccounted for but, Blair claimed, was 'almost certainly used for his weapons programmes' (2002d, p. 2). At the same time, Saddam's flawed implementation of sanctions had left

60 per cent of his people dependent on food aid, and 50 per cent of Iraq's rural population without access to clean water (Blair, 2003a, p. 4). This violated their fundamental right to an adequate standard of living, which is guaranteed by Article 25 of the UDHR, and the international community therefore had a responsibility to act. As Alex Bellamy points out, the options available to the international community at the time were to continue with its policy of containment, or to declare war on Iraq. Because sanctions had seemingly failed to achieve their objective of disarming Saddam and, moreover, were harming Iraqi civilians, it followed that military action was justified, given that it would 'simultaneously achieve the coalition's material goals and ease the suffering of the Iraqi people' (2004, p. 136).

The second strand of Blair's deontological argument focused on the brutal nature of Saddam's regime and its crimes against the people of Iraq. According to Blair, Saddam was an individual who 'operate[d] without any sense of democratic values, without any regard for the sanctity of human life' (2002e, p. 8). Despite UN condemnation, he had systematically abused the human rights of his people; indeed, 'the death and torture camps, the barbaric prisons for political opponents, the routine beatings for anyone or their families suspected of disloyalty are well documented' (Blair, 2003b, p. 11). Such brutality should not be permitted to continue, and the international community therefore had a duty to intervene. Using the above account of New Labour's core values in an international context, we can say that because Saddam had violated the basic rights of the Iraqi people, and thus failed to respect their equal worth as human beings, he had contravened his obligations under international law. In consequence, Iraq had forfeited its right to self-determination, while the international community had a responsibility to end the suffering of its population. As Blair put it, 'ridding the world of Saddam would be an act of humanity. It is leaving him there that is in truth inhumane' (2003a, p. 6). The deontological argument was, Bellamy believes, the more persuasive of the two cases for humanitarian intervention in Iraq (2004, p. 137), and in the following section I evaluate the effectiveness of Blair's argumentative and rhetorical strategies in persuading MPs and the public to support the war.

New Labour's strategies for winning hegemonic advantage

One of the main points of contention in the debate over Iraq was the role played by the intelligence, which was peripheral in Blair's decision to resort to war and yet was a central component of his argumentative strategy (Bluth, 2004, p. 890). In his *Foreword* to the September dossier, for instance, Blair highlighted the difficulties involved in gathering intelligence within a secretive state such as Iraq, and expressed his belief that people would understand why the intelligence services could not identify their sources (on which the judgements presented in the dossier were based), and why 'we cannot publish everything we know'. The government was also unable to make the detailed raw intelligence public, but Blair claimed he and other ministers had received thorough briefings on the intelligence and were 'satisfied as to its authority' (2002a, p. 3).

Blair's statements regarding the intelligence on Iraq are an example of epistemic legitimization. In using this technique, the speaker claims to have superior knowledge of a situation than his or her opponents, and hence to be in a better position to grasp its implications. Epistemic claims are often supported by sources that the speaker believes their audience will accept as reliable (Chilton, 2004, p. 117), and Blair utilized the findings of the intelligence agencies to perform this role. In doing so, as Craig McLean and Alan Patterson correctly point out, he 'made his case for action on the basis of *certainty* and *facts*' (2006, p. 363), which were derived from information that could not be made public for security reasons, and was therefore unavailable for public scrutiny. Blair's privileged knowledge of the situation also contributed to an *ethos* of authority, which gave his WMD argument additional force.

Blair's 'better knowledge' of the situation in Iraq enabled him to construct a scenario in which the threats of terrorist groups and rogue states with WMD had converged, and the international community had failed to prevent them from doing so. He began by inviting his listeners to imagine that, on 10 September 2001, he had told them:

> There is a terrorist network called al-Qaeda. It operates out of Afghanistan. It has carried out several attacks and we believe it is planning more. It has been condemned by the UN in the strongest terms. Unless it is stopped, the threat will grow. And so I want to take action to prevent that. (2002d, p. 1)

Blair then suggested that they, like most people, would have been reluctant to tackle al-Qaeda at that time – least of all by taking military action – and proceeded to compare this response to the scepticism surrounding the invasion of Iraq (2002d, p. 1). He therefore left open the inference that, in the same way as the 9/11 attacks would have absolved his decision to deal with al-Qaeda in the hypothetical situation described above, a future catastrophe would vindicate his policy of disarming Saddam. This suggestion was made explicit in Blair's assertion that if the international community does not act to neutralize the threat from Saddam, 'it may not erupt and engulf us this month or next; perhaps not even this year or the next. But it will at some point'. That the listener was expected to attribute Blair's certainty to his superior understanding of the situation in Iraq is made clear in his next sentence: 'I do not want it on my conscience that we *knew* the threat, saw it coming and did nothing' (2002d, p. 3, emphasis added).

In addition to these techniques, Blair used the tactic of emotive coercion in making both the consequentialist and the deontological case for war. In the former argument, Blair may have intended to induce fear in his listeners by making truth claims about the causal effects of allowing Saddam to continue unchecked in his efforts to develop WMD. Such effects included the regional – and ultimately global – instability that would result if Saddam deployed WMD against neighbouring states; the disastrous consequences of the convergence of WMD and terrorist groups; and the undermining of the authority of UN. To reinforce the fearful response that his claims produced, Blair repeatedly used such terms as 'threat' and 'evil' in making the consequentialist case for war, while presenting military action against Iraq as the only feasible means of averting these outcomes.

Turning now to the deontological argument, Blair perhaps sought to appeal to his listeners' sense of justice and compassion by emphasizing Saddam's violations of human rights. To this end, he substantiated the findings of the intelligence services with anecdotal evidence in the form of letters and emails from Iraqi exiles. In his Glasgow speech, for instance, he quoted from a letter he received from a Dr Safa Hashim, who said the suffering of the Iraqi people under Saddam was 'beyond anything that British people can possibly envisage, let alone understand his obsession to develop and possess weapons of mass destruction'. This suffering, Dr Hashim believed, could be ended only by the removal of Saddam (quoted in Blair, 2003a, p. 5). After his address, Blair circulated the full transcript of an email from another Iraqi exile to delegates, telling them, 'It is the reason why I do not shrink from action against Saddam if it proves necessary' (BBC, 2003a). Here, Blair employed the rhetorical technique of *exemplum*, where a speaker tells stories to illustrate or prove their claims. This is a powerful tool because personal experience is often seen as more immediate and authentic than official sources (see Livingstone and Lunt, 1994, pp. 101–6), and thus as having greater persuasive force. Indeed, Blair's frequent use of *exemplum* in making his deontological case for war may help to explain why this argument won more support than the consequentialist strategy.

The availability of two moral arguments proved useful to Blair, as it enabled him to emphasize one strand over another at different times and to different audiences. Initially, the consequentialist argument won support from a number of areas, including the then Conservative leader Iain Duncan Smith (Hansard, 24 September 2002, c.7–9), many Conservative MPs and the Murdoch press (Greenslade, 2003). However, it was clear in early February 2003 that the public remained stubbornly opposed to war, with only 25 per cent believing it was justified (BBC, 2003b), so Blair changed his strategy to emphasize the deontological case. The Glasgow speech, in which Blair made this shift, was reported favourably in the media and, moreover, gave comfort to those Number 10 insiders who were struggling with the prospect of war (Seldon, 2007, p. 153). Indeed, as Paul Hoggett points out, 'there is no doubt that this "moral case"...was instrumental in swinging the votes of a number of the undecided in the crucial Commons debate [of 18 March 2003]' (2005, pp. 421–2).

Prior to this important debate, Blair and his supporters sought to win the backing of sceptical Labour MPs by identifying and deploying the particular argument they believed might persuade them to vote in favour of the invasion. Some MPs were given the consequentialist case for war, while others were presented with the deontological argument. Additionally, some were told the invasion was about 'saving the integrity of the UN', while yet others were reminded of 'the domestic political implications, that the government could be in peril' (Kampfner, 2004, pp. 306–7).[8] In Bastow and Martin's words, this was an 'exercise in rhetorical inventiveness, manipulation and audacity, as different, sometimes deeply contradictory, demands and expectations [were] brought together' (2003, p. 64) behind Blair's case for military action. This strategy ultimately proved successful, as a Commons cross-party motion stating that the government had not yet made the case for war was defeated by 396 votes to 217 and, 'in one of the most skilful sleights of hand by Alastair Campbell...was trumpeted in the media as representing a victory for the Prime Minister' (Kampfner, 2004, p. 309).

The question arises, however, of why so many MPs backed the government, despite their deep-seated reservations about the invasion. A possible response comes from Ronald Krebs and Jennifer Lobasz, whose analysis of the Iraq debate in the USA reveals that critics of the war were the 'victims of successful "rhetorical coercion" – a strategy that seeks to rhetorically constrain political opponents and manoeuvre them into public assent to one's preferred terms of debate and ideally to one's policy stance' (2007, p. 412). This claim is equally applicable to the situation in Britain, as I will now demonstrate. As in the USA, the British government's case for war on Iraq was set against the backdrop of the post-September 11 'war on terror', which functioned as an organizing discourse, or background narrative (Krebs and Lobasz, 2007, p. 423). Because the nature and scale of the 9/11 attacks were unprecedented, both Blair and George W. Bush needed to construct a new discourse that would make sense of these events and unify their shocked communities. To this end, they employed epideictic rhetoric which, as Krebs and Lobasz explain, 'defines situations and fixes meaning...[and thereby] creates the foundation upon which later deliberative argumentation proceeds' (2007, p. 439). Although other discourses offered competing explanations of the crisis, it was the 'war on terror' narrative that was eventually accepted as common sense, and thus achieved hegemonic status.

According to Krebs and Lobasz, one of the functions of the 'war on terror' narrative was to generate insecurity (2007, p. 413). This is evident in Blair's speech to the Labour Party conference held just three weeks after September 11, where he used metaphor to express his view that the attacks marked a defining moment in history: 'The kaleidoscope has been shaken. The pieces are in flux' (2001b, p. 13). While he understood that 'people are anxious, even a little frightened', Blair claimed this period of upheaval presented an opportunity to 're-order this world around us' before the pieces settled again (2001b, pp. 1, 13). A key part of this process was the promotion of democracy and freedom around the world, and the 'war on terror' thus became a 'battle of values' between those who share 'our way of life', and the 'fanatics' who wished to destroy it (Blair 2001b, pp. 11, 1). Here, we can see that the conceptual metaphors MORALITY IS CONFLICT and POLITICS IS ETHICS contributed to a rhetoric of legitimization that Blair employed to justify the 'war on terror', and eventually the invasion of Iraq. To reinforce this strategy, he invoked the myth of good versus evil to create a contrast between the September 11 atrocities and his vision of a new world order:

> Out of the shadow of this evil, should emerge lasting good: destruction of the machinery of terrorism wherever it is found...and above all justice and prosperity for the poor and dispossessed, so that people everywhere can see the chance of a better future through the

hard work and creative power of the free citizen, not the violence and savagery of the fanatic. (2001b, p. 1)

This combination of conceptual metaphors and ethical contrasts enabled Blair to produce a Conviction Rhetoric that allowed him to represent himself as a moral arbiter, and thereby gave his argument additional persuasive force (see Charteris-Black, 2005, pp. 142–68).

Like Bush, Blair created a connection between the 'war on terror' and the danger posed by Saddam (Krebs and Lobasz, 2007, p. 413). This is evident in his consequentialist case for war, in which he often brought the two discourses together.[9] The following extract from his speech to the TUC conference in 2002 is a typical example: 'Terrorism and weapons of mass destruction combine modern technology with political or religious fanaticism. If unchecked they will, as September 11 showed, explode into disorder and chaos' (2002d, p. 3). This is not to suggest that Blair believed Saddam's regime and al-Qaeda were cooperating with regard to WMD. Rather, the point is that he constructed a chain of equivalence between terrorism, rogue states and WMD, in order to resignify them as constituent elements of a single threat. The construction of Saddam as an evil dictator that was central to both the consequentialist and the deontological arguments enabled Blair to link this equivalential chain to the promotion of democracy, and thus to bring it into an antagonistic relation with nations that share 'our values'. In his Glasgow speech, for instance he argued that terrorism and rogue states in possession of WMD 'are answerable to no democratic mandate, so are unrestrained by the will of ordinary people. They are extreme and inhumane. They detest and fear liberal, democratic and tolerant values. And their aim is to destabilise us' (2003a, p. 1). This linkage of the threat of Iraqi WMD and Saddam's human rights abuses enabled Blair to offer regime change as a single solution to these two problems.

By establishing the 'war on terror' as the organizing discourse in foreign policy and combining it with the depiction of Saddam as a force for evil, Blair and his followers left their opponents 'without access to the rhetorical materials needed to craft an acceptable rebuttal'. As a result, their opposition was limited to questions about the circumstances and timing of the war (Krebs and Lobasz, 2007, p. 445), which indeed featured significantly in the Commons debate of 18 March 2003. The first line of questioning typically focused on the need for UN backing, with the Labour MP John Denham (among others) arguing that because the war on Iraq was pre-emptive, it required 'even greater international support and consensus than other sorts of intervention' (Hansard, 18 March 2003a, c.798). Meanwhile, the second called into question the timing of the war, with MPs such as Joyce Quin claiming that the UN weapons inspectors could be given more time to do their work (Hansard, 18 March 2003b, c.806).[10] Although these objections struck a chord with the public, with 86 per cent supporting Quin's position (BBC, 2003b), for instance, they were relatively modest and easily rebutted by reference to the grave consequences of inaction. Thus, in his closing statement, the then Foreign Secretary, Jack Straw, said:

> The different positions that we have taken all come from the best, not the worst, of intentions. But as elected Members of Parliament, we all know that we will be judged not only on our intentions, but on the results, the consequences of our decisions. The consequences of the amendment would be neither the containment nor the disarmament of Saddam's regime, but an undermining of the authority of the United Nations, the rearmament of Iraq, a worsening of the regime's tyranny, an end to the hopes of millions in Iraq, and a message to tyrants elsewhere that defiance pays. (Hansard, 18 March 2003c, c.902)

The objections of the government's critics appeared insignificant in the light of Straw's statement, which in turn suggests that rhetorical coercion had left them unable to mount a convincing challenge against the invasion of Iraq.

Although Blair successfully used rhetorical coercion to limit the scope for criticism of the war, the same strategy also committed him to a course of action from which there was no escape. This situation arose because Blair accepted the background narrative that the events of 9/11 marked the beginning of a 'war on terror'; that the greatest threat to global security was posed by an 'axis of evil' comprising Iran, Iraq and North Korea; and that certain regimes were 'too dangerous to be left in place, and that it was essential that the international community take action to contain or remove them' (Coates and Krieger, 2009, p. 249). By early 2003, however, Saddam was still in power, but there was no international coalition to remove him. Blair was therefore committed to unilateral action against Iraq, on pain of leaving a dangerous dictator 'strengthened beyond measure' and endangering Britain's 'special relationship' with the USA (Blair, 2003b, p. 12; Coates and Krieger, 2009, p. 249). In short, Blair was trapped by his own rhetoric in the pursuit of a policy that proved to be his undoing.

Although the swift overthrow of Saddam's regime initially appeared to vindicate the decision to go to war, the subsequent deterioration of Iraq's security situation and accusations that the government had overstated the threat were deeply damaging (Freedman, 2007, p. 628). Indeed, the next two years saw four government inquiries into aspects of the war, the most notable of which was Lord Butler's report, published in July 2004, on the intelligence about Iraq's weapons of mass destruction. This inquiry was more critical of the government than its predecessors, and suggested that Blair 'pursued a policy of threat exaggeration in a bid to persuade the British public and members of the UN Security Council of the necessity and urgency of war' (Doig and Phythian, 2005, p. 369). The question of whether Blair overstated the strength of the intelligence was deeply injurious to his carefully constructed *ethos* of honesty, which gradually eroded his popularity and led to his eventual resignation on 27 June 2007 (Bromund, 2009, p. 269).

Conclusion

This chapter has considered Blair's moral arguments and the range of rhetorical techniques he deployed in his efforts to win support for the invasion of Iraq. The examination of the 'context of ideology' reveals that Blair's case for military action was broadly consistent with his conception of international affairs, which I extended to accommodate New Labour's core concept of reciprocal rights and responsibilities. However, the decision to go to war without the backing of the UN violated Blair's commitment to an international community whose members worked together to deal with common problems. Meanwhile, an analysis of the 'context of argumentation' shows that Blair's use of consequentialist reasoning was appropriate to his arguments about the threat of Saddam's WMD, while deontological language was suitable for making the case for intervention on humanitarian grounds.

The 'context of hegemonic competition' reveals that Blair was faced with the 'difficult rhetorical task of persuading a reluctant House of Commons and general public to support direct military intervention in Iraq' (Charteris-Black, 2005, p. 166). To this end, he employed a variety of rhetorical strategies – including epistemic legitimization, emotive coercion and *exemplum* – to make his case, and presented different arguments at different times and to different audiences in an effort to unite competing viewpoints behind his cause. Perhaps the most interesting of these strategies was Blair's use of Conviction Rhetoric, which he combined with rhetorical coercion to limit the arguments available to his opponents, thereby leaving them unable to mount a convincing challenge against him. At the same time, however, Blair 'locked [himself] into a confrontation with Iraq from which he could not escape without cost' (Coates and Krieger, 2009, p. 249). In his Glasgow speech, Blair told delegates: 'I do not seek unpopularity as a badge of honour. But sometimes it is the price of leadership. And the cost of conviction' (2003a, p. 4S). His words were to prove prophetic, as the aftermath of the war did irreparable damage to his *ethos* and his popularity, and ultimately contributed to the decline of the New Labour project.

Conclusion

The primary objective of this book was to construct a theoretical framework for investigating how politicians use moral arguments to win support for their policy programmes. Taking into account the requirements of ideology, argumentation and hegemonic competition, this framework enabled us to analyse the process by which New Labour selected, modified and applied such arguments in the areas of welfare, rights and constitutional reform, community and foreign policy. I begin this concluding chapter with a general account of the argumentative strategies that New Labour employed during Blair's premiership. Next, I outline the policies introduced by the Brown government in the four areas and the arguments used to promote them, and I compare them with those examined elsewhere in this book. In the final section, I consider the implications of the case of New Labour for our understanding of the process of political justification.

The moral arguments employed by the Blair governments

Perhaps the most successful of New Labour's argumentative strategies was its case for the New Deals. This argument, which drew primarily on consequentialist reasoning, was broadly consistent with New Labour's ideological commitments and, in conjunction with a number of rhetorical techniques, won sufficient parliamentary support to ensure the passage of the New Deals onto the statute book. Indeed, the failure of the Conservatives to offer an original alternative indicated that New Labour had set the agenda on welfare policy, and the schemes celebrated their tenth anniversary in 2008. However, a number of difficulties arising from their implementation meant the New Deals did not deliver everything that was promised of them. For instance, they failed to provide adequate skills training for many participants and, moreover, had little impact on the problems of child and in-work poverty. Nonetheless, New Labour's rhetoric proceeded as if the policies had achieved their stated aims, which perhaps contributed to the longevity of the New Deals and, further, allowed the party to maintain hegemonic advantage in the area of welfare policy.

However, New Labour's deontological argument in favour of the Human Rights Act was less effective. Although the Act was successfully enshrined in UK law, it proved unpopular with MPs and the public alike, despite the widespread acceptance of the notion of basic human rights. The framework enabled us to attribute this lack of support to New Labour's emphasis on individual rights at the expense of civic responsibilities, which was present in the legislation itself and in the argumentative strategies used to promote it. This imbalance violated New Labour's ideological commitment to the value of reciprocal rights and responsibilities, and risked turning citizens into individualist consumers. A failure to provide the courts with sufficient guidance on how to interpret the legislation compounded New Labour's difficulties, leading to several controversial rulings and hostile coverage of the Act in the media. More seriously, the neglect of responsibilities had created a culture in which both the HRA and the concept of human rights itself were rapidly becoming devalued.

One of New Labour's key commitments on entering office in 1997 was to be 'tough on crime, tough on the causes of crime'. This mantra marked a new approach to law and order, and underpinned New Labour's efforts to tackle anti-social behaviour through a combination of punishment and early intervention. The goal of these initiatives was to inculcate respect and responsibility in people who behaved anti-socially, and New Labour used an argumentative strategy based on virtue theoretic principles to promote them. While this argument was appropriate for the policy programme, New Labour's emphasis on individual weakness in its account of the causes of crime helped to tip the balance in favour of punishment and away from prevention. This shift was compounded by the increasing scope of the concept of anti-social behaviour itself, which fuelled public concern about the issue even as crime rates fell. Instead of reassuring the electorate, however, New Labour responded by introducing tough-sounding but ultimately ineffective measures to address the problem. This was to cost New Labour its hegemonic advantage, and ultimately enabled the Conservatives to reclaim the centre ground on the issue of law and order.

The invasion of Iraq in 2003 was arguably the defining issue of New Labour's foreign policy, and was without doubt the most controversial. Blair offered two moral arguments in favour of the war, which drew on consequentialist and deontological principles and emphasized the threat posed by Iraqi WMD and Saddam's human rights abuses respectively. These arguments were supported by a wide range of rhetorical strategies, which was perhaps indicative of the scale of the task facing Blair as he attempted to persuade Parliament and the public that military action was justified. Despite their reluctance, many MPs nonetheless voted for the war, and an analysis of the 'context of hegemonic competition' suggests they were 'rhetorically coerced' into doing so. At the same time, however, Blair inextricably committed himself to the invasion, even in the absence of a second UN resolution. This, together with the charge that he overstated the strength of the intelligence about Saddam's WMD, inflicted irreparable damage on Blair's *ethos*, and indeed was a key factor in the decline of the New Labour project.

As we have seen, New Labour's arguments for its anti-social behaviour agenda and the Iraq war were founded on the notion of community, which Gould identifies as Blair's guiding concept (1999, p. 218). Squires attributes Blair's belief in this principle to his perception that British society at the end of the twentieth century was changing rapidly, and that it was necessary to 'assert the values of community and social inclusion more forcefully' as a result (2008, p. 305). This in turn could account for New Labour's 'growing commitment to use public power to try to change the behaviour of citizens individually and of publics collectively' in areas ranging from health to neighbourhood renewal (6, Fletcher-Morgan and Leyland, 2010, p. 428). Central to many – if not all – of these attempts was New Labour's core value of reciprocal rights and responsibilities, which it viewed as a prerequisite for the creation of a strong, cohesive community. The concept of rights and responsibilities had a strong presence in the four policy programmes examined in this book, and we saw in these discussions that New Labour's efforts to promote personal and civic responsibility became increasingly reliant on compulsion. This was evident in the growing conditionality imposed on New Deal participants and the coercion of parents who refused help in dealing with the anti-social behaviour of their children. While these measures proved controversial, with some critics arguing that they represented a move into authoritarianism (e.g. Coates, 2005, p. 142), an analysis of the 'context of ideology' revealed that this shift was in means only; New Labour remained committed to the social democratic values of community cohesion and social justice.

It is interesting to note that Blair used Conviction Rhetoric to win support for the two policies that were based on his guiding principle of community. In arguing for both the anti-social behaviour agenda and the invasion of Iraq, Blair identified a specific entity as the embodiment of evil – the immoral underclass and Saddam's regime respectively – and cast himself as a force for good that would deal with it. A common feature of these 'evils' was their failure to act in accordance with the values of the community (either domestic or international), and their subsequent exclusion from that community. For Blair, the way to deal with these 'enemies' was to instil in them 'our values', using coercive measures if necessary, and thus to bring them back into the community. This in turn would make the community stronger and more cohesive. In both cases, he believed that pre-emptive intervention was justified if the consequences of inaction were deemed to be more damaging in the long term.

The transference of discourses from New Labour's anti-social behaviour agenda to the Iraq war is indicative not only of a shift in the target of its moral crusade, but also of a remarkable degree of consistency in its overall approach. Although 6 *et al.* are correct in claiming that the desire to change citizens' behaviour was a distinctive feature of the Blair governments' policies, I believe we can go further and identify a commitment to changing the entire *culture*. This bold commitment was present, for example, in New Labour's attempts to create a 'culture of human rights' in the public services; effect a shift from a society in which anti-social behaviour is prevalent to a 'culture of respect' where rights are paired with responsibilities; and bring democracy and the rule of law to the people of Iraq. Although these efforts achieved varying degrees of success, they nonetheless reveal the extent of the Blair-led New Labour governments' ambitions and their belief in their ability to achieve these goals. In contrast, the party's aims under the leadership of Gordon Brown were more modest, as we will see next.

The argumentative strategies of Gordon Brown's government

When Gordon Brown replaced Blair as Prime Minister on 27 June 2007, he promised a 'new government with new priorities' that would meet the concerns and hopes of the British people. His mission, he said, was to provide 'the best of chances for everyone' to realise their talents and fulfil their potential, which in turn would make Britain the 'great global success story of this century' (2007). This statement gave expression to Brown's commitment to the value of equality of opportunity, which provided the impetus behind the welfare-to-work programmes he introduced as Chancellor. It also distinguished his position from that of Blair, whose approach was based on the concept of community (Gould, 1999, p. 218). Both concepts, however, were located within the core cluster of New Labour's ideology, which indicates that Brown was offering a shift in focus, as opposed to radical change.[1] This point is borne out by the following discussion of the Brown government's policies, the moral arguments it used to promote them, and their relationship to Labour's ideological platform.

During its third term in office, Labour introduced the Flexible New Deal (FND), which was based on the notion of 'opportunity for all and responsibility from all' (DWP, 2008c, p. 17). Like its predecessor, the FND was intended to make work pay – to which end it introduced new back-to-work credits – and to help people who can work to find employment while supporting those who cannot. It also sought to remove the barriers that prevent disadvantaged individuals entering the job market, which in turn would enable them to contribute to the nation's prosperity. This active approach to welfare, Peter Hain believed, would realize Labour's vision of an 'inclusive, cohesive and prosperous society with fairness and social justice at its core' (2007, p. 3). Thus, the values of equal worth, opportunity, community, cohesion and social justice all found expression in the FND.

An important difference between the New Deals and the FND was that the latter imposed greater conditionality on jobseekers and training providers alike. For participants, this new approach was summarized as 'more support matched by higher expectations' (DWP, 2008c, p. 16). Hence, they were required to act responsibly by preparing for, searching for, and accepting employment in exchange for the flexible, personalized support they received. Individuals who failed to comply with the scheme were subjected to a tougher sanctions regime, and there was a new requirement for the long-term unemployed to engage in a programme of full-time work experience (DWP, 2008a, p. 37). Providers, meanwhile, were motivated to find work for people by a competition for contracts and payment by results (DWP, 2008c, p. 11). Those who did not meet their targets risked having their contracts terminated early. At first sight, this increased emphasis on reciprocal responsibilities suggests a move to the right in Labour's thinking on welfare. However, when we consider the goals of the programme – namely the creation of a fairer, more cohesive community, in which 80 per cent of people are in work and no child is growing up in poverty (Hain, 2007, p. 3) – it is clear that Labour remained firmly committed to social democratic values.

Labour's arguments for the FND closely resembled the tripartite consequentialist argument that it employed to promote the New Deals. Consequently, its first strand emphasized the benefits of the FND for participants in the scheme, among which were improved well-being, self-esteem, and future prospects. As regards the community, Labour claimed that the FND would improve the job prospects of those who faced the greatest disadvantage, which in turn would promote social inclusion (DWP, 2007, pp. 23, 5). Here, Labour again failed to address the exclusion of the rich, which was a flaw in the original New Deals. Nonetheless, the new focus on job retention and progression in the FND, together with the introduction of new back-to-work credits, were perhaps intended to tackle the problem of in-work poverty that was neglected by its predecessor (DWP, 2008c, p. 38).

Meanwhile, Labour's third consequentialist argument for the FND emphasized its economic benefits. The DWP maintained that, by improving people's skills, the programme would enable Britain to compete more effectively in the global economy by creating more jobs and more growth (2007, p. 27). This renewed commitment to skills was evident in the introduction of increasingly personalized support and training through the FND, which was perhaps a tacit recognition of the limited success of the New Deals in this area. Labour also used a deontological argument to promote the FND, which emphasized the increasing obligations that participants in the scheme must accept in exchange for this support. In the words of the DWP, 'for those who are capable of working, there will be no right to a life on benefits' (2008a, p. 12). A tougher sanctions regime underpinned the responsibility to find work, while the greater conditionality imposed on training providers was designed to improve the efficacy of the scheme. These changes, claimed the DWP, would set the government on course to achieving its targets of an 80 per cent employment rate by 2015, and the eradication of child poverty by 2020 (2008a, p. 26).

In his first statement to Parliament as Prime Minister, Brown announced his government's intention of developing and consulting on a Bill of Rights and Responsibilities. This Bill lay at the heart of Labour's plans for constitutional reform and aimed to 'build on the Human Rights Act [by bringing] out more clearly the responsibilities we owe to each other – above all to observe the law and to respect the rights of others' (Straw, 2007).[2] It would also clarify what people were entitled to expect from both the state and from other people, and supply an ethical framework that gave practical expression to our common values. Labour's new approach was necessitated by the rise of consumerism and the attendant commoditization of rights which, in Straw's words, had 'become perceived as yet more goods to be "claimed"'. This perception stemmed in no small part from the disproportionate emphasis placed on individual rights in the HRA, and Labour sought to rectify this by enshrining the responsibilities we owe to each other in a constitutional document. In this way, Straw argued, the Bill of Rights and Responsibilities would give public recognition to the important role played by responsibilities in the 'healthy functioning of our democracy' (2008).

According to the Green Paper outlining the Bill, these responsibilities could include: the protection and promotion of the welfare of children in our care; the respectful treatment of NHS and other public sector workers; civic participation in the form of voting and jury service; respect for environmental limits; and other, more general, duties such as obedience to the law and the payment of taxes (Ministry of Justice, 2009, p. 9). Like the HRA, a Bill of Rights and Responsibilities would not contain a mechanism for legal enforceability, on the ground that 'the imposition of new penalties is unlikely to be the best way to foster a sense of civic responsibility and encourage respect and tolerance for others and participation in the democratic process' (Ministry of Justice, 2009, p. 10). The Bill would also include a number of new rights, among which were: equality; welfare entitlements; victims' rights within the criminal justice system; and 'principles of sustainable development in relation to our environment' (Ministry of Justice, 2009, p. 9). All citizens are entitled to these rights, and no one is exempt from the obligations they owe in return (Straw, 2008). Thus, the Bill of Rights and Responsibilities manifested the values of equal worth and reciprocal rights and responsibilities, and so was consistent with Labour's core ideological commitments.

As we would expect, Labour's argumentative strategy to promote the Green Paper drew primarily on deontological reasoning. This is evident in Straw and Wills's claim that the issue of rights and responsibilities connects with the fundamental human aspiration to 'live our lives fulfilled, peacefully, free from arbitrary interference and control by others', to the extent that it does not impede the ability of others to do likewise (2009, p. 4). While liberty is always important, claimed the Ministry of Justice, it is arguably more so during times of change, when people need reassurance that their freedoms will be protected. By promoting and safeguarding our basic rights and liberties, therefore, the Bill of Rights and Responsibilities could 'act as an anchor for people in the UK as we enter a new age of anxiety and uncertainty' (Ministry of Justice, 2009, p. 13). Moreover, by giving a clear account of the relationship between rights and responsibilities, the Bill could help people to understand those rights better (Ministry of Justice, 2009, p. 17). This in turn could supply a corrective to the selfish individualism that had hitherto prevailed, and so restore the public's faith in the notion of fundamental human rights.

As we saw in Chapter 7, Labour supplemented its deontological case for the HRA with a virtue theoretic argument that drew on its core values of community and cohesion. It also employed this strategy to promote the Bill of Rights and Responsibilities, though it accorded it greater prominence by emphasizing the 'essential contribution of responsibilities to collective harmony and prosperity' (Ministry of Justice, 2009, p. 18). Straw explained that, by improving our understanding of our rights and the responsibilities we owe in return, the Bill could 'help to foster a stronger sense of shared citizenship' among the British people (2008). After all, an insufficient emphasis on responsibilities can encourage people to assert their rights in a selfish and sometimes aggressive way, which may spoil others' enjoyment of their own rights. If such behaviour is left unchallenged, it will damage social cohesion and stability (Ministry of Justice, 2009, p. 18), which could further aggravate hostility towards human rights legislation. So, in promoting civic responsibility, the Brown government followed in the footsteps of its predecessor by attempting to change not only individual behaviour, but the culture itself.

The concepts of community and reciprocal rights and responsibilities were also present in Labour's policies for tackling anti-social behaviour. However, the Brown government sought to distance itself from the punitive populism that defined Blair's approach, to which end it disbanded the Respect Taskforce and scaled back the use of ASBOs against young offenders (Wintour, 2007).[3] As Ed Balls, the then Children's Secretary, explained, ASBOs are necessary, but 'not right. It's a failure every time a young person gets an ASBO. I want to live in the kind of society that puts ASBOs behind us' (quoted in ePolitix, 2007). The Brown government also set up a Youth Taskforce within the Department for Children, Schools and Families (DCSF), whose remit was to tackle anti-social behaviour through a combination of tough enforcement, support and prevention (Balls, 2008, p. 2). That the new unit was not based at the Home Office indicated that Labour viewed anti-social behaviour as more than just a criminal justice issue and, moreover, that it was keen to correct the imbalance between punishment and prevention that had so damaged the credibility of the Blair governments in this area.

On Alan Johnson's view, Labour failed to sustain its early momentum and, by 2009, had settled into 'a certain degree of complacency' about anti-social behaviour (2009a). Meanwhile, the Conservatives' narrative of the 'broken society' (e.g. Cameron, 2008b) had come to dominate the debate on law and order, and Labour viewed its annual conference as an opportunity to reclaim its advantage. With this in mind, Johnson's first speech as Home Secretary contained commitments to revive ASBOs, reduce delays in securing these orders, and prosecute anyone who breaches an ASBO. Consequently, perpetrators would be subjected to the 'full range of enforcement powers we have introduced, not as a last resort, but as a preventative measure' (2009b). While these initiatives seemed to suggest a return to the Blair governments' approach, the reality was more complex, as Labour also pledged to make young offenders face the consequences of their actions through community reparation and restorative justice. These enforcement measures would be combined with intensive support, which would enable perpetrators to 'address the underlying problems with their behaviour and help to turn their lives around' (Home Office, Ministry of Justice, Cabinet Office and DCSF, 2008, pp. 50, 5).

Labour's Family Intervention Projects (FIPs) lay at the heart of its strategy to support families, and in his conference address Brown promised to extend them to the 50,000 most chaotic families in Britain. The aim of these schemes was to tackle the underlying causes of anti-social behaviour by providing 'help for those who want to change' in the form of, for instance, parenting classes and drug treatment programmes, and 'proper penalties for those who don't or won't'. Moreover, Brown claimed, they were effective: 'They change lives, they make our communities safer and they crack down on those who're going off the rails' (2009a). Unlike the early intervention programmes introduced by the Blair governments, FIPs did not seek to instil respect and responsibility in young people who behave anti-socially, but to support and challenge parents to take their responsibilities seriously. This shift of focus was mirrored in Labour's rejection of Blair's virtue theoretic argument in favour of a consequentialist strategy, which emphasized the benefits of the schemes for participants and communities alike. Therefore, the DCSF claimed that FIPs increased young people's attendance at school, addressed their risky behaviours, and stabilised the tenancies of 80 per cent of the families who took part (2008, p. 18). Moreover, by improving outcomes for vulnerable young people, the programmes would reduce the likelihood that they would engage in anti-social behaviour, which would promote public safety (Home Office et al., 2008, pp. 8–9) and help Labour to 'deliver fairness and prosperity to all communities' (Smith, Balls and Straw, 2008, p. 1).

In June 2009, Brown announced the establishment of an independent inquiry, chaired by Sir John Chilcot, into the 2003 invasion of Iraq war (2009b). The remit of this fifth inquiry was to examine 'the period from summer 2001 before military operations began in March 2003, and our subsequent involvement in Iraq until the end of July [2009]', and to identify the lessons to be learned in each of these areas. By doing so, Brown continued, it would enable the government to 'strengthen the health of our democracy, our diplomacy and our military' (2009b). Although the inquiry was ongoing at the time of writing, it is worth noting Blair's insistence that the intelligence indicated the threat posed by Iraq's WMD was 'growing', and that if the coalition had not deposed Saddam in 2003, it would have had to deal with him at some later time, 'possibly in circumstances where the threat was worse' (quoted in Sparrow, 2010). When asked if he had any regrets, Blair replied that he felt 'responsibility, but not a regret for removing Saddam Hussein', on the ground that 'I do genuinely believe that the world is safer as a result'. The inquiry is due to publish its report in late 2010.

Overall, it seems that a unifying aim of the policies considered in this section was to put right the mistakes of the Blair-led governments. While these initiatives were undoubtedly consistent with Labour's core values, they were widely criticized for their lack of originality.[4] Indeed, following Brown's decision not to call a general election in autumn 2007, Falconer warned that

> If we...do not set out, in the coming months, our vision for the future of the UK, a vision which represents the progressive view of politics, then we will be offering drift not leadership, and the past not the future. (quoted in Hennessy, 2007)

This admonition proved prophetic, as no such vision was forthcoming and Brown's influence steadily declined. He eventually called a general election for 6 May 2010 and, after a faltering campaign, Labour lost power after 13 years in government.

Political justification and the case of New Labour

So what are the implications of the case of New Labour for our understanding of the process of political justification? We saw in Part II of the book that its core values remained remarkably consistent throughout its time in office, which in turn gave an underlying coherence to its policy programmes across a range of areas. Underpinning these commitments was a desire to move beyond the antagonisms that characterized the 'old' politics, and to reconcile, for instance, individual *and* society, rights *and* responsibilities, and economic efficiency *and* social justice. However, it quickly became apparent from an examination of the four policies that although New Labour achieved this goal on an ideological level, it was less successful in practice; its policies often emphasized one element over the other. The Human Rights Act is a good example of this, as New Labour's focus on individual rights in both the legislation itself and its supporting arguments marginalized the responsibilities that were intended to accompany them. As we have seen, this contributed to the growth of a culture of selfish individualism that eventually undermined the Act itself.

The case of New Labour also allows us to make some more general points concerning the use of moral argument in political justification. We saw in Chapter 2 that a key feature of consequentialist reasoning is the maximization of expectation, and this was certainly true of the argumentative strategy that New Labour used to promote the New Deals. Here, New Labour emphasized the benefits of the programmes for individuals, the economy and society as a whole, claiming that they would promote social justice and economic growth, and thus realize its goal of a fairer, more inclusive society. In practice, however, the schemes did not meet these high expectations, while the difficulties arising from their implementation created tension within the core cluster of New Labour's ideology. This left New Labour vulnerable to the accusation that it had failed to deliver on its promises, which in turn was damaging to its credibility.

Consequentialist arguments can also be employed to maximize risk, as evidenced by New Labour's claims about the consequences of inaction on anti-social behaviour and Blair's WMD argument for the 2003 Iraq war. In both cases, New Labour identified a potential threat and made truth claims about the consequences that would ensue if it was left unchecked. This is an example of emotive coercion, which New Labour perhaps employed to induce fear in its audience, and thus to persuade them to support its policies. However, we saw in Chapter 8 that this strategy was arguably too successful with regard to anti-social behaviour, as it fuelled public concern about crime even as rates fell. Blair's use of this technique in his argument for the invasion of Iraq also proved problematic, as it led to charges that he had exaggerated the threat posed by Saddam in order to persuade Parliament and the public that military action was necessary.

This discussion highlights the need for politicians to exercise caution when employing consequentialist strategies to promote their policies. Although it is easy to make grand claims about the benefits a new initiative will produce, or about the ill-effects that will follow if a particular threat is not addressed, the risks involved in doing so can be high. Indeed, Blair discovered this to his cost, as the allegation that he had deceived the public about Iraqi WMD not only did grave damage to his credibility, but it weakened support for his party and fuelled public cynicism about the practice of politics itself. A similar difficulty can arise if a party employs two seemingly opposing arguments to promote a single policy. We saw in Chapter 7 that New Labour utilized this strategy in making the case for the Human Rights Act, with Cooper describing it as an important constitutional change and Straw portraying it as a 'tidying-up exercise'. The inevitable reporting of both arguments in the media helped to create a climate of suspicion and confusion around the Act, and was almost certainly a factor in its unpopularity.

While the analysis of New Labour's argumentative strategies has highlighted some of the dangers inherent in political justification, it also sheds light on the relationship between rhetoric and the performance of leadership. For Andrew Sparrow, 'Blair was probably the best advocate/communicator of his political generation' (2010), and the present study supports Fairclough's thesis that one of the keys to his success was his ability to alternate between the figure of the 'normal person', who used colloquial phrases and articulated his government's policies in a personal manner, and the 'conviction politician', who blended ethical discourse with the myth of good and evil to represent himself as a moral arbiter. This combination of *ethos* and *pathos* – the 'personalisation of messages by reference to [one's] own experience' – gave Blair's rhetoric its persuasive power (Charteris-Black, 2005, p. 144) which, although vital to his success, ultimately contributed to his downfall.

Overall, the application of the analytical framework presented in this book has offered a number of insights into the process by which politicians select, modify and apply moral arguments in their efforts to win support for their policy programmes. It has also allowed us, through reference to the imperatives provided by the three aspects of the 'context of justification', to explain why these argumentative strategies developed as they did. However, the utility of the framework goes beyond the case study analysed here. It could, for instance, facilitate an examination of the ways in which other parties use moral arguments to promote their policy programmes, and thus pave the way for a comparative analysis. Equally, the framework could provide a starting-point for a study of the modes of moral argument used by politicians in democratic societies beyond Britain, though further research may be necessary. This could further contribute to our understanding of the complex and under-theorized process of moral justification in contemporary politics.

Notes

Introduction

1. Following Charteris-Black, and in accordance with the convention in cognitive linguistics, I use upper case to distinguish the underlying conceptual metaphors from 'surface' metaphors.

1 The Context of Ideology

1. Kenneth Smith claims to find within Gallie's work the notions of 'mutually contesting and contested concepts', and their widely accepted standard general use (2002, p. 329). He explains that, in contrast with essentially contested concepts, the distinguishing feature of mutually contested concepts is that the disputing parties both acknowledge and *accept* '(a) that they are either using *different* concepts in the *same* way or *similar* concepts in *different* ways, and that (b) "these mutually contesting, mutually contested uses of the concept [make] up together its standard general use" [Gallie, 1956, p. 167], about which there is little or no disagreement' (2002, p. 332).
2. In contrast, 'extension' refers to 'the referents, in the external (including social) world, to which the concept applies' (Freeden, 1996, p. 57 n. 17).
3. Freeden explains that this 'is not epistemological ineliminability: it is not underpinned by the absoluteness of knowledge itself. Instead, it will always be internal to, and conditional on, the survival of the thought-pattern that has gained general currency' (2003, p. 11).
4. Similarly, Vincent defines ideologies as 'bodies of concepts, values and symbols which incorporate conceptions of human nature and thus indicate what is possible or impossible for humans to achieve; critical reflections on the nature of human interaction; the values which humans ought either to reject or aspire to; and the correct technical arrangements for social, economic and political life which will meet the needs and interests of human beings' (1995, p. 16).
5. Freeden notes that philosophical accounts of coherence frequently link it to the ascertainment of truth; but 'truth-status is optional for analysts of ideology, even when given ideas are specifically, or vaguely, held as true by ideological producers and practitioners' (2005, p. 4).
6. As Vincent puts it, 'the same basic unit, idea, argument, technique or thinker will [often] be used by apparently quite alien ideologies for different reasons and outcomes' (1995, p. 18). This statement counters Bevir's objection that Vincent 'tends to see [ideologies] as mutually exclusive' (2000, pp. 278–9).
7. In brief, multiculturalism recognizes the 'just claims of ethnic and cultural groups *because* ethnicity and culture, and not only choice and wealth, are coming to be regarded as crucial elements of human self-understanding and dignity' (Freeden, 2003, p. 5).

2   The Context of Argumentation

1. It is worth noting, however, that there is no consensus on what the virtues are. While Christianity holds that humility is an important virtue because it 'prepares the righteous believer to stand in an appropriate relationship of awe, obedience, and worship to a creator God', this view was rejected by Hume and Nietzsche (Button, 2005, pp. 842–8), as well as by the ancient Greeks (MacIntyre, 1985, p. 136). Likewise, the quality of cunning is viewed as praiseworthy in the Homeric poems, due to its connection with the virtue of courage. However, cunning is not regarded as a virtue in today's society, perhaps because it has come to be associated with deceit. For an examination of a number of attempts to catalogue the virtues, see MacIntyre, 1985, pp. 181–203.

2. It is important to point out that, for Barry, it is a 'fallacy to say that any theory which holds that the fulfilment of some wants is (in a very special sense) without value is an ideal-regarding theory. It is not an ideal-regarding theory if all it says is that the fulfilment of desires *incompatible with the criteria of distribution laid down in the theory* is without value. Indeed, that is precisely what is meant when one says that a want-regarding theory is not purely aggregative but includes distributive criteria' (1973, p. 139).

3. Distributive principles can be further classified into comparative and absolute distributive principles. The former type, explains Barry, 'involve in their application to one person a comparison with the position of some other man or men', while the latter enable us to specify what an individual should get without reference to someone else's position (1990, p. 44).

4. Rawls defines a 'conception of the good' as an 'ordered scheme of final ends' (1980, p. 524). Particular conceptions of the good are those which lead people to have 'different ends and purposes' (Rawls, 1999, p. 110).

5. This right finds expression in the 'principle of non-intervention'. For an examination of the relationship between the Kantian conception of the person and humanitarian intervention, see Beitz, 1983.

6. The Civil Authorities (Special Powers) Act (Northern Ireland) 1922 authorized the issue of an Internment Order against an individual 'who is suspected of acting or having acted or being about to act in a manner prejudicial to the preservation of the peace and the maintenance of order in Northern Ireland' (quoted in Spjut, 1986, p. 713).

7. In so doing, I follow in the footsteps of such theorists as Laclau and Mouffe (2001), who adopt Gramsci's concept of hegemony but reject his historical materialism.

3   The Context of Hegemonic Competition

1. It is clear from this definition that the concept of discourse is distinct from that of ideology, though the two terms are sometimes used interchangeably (Purvis and Hunt, 1993, p. 473). For an example of this usage, see Townshend, 2004, esp. p. 270.

2. As Benjamin Bertram points out, nodal points 'replace the Gramscian formation of historical blocs [in Laclau and Mouffe's approach] and allow for

greater dispersion in political formations' (1995, p. 96). See Rosenthal (1988) for a detailed analysis of the relationship between the work of Gramsci and the discourse theory of Laclau and Mouffe.
3. In contrast, a 'war of manoeuvre' is a 'single front that is mobilised directly against the single power centre' (Smith, 1998, p. 165).

5 The Ideology of New Labour

1. However, Freeden notes – correctly I believe – that it is overly simplistic to view 'Old' Labour and Thatcherism in this way. He explains that if the first way drew on the new liberalism of the early twentieth century, it 'coexisted with a number of British socialist currents which cannot be reduced to social liberalism: Fabianism, ethical socialism, and a trade-union-oriented Labourism'. Meanwhile, if the second way broadly corresponds to Thatcherism, Freeden continues, it ignores the strong Tory beliefs that sustained a large proportion of middle England in the recent past, and indeed continue to do so (1999, p. 44).
2. Clause IV, Part Four of its Constitution committed the Labour party to 'secure for the workers by hand or by brain the full fruits of their industry, and the most equitable distribution thereof that may be possible, upon the basis of the common ownership of the means of production and the best obtainable system of popular administration and control of each industry or service' (quoted in Jones, 1996, p. 4).
3. Purdy explains that Old Labour conceived of full employment as 'a condition of the labour market in which the number of unemployed jobseekers equals the number of unfilled job vacancies or, alternatively, as the lowest rate of unemployment compatible with a stable rate of inflation, [so] the aim of public policy is now to maximise labour force participation and enhance the employability of socially disadvantaged groups' (2000, p. 187).
4. In a similar vein, Michael Harris writes that 'New Labour is born of the recognition ... of how distanced the Labour party, and the left generally, was from the mainstream political, social and economic perspectives of the mass of the public, or what we might term the "dominant political culture". The landslide general election victory of 7 May 1997 was achieved because of this recognition' (1999, p. 55).

6 New Labour's Welfare Reforms: The New Deals

1. By 1995–6, 23 per cent of the social security budget was spent on means-tested benefits, and this figure grew to over 30 per cent with the inclusion of housing benefits. 'National Insurance benefits still accounted for just under half the total, compared with almost two-thirds in 1979–80, but three-quarters of these payments went on retirement pensions' (Purdy, 2000, pp. 182–3).
2. Estimates vary as to the amount of money raised by the windfall tax. Adrian Harvey, for instance, states that it netted the government £4.5 billion (2001, p. 6), while Purdy claims that it raised £5.2 billion, of which £3.6 billion was used to fund the New Deal programme (2000, p. 186).

3. The National Minimum Wage, the Working Families Tax Credit (WFTC) and the Disabled Person's Tax Credit were launched in 1999, while the Child Tax Credit and the Working Tax Credit were introduced in April 2003. Johnson notes that although WFTC was heralded as a 'major new policy innovation, this is effectively a more generous version of the Family Credit benefit introduced and expanded by the Conservatives'. However, he identifies the introduction of the 'childcare credit' as a significant development that could substantially improve work incentives for lone parents in particular (2001, p. 69).

4. According to the DWP, Jobcentre Plus has 'merged the Employment Service and the working age parts of the Benefits Agency and will...provide a work-focused service to all people making a claim to benefit' (2002, p. 21). Meanwhile, New Labour published its National Skills Strategy in 2003, which aimed to 'ensure employers have the right skills to support the success of their businesses, and individuals have the skills they need to be both employable and personally fulfilled' (HM Treasury, DWP and DfES, 2004, p. 47). The drive to improve skills was a key element of New Labour's welfare policy, on the ground that, as Brown observes, 'the concentration of long-term unemployment among the badly educated suggests that inadequate skills must be an important part of the reason for persistent unemployment' (1994, p. 9).

7   Rights and Constitutional Reform: The Human Rights Act of 1998

1. Further, as Lord Falconer observes, Article 5 of the Human Rights Act means that individuals who have been sectioned under the Mental Health Act 'no longer have to wait a standard eight weeks for their reviews to be heard by a tribunal because of "administrative convenience"' (2004a, p. 4).

2. One such case was that of Max Mosley vs. the *News of the World*, in which Mosley sued the paper for breach of privacy after it accused him of participating in a Nazi-themed orgy with five prostitutes. Despite the paper's claims that its exposé was in the public interest, Mosley won the case and was awarded £60,000 in damages (Dowell, 2008). On this basis, we can say that Mosley's right to privacy under Article 8 of the Human Rights Act overrode the *News of the World*'s right to free expression under Article 10.

3. Article 29 Section 1 of the Universal Declaration of Human Rights states that 'everyone has duties to the community in which alone the free and full development of his personality is possible' (General Assembly of the United Nations, 1948).

4. According to Brian Mawhinney, 'it is not about whether hon. Members support human rights for UK citizens; we do. It is not about whether we support the convention and its interpretation by the European Court of Human Rights; we support the former, and most of the time the latter' (Hansard, 16 February 1998d, c.793).

5. Examples of such newspaper headlines are '"Traitor wins Human Rights Payout", "Ordinary Britons deserve human rights too", "Human rights, social wrongs", "Terrorists' Charter"' (Falconer, 2007, p. 4).

6. In this case, the European Court judged that Article 3 of the Convention, which guarantees the right to protection from torture, includes in every case the right not to be expelled or extradited to a country where you face a genuine risk of being tortured or subjected to inhuman treatment (Dworkin, 2008, p. 1).
7. Marcel Berlins sums up the dilemma as follows: 'It is wrong to send people back to a country where they will be tortured or killed. It is equally repugnant that the Afghans should be rewarded for committing an appalling criminal act, and that the message goes out that serious criminality is no bar to a future life in Britain' (2006).
8. Lord Goldsmith, for instance, claimed that Cameron's proposals 'would lead to more, not less, confusion about the best way to strike a balance between protecting the public and individual liberties' (quoted in Carlin, 2006).

8 Community: New Labour's Policies on Anti-Social Behaviour

1. The remit of the ASBU was to 'add value to the existing measures to tackle anti-social behaviour and to drive forward new policy, practice and action' (Home Office, 2003b, p. 5).
2. YOTs are made up of police officers, social workers, probation officers and staff from the education and health authority, and are run by a YOT manager. Their role is to identify and address the underlying causes of a young person's offending behaviour, with the aim of preventing them from re-offending in the future (Home Office, 1997b, pp. 35–6).
3. Philip Gould explains that 'most people believe in punishment, they believe in right and wrong, they believe in discipline and order. That for so long Labour denied this, that they sought to excuse the inexcusable on grounds of education, class or other disadvantages, was unacceptable to large numbers of the electorate who suffered the consequences of crime on a daily basis'. While Blair's new approach succeeded in winning these people round, it nonetheless seemed iconoclastic to many on the Left (1999, pp. 188–9).
4. According to the Respect Task Force, 'anti-social behaviour and offending by men have their origins in early childhood in 90 per cent of cases' (2006, p. 17).
5. The most popular intervention in the same period was the Acceptable Behaviour Contract, which is a less formal version of an ASBO. 8,654 ABCs were handed out between 1 October 2004 and 30 September 2005, up from 5,094 in 2003–4 (Margo and Stevens, 2008, p. 67).
6. A Home Office study has shown that the risk of being a victim of crime fell from 40 per cent in 1995 to 24 per cent in 2007 (2007, p. 1).
7. See Allen, 2004. This study also found that 'almost everybody, including tabloid readers, takes the view that drug addicts should be treated, rather than punished', which suggests that public attitudes towards crime are more complex than opinion polls suggest (Margo and Stevens, 2008, p. 18).
8. The 'hoodie' is a mutation of the 'feral youth' folk devil, whose hooded top has come to symbolize urban decay and the threat of violence. Following Cameron's call for a greater understanding of young people's problems, some

Labour figures attempted to delegitimize his position by referring to his address as the 'hug a hoodie' speech.

9. The concern that New Labour's approach was criminalizing a generation of young people was shared by some within the Party and may have been a factor in the downgrading of the Respect Bill to an action plan in December 2005, though the official reason was given as a 'lack of consensus across Whitehall over what it should contain' (Travis, 2005). Indeed, Rhodri Morgan cited this fear as one of the reasons behind his resignation as head of the Youth Justice Board in January 2007 (Squires, 2008, p. 319).

9 Foreign Policy: The Iraq War of 2003

1. According to Seldon, 'a dossier had been due to be published in March 2002 based on SIS intelligence examining Iraq's WMD capabilities, but had been held back for fear it was insufficiently convincing' (2005, p. 581). The intelligence community strengthened and updated this dossier, and it was eventually published on 24 September 2002.

2. Saddam's human rights abuses formed a small proportion of the first dossier – a total of eight pages out of 55. The majority of the document was devoted to the subject of WMD.

3. As Seldon notes, the Coalition Information Centre was based in the FCO but 'reported direct to [Alastair] Campbell, with little oversight' (2007, p. 151).

4. See Atkins, 2006 for a critical examination of the assumptions underlying Blair's 'doctrine of the international community'.

5. As Michael Clarke points out, 'the values/interests nexus was backed up by a belief in further liberalisation within the world economy. Only economic liberalism would allow societies to cope with globalisation and benefit from it; for the poor as well as the rich, disruptive as that may be for both' (2007, p. 598). As such, Blair's view of the relationship between interests and values in the international order is founded upon the Third Way assumption that globalization has had a significant impact on the world as a whole.

6. For cosmopolitan thinkers, this argument evokes a 'humanitarian exception' to the prohibition of the use of force propounded in positive international law. Alex Bellamy explains that these writers believe 'there is agreement in international society about what constitutes a "supreme humanitarian emergency" and that in such cases states not only have a right to intervene to halt human suffering, they have a moral duty to do so' (2004, p. 137).

7. This march was held on 15 February 2003 and up to one million people participated in it, including relatives of some of Blair's closest allies (Seldon, 2007, p. 152).

8. Blair also presented the latter argument in his statement opening the Iraq debate, saying, 'here we are: the Government with its most serious test, its majority at risk, the first Cabinet resignation over an issue of policy. The main parties divided' (2003b, p. 1).

9. McLean and Patterson's view that 'it could be argued that Saddam's fate was sealed, not by some putative connection to weapons of mass destruction (WMD), human rights abuses, connections to international terrorism, or even his threat to neighbouring states, but rather by the new international reality of the post-9/11 world' (2006, p. 359) lends support to this interpretation.

10. Similarly, the Conservative MP John Baron asked, 'what is to be lost by giving the UN inspectors what they want: a few more months to see whether the task can be completed?' (Hansard, 18 March 2003d, c.834).

Conclusion

1. Giddens supports this point with his prediction that Brown would 'certainly follow – and further develop – the main framework of Third Way political thinking' (2007, p. 1).
2. In this way, Labour's policy differed from that of the Conservatives, who were committed to repealing the Human Rights Act and replacing it with a British Bill of Rights. For criticisms of this approach, see Straw, 2008.
3. According to Alan Travis, writing in the *Guardian*, 'the number of new orders issued dropped by more than a third from 4,123 in 2005 to 2,706 in 2006. Although no official figures have been published since, it is believed that the downward trend has continued over the past three years' (2009).
4. The Conservatives repeatedly attacked Labour on this point. See, for instance, George Osborne's comments in Webster, 2008 and Cameron's words in BBC, 2010.

Bibliography

6, P., Fletcher-Morgan, C. and Leland, K. (2010) 'Making People More Responsible: The Blair Governments' Programme for Changing Citizens' Behaviour', *Political Studies*, 58, 427–49.

Allen, R. (2004) *Rethinking Crime and Punishment: The Final Report* (London: Esmée Fairbairn Foundation).

Althusser, L. (2005) 'Contradiction and Overdetermination' in *For Marx* (London: Verso).

Aristotle (1998) *The Nicomachean Ethics* (Oxford: Oxford University Press).

Atkins, J. (2006) 'A New Approach to Humanitarian Intervention? Tony Blair's "Doctrine of the International Community"', *British Politics*, 1, 274–83.

Atkins, J. (2010) 'Assessing the Impact of the Third Way' in S. Griffiths and K. Hickson (eds) *British Party Politics and Ideology after New Labour* (Basingstoke: Palgrave Macmillan).

Atkinson, P. and Coffey, A. (1997) 'Analysing Documentary Realities' in D. Silverman (ed.) *Qualitative Research: Theory, Method and Practice* (London: SAGE Publications Ltd).

Avineri, S. and de-Shalit, A. (1992) 'Introduction' in S. Avineri and A. de-Shalit (eds) *Communitarianism and Individualism* (Oxford: Oxford University Press).

BBC (2002) *Q and A: On-the-spot fines*, 12 August, http://news.bbc.co.uk/1/hi/uk/2187565.stm

BBC (2003a) *For and against: The Iraqi Exile*, 16 February, http://news.bbc.co.uk/1/hi/uk/2768747.stm

BBC (2003b) *Polls Find Europeans Oppose Iraq War*, 11 February, http://news.bbc.co.uk/1/hi/world/europe/2747175.stm

BBC (2005a) *Eight Terror Detainees Released*, 11 March, http://news.bbc.co.uk/1/hi/uk/4338849.stm

BBC (2005b) *Feral Youths on 'Rampage of Fear'*, 17 May, http://news.bbc.co.uk/1/hi/england/manchester/4554611.stm

BBC (2007) *Brown is UK's New Prime Minister*, 27 June, http://news.bbc.co.uk/1/hi/uk_politics/6245682.stm

BBC (2010) *Labour 'Will Pledge Not to Raise Income Tax Rates'*, 11 April, http://news.bbc.co.uk/1/hi/uk_politics/election_2010/8613798.stm

Balls, E. (2008) 'Foreword by the Secretary of State for Children, Schools and Families' in Department for Children, Schools and Families *Youth Taskforce Action Plan* (London: HM Government).

Barry, B. (1973) 'Liberalism and Want-Satisfaction: A Critique of John Rawls', *Political Theory*, 1, 134–53.

Barry, B. (1990) *Political Argument: A Reissue with a New Introduction* (Berkeley and Los Angeles, CA: University of California Press).

Bastow, S. and Martin, J. (2003) *Third Way Discourse: European Ideologies in the Twentieth Century* (Edinburgh: Edinburgh University Press).

Beech, M. (2009) 'No New Vision: The Gradual Death of British Social Democracy?' *Political Quarterly*, 80, 526–32.

Beitz, C.R. (1979) *Political Theory and International Relations* (Princeton, NJ: Princeton University Press).

Beitz, C.R. (1983) 'Cosmopolitan Ideals and National Sentiment', *Journal of Philosophy*, 80, 591–600.

Bell, D. (2000) *The End of Ideology: On the Exhaustion of Political Ideas in the Fifties* (Cambridge, MA: Harvard University Press).

Bell, D.N.F. and Blanchflower, D.G. (2010) *Youth Unemployment: Déjà Vu?* Stirling Economics Discussion Paper 2010-04, http://www.economics.stir.ac.uk

Bellamy, A. (2004) 'Ethics and Intervention: The "Humanitarian Exception" and the Problem of Abuse in the Case of Iraq', *Journal of Peace Research*, 41, 131–47.

Berlins, M. (2006) 'Stop Blaming the Human Rights Act', *Guardian*, 15 May, http://www.guardian.co.uk/commentisfree/2006/may/15/uk.politics

Bertram, B. (1995) 'New Reflections on the "Revolutionary" Politics of Ernesto Laclau and Chantal Mouffe', *Boundary 2*, 22, 81–110.

Bevir, M. (2000) 'New Labour: A Study in Ideology', *British Journal of Politics and International Relations*, 2, 277–301.

Bevir, M. (2005) *New Labour: A Critique* (Abingdon: Routledge).

Bevir, M. and Rhodes, R.A.W. (1999) 'Studying British Government: Reconstructing the Research Agenda', *British Journal of Politics and International Relations*, 1, 215–39.

Blair, T. (1993) 'Why Crime is a Socialist Issue', *New Statesman*, 25 January.

Blair, T. (1994a) *Speech to the Family Breakdown and Criminal Activity Conference*, 24 May.

Blair, T. (1994b) *Speech to the Labour Party Conference*, 4 October.

Blair, T. (1995a) *Let Us Face the Future – the 1945 Anniversary Lecture* (London: Fabian Society).

Blair, T. (1995b) 'Power with a Purpose' in P. Richards (ed.) *Tony Blair: In His Own Words* (London: Politico's Publishing).

Blair, T. (1996a) *New Britain: My Vision of a Young Country* (London: Fourth Estate Limited).

Blair, T. (1996b) *Speech to the Labour Party Conference*, 1 October.

Blair, T. (1996c) 'Introduction to *What Needs to Change*' in P. Richards (ed.) *Tony Blair: In His Own Words* (London: Politico's Publishing).

Blair, T. (1997a) 'Preface by the Prime Minister' in Home Office *Rights Brought Home: The Human Rights Bill*, Cm 3782 (London: HMSO), p. 3.

Blair, T. (1997b) *Speech at the Aylesbury Estate*, 2 June.

Blair, T. (1997c) *Speech on 'Bringing Britain Together'*, 8 December.

Blair, T. (1998a) *The Third Way: New Politics for the New Century* (London: Fabian Society).

Blair, T. (1998b) *Speech to the Labour Party Conference*, 29 September.

Blair, T. (1999a) *Beveridge Lecture*, 18 March.

Blair, T. (1999b) *Doctrine of the International Community at the Economic Club, Chicago*, 22 April.

Blair, T. (2000) *Speech to the Labour Party Conference*, 26 September.

Blair, T. (2001a) *Speech to the Christian Socialist Movement at Westminster Central Hall*, 29 March.

Blair, T. (2001b) *Speech to the Labour Party Conference*, 2 October.

Blair, T. (2002a) 'Foreword by the Prime Minister' in Joint Intelligence Committee *Iraq's Weapons of Mass Destruction: The Assessment of the British Government*, pp. 3–4.

Blair, T. (2002b) *Prime Minister's Iraq statement to Parliament*, 24 September.

Blair, T. (2002c) *Speech at the George Bush Senior Presidential Library*, 7 April.

Blair, T. (2002d) *Prime Minister's speech to TUC conference in Blackpool*, 10 September.

Blair, T. (2002e) *Interview Given by Prime Minister Tony Blair for NBC*, 4 April.

Blair, T. (2003a) *Speech to the Labour Party Conference*, 15 February.

Blair, T. (2003b) *Prime Minister's Statement Opening Iraq Debate*, 18 March.

Blair, T. (2003c) *Prime Minister's Statement Following the Azores Summit*, 16 March.

Blair, T. (2003d) *Prime Minister's Address to the Nation*, 20 March.

Blair, T. (2004) *Prime Minister Warns of Continuing Global Terror Threat*, 5 March.

Blair, T. (2005a) 'Our Citizens Should not Live in Fear', *Observer*, 11 December.

Blair, T. (2005b) *Speech on Improving Parenting*, 2 September.

Blair, T. (2006a) *Our Nation's Future – Social Exclusion*, 5 September.

Blair, T. (2006b) *Speech to the Labour Party Conference*, 26 September.

Blunkett, D. (2003a) 'Foreword' in Home Office *Together: Tackling Anti-Social Behaviour* (London: Home Office), 1.

Blunkett, D. (2003b) 'Ministerial Foreword' in Home Office, *Respect and Responsibility – Taking a Stand Against Anti-Social Behaviour*, Cm 5778 (London: HMSO), 3–4.

Bluth, C. (2004) 'The British Road to War: Blair, Bush and the Decision to Invade Iraq', *International Affairs*, 80, 871–92.

Bogdanor, V. (2001) 'Constitutional Reform' in A. Seldon (ed.) *The Blair Effect: The Blair Government 1997–2001* (London: Little, Brown).

Booth, C. and Singh, R. (2000) 'Law That Will Turn Dreams of Equality into Reality', *Telegraph*, 7 August, http://www.telegraph.co.uk/news/uknews/1351718/Law-that-will-turn-dreams-of-equality-into-reality.html

Bromund, T. (2009) 'A Just War: Prime Minister Tony Blair and the End of Saddam's Iraq' in T. Casey (ed.) *The Blair Legacy: Politics, Policy, Governance, and Foreign Affairs* (Basingstoke: Palgrave Macmillan).

Brown, G. (1994) *Fair Is Efficient – a Socialist Agenda for Fairness* (London: Fabian Society).

Brown, G. (1996) 'Tough Decisions', *Fabian Review*, 108 (3), 1–3.

Brown, G. (2007) *Speech Outside Downing Street*, 27 June.

Brown, G. (2009a) *Speech to the Labour Party Conference*, 29 September.

Brown, G. (2009b) *Statement on Iraq Inquiry*, 15 June.

Brown, G. and Darling, A. (2001) 'Foreword' in HM Treasury and Department for Work and Pensions, *The Changing Welfare State: Employment Opportunity for All* (London: HMSO), iii–iv.

Brown, G. and Smith, A. (2003) 'Foreword' in HM Treasury and Department for Work and Pensions, *Full Employment in Every Region* (London: HMSO), i.

Browne, A. (2006a) 'New Deal Not Working for Youths', *The Times*, 21 December, http://www.timesonline.co.uk/tol/news/uk/article759561.ece

Browne, A. (2006b) 'No School, No Work and Little Hope for 1.24m Young Britons', *The Times*, 11 December, http://www.timesonline.co.uk/tol/news/politics/article667300.ece

Buckler, S. (1993) *Dirty Hands: The Problem of Political Morality* (Aldershot: Avebury).

Buckler, S. (2007) 'Theory, Ideology, Rhetoric: Ideas in Politics and the Case of "Community" in Recent Political Discourse', *British Journal of Politics and International Relations*, 9, 36–54.

Buckler, S. and Dolowitz, D.P. (2000) 'Theorizing the Third Way: New Labour and Social Justice', *Journal of Political Ideologies*, 5, 301–20.

Burch, M. and Holliday, I. (2000) 'New Labour and the Constitution' in D. Coates and P. Lawler (eds) *New Labour in Power* (Manchester: Manchester University Press).

Burnham, P., Gilland, K., Grant, W. and Layton-Henry, Z. (2004) *Research Methods in Politics* (Basingstoke: Palgrave Macmillan).

Button, M. (2005) ' "A Monkish Kind of Virtue"? For and Against Humility', *Political Theory*, 33, 840–68.

Cabinet Office (2006) *Reaching Out: An Action Plan on Social Exclusion* (London: Cabinet Office).

Cameron, D. (2006a) *Balancing Freedom and Security – A Modern British Bill of Rights*, 26 June.

Cameron, D. (2006b) *Speech to the Centre for Social Justice*, 10 July.

Cameron, D. (2008a) 'Foreword' in Conservative Party *Work for Welfare: REAL Welfare Reform to Help Make British Poverty History* (Policy Green Paper No. 3), 1–2.

Cameron, D. (2008b) *Speech to the Conservative Party Conference*, 1 October.

Carlin, B. (2006) 'Rip Up Human Rights Act, Says Cameron', *Telegraph*, 26 June, http://www.telegraph.co.uk/news/uknews/1522326/Rip-up-Human-Rights-Act%2C-says-Cameron.html

Chakrabarti, S. (2005) 'There is No Halfway House on Human Rights', *The Times*, 1 February, http://business.timesonline.co.uk/tol/business/law/article 507956.ece

Charteris-Black, J. (2005) *Politicians and Rhetoric: The Persuasive Power of Metaphor* (Basingstoke: Palgrave Macmillan).

Chilton, P. (2004) *Analysing Political Discourse: Theory and Practice* (Abingdon: Routledge).

Clarke, K. (2007) 'New Labour: Family Policy and Gender' in C. Annesley, F. Gains and K. Rummery (eds) *Women and New Labour: Engendering Politics and Policy?* (Bristol: The Policy Press).

Clarke, M. (2007) 'Foreign Policy' in A. Seldon (ed.) *Blair's Britain, 1997–2007* (Cambridge: Cambridge University Press).

Coalition Information Centre (2003) *Iraq – Its Infrastructure of Concealment, Deception and Intimidation*, http://www.number-10.gov.uk/files/pdf/Iraq.pdf

Coates, D. (2005) *Prolonged Labour: The Slow Birth of New Labour Britain* (Basingstoke: Palgrave Macmillan).

Coates, D. and Krieger, J. (2009) 'The Mistake Heard Round the World: Iraq and the Blair Legacy' in T. Casey (ed.) *The Blair Legacy: Politics, Policy, Governance, and Foreign Affairs* (Basingstoke: Palgrave Macmillan).

Conservative Party (2006) *David Cameron Unveils the Real Respect Agenda*, 10 January, http://m.conservatives.com/News/News_stories/2006/01/David_Cameron_unveils_the_Real_Respect_agenda.aspx

Conservative Party (2008) *Work for Welfare: REAL Welfare Reform to Help Make British Poverty History* (Policy Green Paper No. 3).

Cook, R. (1997) *Speech on the Government's Ethical Foreign Policy, Guardian*, 12 May.

Cook, T.E. (1980) 'Political Justifications: The Use of Standards in Political Appeals', *The Journal of Politics*, 42, 511–37.

Cooper, Y. (2003) *Keynote Speech at the Liberty Annual Conference: Championing the Values of Human Rights*, 10 May.

D'Andrea, T.D. (2006) *Tradition, Rationality, and Virtue* (Aldershot: Ashgate Publishing Limited).

Darling, A. (1999) 'Rebuilding the Welfare State: The Moral Case for Reform' in Kelly, G. (ed.) *Is New Labour Working?* (London: The Fabian Society).

Day, J.P. (1968) 'Review of *Political Argument* by Brian Barry', *Mind*, 77 (308), 593–601.

Department for Children, Schools and Families (2008) *Youth Taskforce Action Plan* (London: HM Government).

Department for Constitutional Affairs (2006) *A Guide to the Human Rights Act 1998: Third Edition*, http://www.dca.gov.uk/peoplesrights/humanrights/index. htm

Department for Social Development (2006) *New Deal for 18 to 24 Year Olds*, http://www.dsdni.gov.uk/ssa/benefit_information/new_deals/new_deal_ for_18_to_24_year_olds.htm

Department for Work and Pensions (2002) *Pathways to Work: Helping People into Employment*, Cm 5690 (London: HMSO).

Department for Work and Pensions (2006a) *A New Deal for Welfare: Empowering People to Work*, Cm 6730 (London: HMSO).

Department for Work and Pensions (2006b) *A New Deal for Welfare: Empowering People to Work (Consultation Report)*, Cm 6859 (London: HMSO).

Department for Work and Pensions (2007) *In Work, Better Off: Next Steps to Full Employment*, Cm 7130 (London: HMSO).

Department for Work and Pensions (2008a) *No One Written Off: Reforming Welfare to Reward Responsibility*, Public consultation, Cm 7363 (London: TSO).

Department for Work and Pensions (2008b) *Transforming Britain's Labour Market: Ten Years of the New Deal* (London: DWP).

Department for Work and Pensions (2008c) *Raising Expectations and Increasing Support: Reforming Welfare for the Future*, Cm 7506 (London: HMSO).

Department of Health (2007) *Why Go Smokefree?* http://smokefree.nhs.uk/why-go-smokefree/

Doig, A. and Phythian, M. (2005) 'The National Interest and the Politics of Threat Exaggeration: The Blair Government's Case for War Against Iraq', *Political Quarterly*, 76, 368–76.

Dorey, P. (2007) 'A New Direction or Another False Dawn? David Cameron and the Crisis of British Conservatism', *British Politics*, 2, 137–66.

Dowell, B. (2008) 'Max Mosley v. *News of the World* timeline', *Guardian*, 24 July, http://www.guardian.co.uk/media/2008/jul/24/privacy.newsoftheworld

Driver, S. (2004) 'North Atlantic Drift: Welfare Reform and the "Third Way" Politics of New Labour and the New Democrats' in S. Hale, W. Leggett and L. Martell (eds) *The Third Way and Beyond: Criticisms, Futures, Alternatives* (Manchester: Manchester University Press).

Driver, S. and Martell, L. (1997) 'New Labour's Communitarianisms', *Critical Social Policy*, 17 (52), 27–46.

Driver, S. and Martell, L. (1998) *New Labour: Politics after Thatcherism* (Cambridge: Polity Press).

Driver, S. and Martell, L. (2006) *New Labour*, 2nd edn (Cambridge: Polity Press).

Dunne, T. (2004) ' "When the Shooting Starts": Atlanticism in British Security Strategy', *International Affairs*, 80, 893–909.

Dworkin, R. (2005) *Taking Rights Seriously: New Impression with a Reply to Critics* (London: Gerald Duckworth & Co. Ltd).

Dworkin, A. (2008) *European Court of Human Rights Affirms Absolute Ban on Torture*, 29 February, http://www.crimesofwar.org/onnews/news-echr.html

ePolitix.com (2007) *Asbos 'a Sign of Failure' Says Balls*, 27 July, http://www.epolitix.com/latestnews/article-detail/newsarticle/asbos-a-sign-of-failure-says-balls/

Etzioni, A. (2000) *The Third Way to a Good Society* (London: Demos).

Evans, M. (2008) 'New Labour and the Rise of the New Constitutionalism' in M. Beech and S. Lee (eds) *Ten Years of New Labour* (Basingstoke: Palgrave Macmillan).

Fairclough, N. (2000) *New Labour, New Language?* (London: Routledge).

Falconer, C. (2004a) *Using Human Rights in the Voluntary Sector: Speech to the Institute of Public Policy and Research*, 10 December.

Falconer, C. (2004b) *Speech at the Launch of the White Paper on the Commission for Equality and Human Rights*, 12 May.

Falconer, C. (2004c) *Human Rights and Constitutional Reform: Speech to the Law Society and Human Rights Lawyers' Association*, 17 February.

Falconer, C. (2006a) *Speech to the DCA Human Rights Conference*, 30 October.

Falconer, C. (2006b) 'Preface' in Department for Constitutional Affairs (2006) *A Guide to the Human Rights Act 1998: Third Edition*, 4.

Falconer, C. (2007) *The Lord Morris of Borth-y-Gest Memorial Lecture: Human Rights are Majority Rights*, 23 March.

Farrington-Douglas, J. with Durante, L. (2009) *Towards a Popular, Preventative Youth Justice System*, Institute for Public Policy Research, http://www.ippr.org/publicationsandreports/publication.asp?id=673

Feinberg, J. (1970) *Doing and Deserving* (Princeton, NJ: Princeton University Press).

Field, F. and White, P. (2007) *Welfare isn't Working – New Deal for Young People*, http://www.reform.co.uk/Research/Welfare/WelfareArticles/tabid/111/smid/378/ArticleID/630/reftab/72/Default.aspx

Finlayson, A. (2003) *Making Sense of New Labour* (London: Lawrence and Wishart).

Finlayson, A. (2004) 'Political Science, Political Ideas and Rhetoric', *Economy and Society*, 33, 528–49.

Finlayson, A. (2007) 'From Beliefs to Arguments: Interpretive Methodology and Rhetorical Political Analysis', *British Journal of Political and International Relations*, 9, 545–63.

Foreign and Commonwealth Office (2002) *Saddam Hussein: Crimes and Human Rights Abuses*, http://news.bbc.co.uk/nol/shared/spl/hi/middle_east/02/uk_human_rights_dossier_on_iraq/pdf/iraq_human_rights.pdf

Freeden, M. (1996) *Ideologies and Political Theory: A Conceptual Approach* (Oxford: Clarendon Press).

Freeden, M. (1999) 'The Ideology of New Labour', *Political Quarterly*, 70, 42–51.

Freeden, M. (2000) 'Editorial: Political Ideology at Century's End', *Journal of Political Ideologies*, 5, 5–15.

Freeden, M. (2003) 'Editorial: Ideological Boundaries and Ideological Systems', *Journal of Political Ideologies*, 8, 3–12.

Freeden, M. (2004) 'Editorial: Essential Contestability and Effective Contestability', *Journal of Political Ideologies*, 9, 3–11.

Freeden, M. (2005) Editorial: Fundaments and Foundations in Ideologies', *Journal of Political Ideologies*, 10, 1–9.

Freedman, L. (2007) 'Defence' in A. Seldon (ed.) *Blair's Britain, 1997–2007* (Cambridge: Cambridge University Press).

Freud, D. (2007) *Reducing Dependency, Increasing Opportunity: Options for the Future of Welfare to Work* (Leeds: Corporate Document Services).

Fukuyama, F. (1992) *The End of History and the Last Man* (London: Penguin Books Ltd).

Gallie, W.B. (1956) 'Essentially Contested Concepts', *Proceedings of the Aristotelian Society*, 56, 167–98.

Gamble, A. (1988) *The Free Economy and the Strong State* (London: Macmillan).

Garrett, P.M. (2007) 'Making "Anti-Social Behaviour": A Fragment on the Evolution of "ASBO Politics" in Britain', *British Journal of Social Work*, 37, 839–56.

Gearty, C. (2003) 'How did Blair get here?' *London Review of Books*, 25 (4), 20 February, http://www.lrb.co.uk/v25/n04/print/gear01_.html

General Assembly of the United Nations (1948) *Universal Declaration of Human Rights*, http://www.un.org/Overview/rights.html

Ghate, D. and Ramella, M. (2002) *Positive Parenting: The National Evaluation of the Youth Justice Board's Parenting Programme*, Policy Research Bureau http://www.yjb.gov.uk/Publications/Scripts/prodList.asp?eP=

Giddens, A. (2000) *The Third Way and Its Critics* (Cambridge: Polity Press).

Giddens, A. (2007) 'It's Time to Give the Third Way a Second Chance', *Independent*, 28 June, http://www.independent.co.uk/opinion/commentators/anthony-giddens-its-time-to-give-the-third-way-a-second-chance-454966.html

Goldsmith (2006) *Speech to the Royal United Services Institute*, 10 May.

Goodchild, S. (2006) 'Demonised: We Lock Them Up. We Give Them Asbos. But is Our Fear of Kids Making Them Worse?' *Independent*, 23 April, http://www.independent.co.uk/news/uk/crime/demonised-we-lock-them-up-we-give-them-asbos-but-is-our-fear-of-kids-making-them-worse-475273.html

Goode, E. and Ben-Yehuda, N. (1994) *Moral Panics: The Social Construction of Deviance* (Oxford: Blackwell).

Gould, P. (1999) *The Unfinished Revolution: How the Modernisers Saved the Labour Party* (London: Abacus).

Gramsci, A. (1971) *Selections from the Prison Notebooks* (London: Lawrence and Wishart).

Grayling, A.C. (2006) 'The Right Kind of Inconvenience', *Guardian*, 26 June, http://www.guardian.co.uk/commentisfree/2006/jun/26/cameronadnhumanrights

Greenslade, R. (2003) 'Their Master's Voice', *Guardian*, 17 February, http://www.guardian.co.uk/media/2003/feb/17/mondaymediasection.iraq/

HM Treasury (1997) *The Modernisation of Britain's Tax and Benefit System: Number One. Employment Opportunity in a Changing Labour Market* (London: HM Treasury).

HM Treasury (2000) *The Goal of Full Employment: Employment Opportunity for all throughout Britain* (London: HMSO).

HM Treasury and Department for Work and Pensions (2001) *The Changing Welfare State: Employment Opportunity for All* (London: HMSO).

HM Treasury and Department for Work and Pensions (2003) *Full Employment in Every Region* (London: HMSO).

HM Treasury, Department for Work and Pensions and Department for Education and Skills (2004) *Supporting Young People to Achieve: Towards a New Deal for Skills* (London: HMSO).

Hain, P. (2007) 'Ministerial Foreword' in Department for Work and Pensions, *Ready for Work: Full Employment in Our Generation*, Cm 7290 (London: HMSO), 3–5.

Hale, S. (2005) *Communitarian Influence? Amitai Etzioni and the Making of New Labour*, http://aladinrc.wrlc.org/bitstream/1961/608/1/Sarah-Hale-2005.pdf

Hall, S. (1988) *The Hard Road to Renewal: Thatcherism and the Crisis of the Left* (London: Verso).

Hall, S. (1998a) 'The Rediscovery of "Ideology" ' in J. Rivkin and M. Ryan (eds) *Literary Theory: An Anthology* (London: Blackwell).

Hall, S. (1998b) 'The Great Moving Nowhere Show', *Marxism Today*, November/December, 9–14.

Hansard (1997) *House of Commons Hansard Debates for 19 December*, http://www.publications.parliament.uk/pa/cm199798/cmhansrd/vo971219/debtext/71219-20.htm

Hansard (1998a) *House of Commons Hansard Debates for 16 February*, http://www.publications.parliament.uk/pa/cm199798/cmhansrd/vo980216/debtext/80216-10.htm#80216-10_spnew5

Hansard (1998b) *House of Commons Hansard Debates for 16 February*, http://www.publications.parliament.uk/pa/cm199798/cmhansrd/vo980216/debtext/80216-07.htm

Hansard (1998c) *House of Commons Hansard Debates for 16 February*, http://www.publications.parliament.uk/pa/cm199798/cmhansrd/vo980216/debtext/80216-14.htm

Hansard (1998d) *House of Commons Hansard Debates for 16 February*, http://www.publications.parliament.uk/pa/cm199798/cmhansrd/vo980216/debtext/80216-13.htm

Hansard (2002) *House of Commons Hansard Debates for 24 September*, http://www.publications.parliament.uk/pa/cm200102/cmhansrd/vo020924/debtext/20924-02.htm#20924-02_spnew0

Hansard (2003a) *House of Commons Hansard Debates for 18 March*, http://www.publications.parliament.uk/pa/cm200203/cmhansrd/vo030318/debtext/30318-16.htm#30318-16_spnew5

Hansard (2003b) *House of Commons Hansard Debates for 18 March*, http://www.publications.parliament.uk/pa/cm200203/cmhansrd/vo030318/debtext/30318-18.htm

Hansard (2003c) *House of Commons Hansard Debates for 18 March*, http://www.publications.parliament.uk/pa/cm200203/cmhansrd/vo030318/debtext/30318-46.htm#30318-46_spnew9

Hansard (2003d) *House of Commons Hansard Debates for 18 March*, http://www.publications.parliament.uk/pa/cm200203/cmhansrd/vo030318/debtext/30318-27.htm#30318-27_spnew0

Hansard (2007) *House of Commons Hansard Debates for 18 January*, http://www.publications.parliament.uk/pa/cm200607/cmhansrd/cm070118/debtext/70118-0008.htm#07011841001124

Harris, M. (1999) 'New Labour: Government and Opposition', *Political Quarterly*, 70, 52–61.

Harvey, A. (2001) 'Social Justice' in A. Harvey (ed.) *Transforming Britain: Labour's Second Term* (London: Fabian Society).

Hay, C. (1997) 'Blaijorism: Towards a One-Vision Polity?' *Political Quarterly*, 68, 372–8.

Hay, C. (1999) *The Political Economy of New Labour: Labouring Under False Pretences?* (Manchester: Manchester University Press).

Hennessy, P. (2007) 'Gordon Brown Hit by Tory Poll Surge', *Telegraph*, 13 October, http://www.telegraph.co.uk/news/newstopics/politics/1566048/Gordon-Brown-hit-by-Tory-poll-surge.html

Hensher, P and Younge, G. (2006) 'Does the Right to Freedom of Speech Justify Printing the Danish Cartoons?' *Guardian*, 4 February, http://www.guardian.co.uk/Columnists/Column/0,,1701986,00.html

Herbert, N. (2008) *Rights without Responsibilities – a Decade of the Human Rights Act*, speech to the British Institute of Human Rights, 24 November.

Heywood, A. (2003) *Political Ideologies: An Introduction*, 3rd edn (Basingstoke: Palgrave Macmillan).

Hickson, K. (2004) 'Equality' in R. Plant, M. Beech and K. Hickson (eds) *The Struggle for Labour's Soul: Understanding Labour's Political Thought Since 1945* (London: Routledge).

Hoggett, P. (2005) 'Iraq: Blair's Mission Impossible', *British Journal of Politics and International Relations*, 7, 418–28.

Home Office (1997a) *Rights Brought Home: The Human Rights Bill*, Cm 3782 (London: HMSO).

Home Office (1997b) *No More Excuses: A New Approach to Tackling Youth Crime in England and Wales*, Cm 3809 (London: HMSO).

Home Office (2003a) *Respect and Responsibility – Taking a Stand Against Anti-Social Behaviour*, Cm 5778 (London: HMSO).

Home Office (2003b) *Together: Tackling Anti-Social Behaviour* (London: Home Office).

Home Office (2004) *Defining and Measuring Anti-Social Behaviour* (London: Research, Development and Statistics Directorate).

Home Office (2007) *Crime in England and Wales 2006/07*, 4th edn (London: Home Office).

Home Office (2008) *Crime in England and Wales: Quarterly Update to December 2007*, 04/08 (London: Home Office).

Home Office, Ministry of Justice, Cabinet Office and Department for Children, Schools and Families (2008) *Youth Crime Action Plan 2008* (London: HM Government).

Hursthouse, R. (1997) 'Virtue Theory and Abortion' in R. Crisp and M. Slote (eds) *Virtue Ethics* (Oxford: Oxford University Press).

Johnson, A. (2009a) *Speech on Crime and Communities*, 2 July.

Johnson, A. (2009b) *Speech to the Labour Party Conference*, 30 September.

Johnson, N. (2004) 'The Human Rights Act 1998: A Bridge between Citizenship and Justice?' *Social Policy & Society*, 3, 113–21.

Johnson, P. (2001) 'New Labour: A Distinctive Vision of Welfare Policy?' in S. White (ed.) *New Labour: The Progressive Future?* (Basingstoke: Palgrave Macmillan).

Joint Committee on Human Rights (2003) *Sixth Report: The Case for a Human Rights Commission*, http://www.publications.parliament.uk/pa/jt200203/jtselect/jtrights/67/6703.htm

Joint Intelligence Committee (2002) *Iraq's Weapons of Mass Destruction: The Assessment of the British Government*, http://www.number-10.gov.uk/files/pdf/iraqdossier.pdf

Jones, G. (2006) 'New Deal is "Revolving Door Back to Welfare"', *Telegraph*, 22 December, http://www.telegraph.co.uk/news/uknews/1537579/New-Deal-is-revolving-door-back-to-welfare.html

Jones, T. (1996) *Remaking the Labour Party: From Gaitskell to Blair* (London: Routledge).

Kampfner, J. (2004) *Blair's Wars* (London: The Free Press).

Kant, I. (1997) *Groundwork of the Metaphysics of Morals*, trans. M. Gregor (Cambridge: Cambridge University Press).

Kenway, P. (2008) *Addressing In-Work Poverty* (York: Joseph Rowntree Foundation).

Klug, F. (2006) 'Enshrine these Rights', *Guardian*, 27 June, http://www.guardian.co.uk/commentisfree/2006/jun/27/comment.politics1

Krebs, R.R. and Lobasz, J.K. (2007) 'Fixing the Meaning of 9/11: Hegemony, Coercion and the Road to War in Iraq', *Security Studies*, 16, 409–51.

Labour Party (1997) *New Labour: Because Britain Deserves Better*, http://www.psr.keele.ac.uk/area/uk/man/lab97.htm

Labour Party (2001) *Ambitions for Britain: Labour's Manifesto 2001*, http://www.psr.keele.ac.uk/area/uk/e01/man/lab/lab01.htm

Labour Party (2005) *Britain Forward not Back*, http://image.guardian.co.uk/sys-files/Politics/documents/2005/04/13/labourmanifesto.pdf

Laclau, E. (1990) 'New Reflections on the Revolution of Our Time' in E. Laclau (ed.) *New Reflections on the Revolution of Our Time* (London: Verso).

Laclau, E. (1996) 'Why do Empty Signifiers Matter to Politics?' in E. Laclau (ed.) *Emancipation(s)* (London: Verso).

Laclau, E. and Mouffe, C. (2001) *Hegemony and Socialist Strategy: Towards a Radical Democratic Politics*, 2nd edn (London: Verso).

Lammy, D. (2003) *Third Anniversary of the Human Rights Act: Speech to the Audit Commission Conference*, 6 November.

Lammy, D. (2004) *Speech on Equality and Human Rights*, 4 February.

Landrum, D. (2002) 'Citizenship, Education and the Political Discourse of New Labour', *Contemporary Politics*, 8, 219–32.

Layard, R. (2001) *Welfare-to-Work and the New Deal* (London: Centre for Economic Performance).

Le Grand, J. (1998), 'The Third Way Begins with Cora,' *New Statesman*, 6 March.

Lister, M.R. (2000), 'To RIO via the Third Way,' *Renewal*, 8 (4): 19–20.

Livingstone, S. and Lunt, P. (1994) *Talk on Television: Audience Participation and Public Debate* (London: Routledge).

MacIntyre, A. (1985) *After Virtue*, 2nd (corrected) edn with Postscript (London: Gerald Duckworth & Co. Ltd).

MacIntyre, A. (1999) *Dependent Rational Animals: Why Human Beings Need the Virtues* (London: Gerald Duckworth).

MacLean, M. (1994) 'The Making of the Child Support Act of 1991: Policy Making at the Intersection of Law and Social Policy', *Journal of Law and Society*, 21, 505–19.

McLean, C. and Patterson, A. (2006) 'A Precautionary Approach to Foreign Policy? A Preliminary Analysis of Tony Blair's Speeches on Iraq', *British Journal of Politics and International Relations*, 8, 351–67.

Major, J. (1996) *Speech to the Conservative Party Conference*, 11 October.

Mandelson, P. and Liddle, R. (1996) *The Blair Revolution: Can New Labour Deliver?* (London: Faber and Faber).

Margo, J. and Stevens, A. (2008) *Make Me a Criminal: Preventing Youth Crime*, Institute for Public Policy Research, http://www.ippr.org.uk/publicationsandreports/publication.asp?id=587

Martell, L. (2004) 'Introduction' in S. Hale, W. Leggett and L. Martell (eds) *The Third Way and Beyond: Criticisms, Futures, Alternatives* (Manchester: Manchester University Press).

Mason, J. (2002) *Qualitative Researching*, 2nd edn (London: Sage).

Mill, J.S. (1998) 'On Liberty' in J. Gray (ed.) *On Liberty and Other Essays* (Oxford: Oxford University Press).

Millar, J. (1994) 'State, Family and Personal Responsibility: The Changing Balance for Lone Mothers in the United Kingdom', *Feminist Review*, 48, 24–39.

Millar, J. (2000) *Keeping Track of Welfare Reform: The New Deal Programmes* (York: York Publishing Services).

Ministry of Justice (2009) *Rights and Responsibilities: Developing Our Constitutional Framework*, Cm 7577 (Richmond: Office of Public Sector Information).

Ministry of Justice, Department for Children, Schools and Families and Youth Justice Board (2007) *Parenting Contracts and Orders Guidance*, revised version, http://publications.teachernet.gov.uk/eOrderingDownload/Parenting-contracts.pdf

Nagel, T. (1991) 'Ruthlessness in Public Life' in T. Nagel (ed.), *Mortal Questions* (Cambridge: Cambridge University Press).

Newburn, T. and Reiner, R. (2007) 'Crime and Penal Policy' in A. Seldon (ed.) *Blair's Britain 1997–2007* (Cambridge: Cambridge University Press).

Newey, G. (2001) 'Philosophy, Politics and Contestability', *Journal of Political Ideologies*, 6, 245–61.

Norton, P. (2007) 'The Constitution' in A. Seldon (ed.) *Blair's Britain, 1997–2007* (Cambridge: Cambridge University Press).

O'Malley, E. (2007) 'Setting Choices, Controlling Outcomes: The Operation of Prime Ministerial Influence and the UK's Decision to Invade Iraq', *British Journal of Politics and International Relations*, 9, 1–19.

Office for National Statistics (2009) *UK Productivity Closer to Leading G7 Countries*, http://www.statistics.gov.uk/pdfdir/icpnr0209.pdf

Organisation for Economic Cooperation and Development (2007) *Activating the Unemployed: What Countries Do*, http://www.oecd.org/dataoecd/2/10/40777063.pdf

Organisation of American States (1969) *American Convention on Human Rights*, http://www.cidh.org/basicos/english/Basic3.American%20Convention.htm

Parmar, I. (2000) 'New Labour and "Law and Order"' in D. Coates and P. Lawler (eds) *New Labour in Power* (Manchester: Manchester University Press).

Pecora, V. (1991) 'Ethics, Politics and the Middle Voice', *Yale French Studies*, 79, 203–30.

Petrongolo, B. and Van Reenen, J. (2010) *Jobs and Youth Unemployment: It's BAD, but Not As Bad As You Might Think*, Centre for Economic Performance Paper No. CEPEA012, http://cep.lse.ac.uk/pubs/download/ea012.pdf

Phillips, M. (2005) 'When Will Our Politicians Wake up to the Fact it's THEY Who Have Done More than Anyone to Create this Culture of Yobbery?' *Daily Mail*, 19 May, http://www.dailymail.co.uk/debate/columnists/article-349247/When-politicians-wake-fact-THEY-create-culture-yobbery.html

Plant, R. (2004) 'Ends, Means and Political Identity' in R. Plant, M. Beech and K. Hickson (eds) *The Struggle for Labour's Soul: Understanding Labour's Political Thought since 1945* (London: Routledge).

Purdy, D. (2000) 'New Labour and Welfare Reform' in D. Coates and P. Lawler (eds) *New Labour in Power* (Manchester: Manchester University Press).

Purvis, T. and Hunt, A. (1993) 'Discourse, Ideology, Discourse, Ideology, Discourse, Ideology...', *British Journal of Sociology*, 44, 473–99.

Rachels, J. (1999) *The Elements of Moral Philosophy*, 3rd edn (London: McGraw Hill).

Rangwala, G. (2003) 'Blair's Crumbling Case for War', *Labour Left Briefing*, March, http://middleeastreference.org.uk/llb030222.html

Rawls, J. (1980) 'Kantian Constructivism in Moral Theory', *Journal of Philosophy*, 77 (9), 515–72.

Rawls, J. (1999) *A Theory of Justice*, revised edn (Oxford: Oxford University Press).

Respect Task Force (2006) *Respect Action Plan* (London: Home Office).

Rosenberg, J. (2000) 'Just War and Intervention: The Challenge of the International for Social and Political Theory', *Papers in Social Theory*, 5, 2–20.

Rosenthal, J. (1988) 'Who Practices Hegemony? Class Division and the Subject of Politics', *Cultural Critique*, 9, 25–52.

Rubinstein, D. (1997) 'How New is New Labour?' *Political Quarterly*, 68, 339–43.

Sandel, M.J. (1992) 'The Procedural Republic and the Unencumbered Self' in S. Avineri and A. de-Shalit (eds) *Communitarianism and Individualism* (Oxford: Oxford University Press).

Scarre, G. (1996) *Utilitarianism* (London: Routledge).

Scheffler, S. (1988) 'Introduction' in S. Scheffler (ed.) *Consequentialism and Its Critics* (Oxford: Oxford University Press).

Scotland (2001) *Citizenship and Justice*, The Roscoe Lecture, 24 October.

Scraton, P. (2005) 'Scant Respect for Children's Rights', *Safer Society*, winter, https://www.nacro.org.uk/data/files/nacro-2008021315-426.pdf#page=19

Scruton, R. (2001) *Kant: A Very Short Introduction* (Oxford: Oxford University Press).

Seldon, A. (2005) *Blair* (London: The Free Press).

Seldon, A. (2007) *Blair Unbound* (London: Simon & Schuster).

Seliger, M. (1976) *Ideology and Politics* (London: George Allen and Unwin).

Shaw, E. (2007) *Losing Labour's Soul? New Labour and the Blair Government 1997–2007* (London: Routledge).

Slote, M. (1997) 'Virtue Ethics' in M.W. Baron, P. Pettit and M. Slote (eds) *Three Methods of Ethics* (Oxford: Blackwell).

Smith, A.M. (1998) *Laclau and Mouffe: The Radical Democratic Imaginary* (London: Routledge).

Smith, J., Balls, E. and Straw, J. (2008) 'Ministerial Foreword' in Home Office, Ministry of Justice, Cabinet Office and Department for Children, Schools and Families *Youth Crime Action Plan 2008* (London: HM Government), 1–2.

Smith, K. (2002) 'Mutually Contested Concepts and Their Standard General Use', *Journal of Classical Sociology*, 2, 329–43.

Smith, N. and Middleton, S. (2007) *A Review of Poverty Dynamics Research in the UK* (York: Joseph Rowntree Foundation).

Sparrow, A. (2010) 'Tony Blair at Iraq inquiry – Live', *Guardian*, 29 January, http://www.guardian.co.uk/politics/blog/2010/jan/29/iraq-war-inquiry-tonyblair

Spjut, R.J. (1986) 'Internment and Detention without Trial in Northern Ireland 1971–1975: Ministerial Policy and Practice', *The Modern Law Review*, 49, 712–40.

Squires, P. (2008) 'The Politics of Anti-Social Behaviour', *British Politics*, 3, 300–23.

Stavrakakis, Y. (1997) 'Green Ideology: A Discursive Reading', *Journal of Political Ideologies*, 2, 259–79.

Straw, J. (1997) 'Preface by Home Secretary' in Home Office, *No More Excuses: A New Approach to Tackling Youth Crime in England and Wales*, Cm 3809 (London: HMSO), 2.

Straw, J. (2007) *Speech to the Labour Party Conference*, 27 September.

Straw, J. (2008) *Towards a Bill of Rights and Responsibility*, 21 January.

Straw, J. and Wills, M. (2009) 'Foreword' in Ministry of Justice *Rights and Responsibilities:Developing Our Constitutional Framework*, Cm 7577 (Richmond: Office of Public Sector Information).

Swanton, C. (1980) 'The Concept of Interests', *Political Theory*, 8, 83–101.

Taylor, R. (2007) 'New Labour, New Capitalism' in A. Seldon (ed.) *Blair's Britain, 1997–2007* (Cambridge: Cambridge University Press).

Temple, M. (2000) 'New Labour's Third Way: Pragmatism and Governance', *British Journal of Politics and International Relations*, 2, 302–25.

Thatcher, M. (1975) *Speech to the Conservative Party Conference*, 10 October.

Thatcher, M. (1980) *Speech to the Conservative Party Conference*, 10 October.

Thatcher, M. (1983) *Speech to the Conservative Party Conference*, 14 October.

Thatcher, M. (1987) *Interview for* Woman's Own *('No Such Thing As Society')*, http://www.margaretthatcher.org/speeches/displaydocument.asp?docid=106689

Thatcher, M. (1993) *The Downing Street Years* (New York: HarperCollins).

Torfing, J. (1999) *New Theories of Discourse: Laclau, Mouffe and Žižek* (Oxford: Blackwell).

Townshend, J. (2004) 'Laclau and Mouffe's Hegemonic Project: The Story So Far', *Political Studies*, 52, 269–88.

Toynbee, P. and Walker, D. (2001) *Did Things Get Better? An Audit of Labour's Successes and Failures* (London: Penguin Books Ltd).

Toynbee, P. and Walker, D. (2005) *Better or Worse? Has Labour Delivered?* (London: Bloomsbury).

Travis, A. (2005) 'Whitehall Divisions Hit Anti-Social Behaviour Bill', *Guardian*, 13 December, http://www.guardian.co.uk/politics/2005/dec/13/ukcrime.prisonsandprobation/print

Travis, A. (2009) 'The Return of the ASBO', *Guardian*, 29 September, http://www.guardian.co.uk/society/2009/sep/29/asbo-brown-crime-crackdown

Verkaik, R. (2005) 'British Detainees May Opt to Stay in Jail', *Independent*, 1 February, http://www.independent.co.uk/news/uk/crime/belmarsh-detainees-may-opt-to-stay-in-jail-489096.html

Vincent, A. (1995) *Modern Political Ideologies*, 2nd edn (Oxford: Blackwell).

Wadham, J. (1999) 'A British Bill of Rights' in R. Blackburn and R. Plant (eds) *Constitutional Reform: The Labour Government's Constitutional Reform Agenda* (London: Longman).

Waltman, J. (2009) 'Reformulating Social Policy: The Minimum Wage, the New Deal, and the Working Families Tax Credit' in T. Casey (ed.) *The Blair Legacy* (Basingstoke: Palgrave Macmillan).

Webster, P. (2008) 'Gordon Brown Hits Back: This is No Time for a Novice', *The Times*, 24 September, http://www.timesonline.co.uk/tol/news/politics/article4813281.ece

White, M. and Addley, E. (2000) 'The Trouble with Mo', *Guardian*, 1 February, http://www.guardian.co.uk/print/0,,3957352-103680,00.html

White, M. and Whitaker, B. (2003) 'UK War Dossier a Sham, Say Experts', *Guardian*, 7 February, http://www.guardian.co.uk/politics/2003/feb/07/uk.internationaleducationnews

Wickham-Jones, M. (2004) 'The New Left' in R. Plant, M. Beech and K. Hickson (eds) *The Struggle for Labour's Soul: Understanding Labour's political thought Since 1945* (London: Routledge).

Williams, B. (1973) 'A Critique of Utilitarianism' in J.J.C. Smart and B. Williams (eds) *Utilitarianism: For and Against* (Cambridge: Cambridge University Press).

Williams, B. (1981) 'Politics and Moral Character' in B. Williams (eds) *Moral Luck: Philosophical Papers 1973–1980* (Cambridge: Cambridge University Press).

Wintour, P. (2007) 'Blair's Respect Agenda Ditched, Claim Tories', *Guardian*, 24 December, http://www.guardian.co.uk/politics/2007/dec/24/uk.publicservices1

Woodward, W. (2006) 'Cameron Promises UK Bill of Rights to replace Human Rights Act', *Guardian*, 26 June, http://www.guardian.co.uk/politics/2006/jun/26/uk.humanrights

Index